abc BRITISH RAILWAYS MOTIVE POWER

CONTENTS

Back Cover: Brush Type 4 No D1505 with a Ferme Park-New England coal empties on 5 July 1963. *Brian Stephenson*

BRITISH RAILWAYS LOCOMOTIVE SHEDS AND SHED CODES

AND PRINCIPAL SIGNING-ON POINTS

All B.R. steam locomotives carry the code of their home depot on a small plate affixed to the smokebox door.

Diesel and electric locomotives carry the plate on the cab side or have the depot name painted on the buffer beam.

LONDON MIDLAND REGION

LMW **Western A.C. Lines**

1A **Willesden**
1B Camden
1C Watford
1D Devons Road (Bow)
1E Bletchley

2A **Rugby**
2B Nuneaton
2E Northampton
2F Woodford Halse

5A **Crewe North**
5B Crewe South
  Gresty Lane
5C Stafford
5D Stoke
5F Uttoxeter

6A **Chester (Midland)**
6B Mold Junction
6C Birkenhead
6F Bidston
6G Llandudno Junction
6H Bangor
6J Holyhead
6K Rhyl

8A **Edge Hill (Liverpool)**
8B Warrington (Dallam)
  Warrington (Arpley)
8C Speke Junction
8D Widnes
8E Northwich
8F Springs Branch (Wigan)
8G Sutton Oak
8H Allerton

9A **Longsight (Manchester)**
9B Stockport (Edgeley)
9D Buxton
9E Trafford Park
  Glazebrook
9F Heaton Mersey
  Gowhole
9G Gorton
  Dinting
  Guide Bridge
  Reddish

12A **Carlisle (Kingmoor)**
12B Carlisle (Upperby)
12C Carlisle (Canal)
12E Barrow
12F Workington
12H Tebay

14A **Cricklewood**
14B Kentish Town
14E Bedford
14F Marylebone

15A **Wellingborough**
15B Kettering
15C Leicester (Midland)
  Market Harborough
  Seaton
15D Coalville
15E Leicester (Central)

16A **Nottingham**
16B Kirkby-in-Ashfield
16D Annesley

17A **Derby**
17B Burton
    Overseal
17C Rowsley
    Cromford
    Middleton
    Sheep Pasture

18A **Toton (Stapleford & Sandiacre)**
18B Westhouses
18C Hasland

21A **Saltley**
21B Bescot
21C Bushbury
21D Aston
21E Monument Lane
21F Walsall

24A **Accrington**
24B Rose Grove
24C Lostock Hall
24D Lower Darwen
24E Blackpool
24F Fleetwood
24G Skipton
24H Hellifield
24J Lancaster (Green Ayre)
24L Carnforth

26A **Newton Heath**
26B Agecroft
26C Bolton
26D Bury
26E Lees (Oldham)
26F Patricroft

27A **Bank Hall**
27B Aintree
27C Southport
27D Wigan
27E Walton-on-the-Hill

EASTERN REGION

30A **Stratford**
30F Parkeston

31A **Cambridge**
    Ely
31B March

32A **Norwich (Thorpe)**
    Cromer Beach
32B Ipswich
32C Lowestoft Central
32D Yarmouth South Town

33B Tilbury
33C Shoeburyness

34A **Kings Cross**
34B Hornsey
34D Hitchin
34E New England
34F Grantham
34G Finsbury Park

36A **Doncaster**
36C Frodingham
36E Retford

40A **Lincoln**
40B Immingham
    Grimsby
    New Holland
40E Colwick
40F Boston
    Sleaford

41A **Sheffield (Darnall)**
41D Canklow
41E Staveley (Barrow Hill)
41F Mexborough
41H Staveley (G.C.)
41J Langwith

NORTH EASTERN REGION

50A **York**
50B Hull (Dairycoates)
 Hull (Alexandra Dock)
50C Hull (Botanic Gardens)
50D Goole
50E Scarborough
50F Malton

51A **Darlington**
51C West Hartlepool
51F West Auckland
51J Northallerton
51L Thornaby

52A **Gateshead**
 Bowes Bridge
52B Heaton
52C Blaydon
 Alston
52D Tweedmouth
 Alnmouth
52E Percy Main
52F North and South Blyth
52G Sunderland
52H Tyne Dock
 Pelton Level
52K Consett

55A **Leeds (Holbeck)**
55B Stourton
55C Farnley
55D Royston
55E Normanton
55F Bradford (Manningham)
 Keighley
55G Huddersfield
55H Leeds (Neville Hill)

56A **Wakefield**
 Knottingley
56B Ardsley
56C Copley Hill
56D Mirfield
56E Sowerby Bridge
56F Low Moor
56G Bradford (Hammerton St.)

SCOTTISH REGION

60A **Inverness (Lochgorm)**
 Dingwall
 Forres
 Kyle of Lochalsh
60B Aviemore
 Boat of Garten
60C Helmsdale
 Tain
60D Wick
 Thurso

61A **Kittybrewster**
 Ballater
 Fraserburgh
 Inverurie
 Peterhead
61B Aberdeen (Ferryhill)
61C Keith
 Banff
 Elgin

62A **Thornton**
 Anstruther
 Burntisland
 Kirkcaldy
 Ladybank
 Methil
62B Dundee
 Arbroath
 Montrose
 St. Andrews
62C Dunfermline
 Alloa
 Kelty

63A **Perth**
 Aberfeldy
 Crieff
 Forfar
63B Fort William
 Mallaig
63C Oban
 Ballachulish

64A **St. Margarets (Edinburgh)**
 Dunbar
 Galashiels
 Granton
 Hardengreen
 Longniddry
 North Berwick
 Seafield
 South Leith
64B Haymarket
64C Dalry Road
64F Bathgate
64G Hawick
64H Leith Central

65A	**Eastfield (Glasgow)**	66A	**Polmadie (Glasgow)**
	Arrochar	66B	Motherwell
65B	St. Rollox	66C	Hamilton
65C	Parkhead	66D	Greenock (Ladyburn)
65D	Dawsholm	66E	Carstairs
	Dumbarton	66F	Beattock
65E	Kipps		
65F	Grangemouth	67A	**Corkerhill (Glasgow)**
65G	Yoker	67B	Hurlford
65H	Helensburgh		Beith
65I	Balloch		Muirkirk
65J	Stirling	67C	Ayr
	Killin	67D	Ardrossan
65K	Polmont	67E	Dumfries
		67F	Stranraer

SOUTHERN REGION

70A	**Nine Elms**	*72C	Yeovil Town
70B	Feltham	*72E	Barnstaple Junction
70C	Guildford		Ilfracombe
	Reading Southern	*72F	Wadebridge
70D	Basingstoke		
70E	Salisbury		
70H	Ryde (I.O.W.)		
71A	**Eastleigh**		
	Andover Junction	73C	Hither Green
	Southampton Terminus	73E	Faversham
	Winchester	73F	Ashford (Kent)
71B	Bournemouth		
	Branksome		
71G	Weymouth		
71I	Southampton Docks		
*72A	**Exmouth Junction**	75A	**Brighton**
	Bude	75B	Redhill
	Callington	75C	Norwood Junction
	Exmouth	75D	Stewarts Lane
	Lyme Regis	75E	Three Bridges
	Okehampton		Horsham
	Seaton	75F	Tunbridge Wells West

**72 district sheds now part of Western Region; not yet recoded*

WESTERN REGION

81A	**Old Oak Common**	82A	**Bristol (Bath Road)**
81B	Slough		Marsh Junction
81C	Southall	82B	St. Phillip's Marsh
81D	Reading		Wells
81E	Didcot		Weston-super-Mare
81F	Oxford		

82C Swindon
  Chippenham
82D Westbury
  Frome
82E Bristol (Barrow Road)
82F Bath (Green Park)
  Highbridge
  Radstock
82G Templecombe

83A **Newton Abbot**
83B Taunton
83C Exeter
  Tiverton Junction
83D Laira (Plymouth)
  Launceston
83E St. Blazey
  Bodmin
83G Penzance
83H Plymouth (Friary)

*84A **Wolverhampton (Stafford Road)**
*84B Oxley (Wolverhampton)
*84C Banbury
*84D Leamington Spa
*84E Tyseley
  Stratford-on-Avon
*84F Stourbridge
*84G Kidderminster
*84H Wellington (Salop)

85A **Worcester**
  Honeybourne
  Kingham
  Ledbury
85B Gloucester (Horton Road)
  Brimscombe
  Cheltenham (Malvern Rd.)
  Lydney
  Ross-on-Wye
85C Gloucester (Barnwood)
  Dursley
85D Bromsgrove
  Redditch

86A **Newport (Ebbw Junction)**
86B Newport (Pill)
86C Hereford
86E Severn Tunnel Junction
86F Aberbeeg
86G Pontypool Road

87A **Neath**
  Glyn Neath
  Neath (N. & B.)
87B Duffryn Yard (Port Talbot)
87C Danygraig (Swansea)
87D Swansea East Dock
  Upper Bank
87E Landore
87F Llanelly
  Llandovery
  Pantyffynnon
  Pembrey
87G Carmarthen
87H Neyland
  Cardigan
  Milford Haven
  Pembroke Dock
  Whitland
87J Goodwick

88A **Canton (Cardiff)**
88B Radyr (Cardiff)
88C Barry
88D Merthyr
  Dowlais Cae Harris
  Rhymney
88E Abercynon
88F Treherbert
  Ferndale
88G Llantrisant
88H Tondu
88J Aberdare
88K Brecon
88L Cardiff East Dock
88M Cathays (Cardiff)

*89A **Shrewsbury**
  Builth Road
  Craven Arms
*89B Croes Newydd
  Bala
  Penmaenpool
*89C Machynlleth
  Aberystwyth
  Aberystwyth (V. of R.)
  Portmadoc
  Pwllheli
*89D Oswestry
  Llanidloes
  Moat Lane

**84 and 89 district sheds now part of London Midland Region; not yet recoded*

Ex-G.W.R. STEAM LOCOMOTIVES
Nos. 7-9799

The numbers of locomotives in service have been checked in W.R. to January 12, 1963, and S.R. to January 30, 1963.

Unclass. V. of R. 2-6-2T

Introduced 1902. Davies and Metcalfe design for Vale of Rheidol 1′ 11½″ gauge.
* Introduced 1923. G.W. development of Vale of Rheidol design.

Weight
25 tons 0 cwt

Gauge
1′ 11½″

Boiler pressure
165 lb sq in NS

Cylinders
(O) 11″ × 17″
(O) 11½″ × 17″*

Driving wheel diameter
2′ 6″

Tractive effort
9,615 lb
10,510 lb*

Valve gear
Walschaerts

7* *Owain Glyndŵr*
8* *Llywelyn*
9 *Prince of Wales*

TOTAL: 3

6MT 1000 4-6-0
"County"

Introduced 1945. Hawksworth design with 280 lb boiler pressure since reduced to 250 lb.
Fitted with double chimney.

Weight
Locomotive: 76 tons 17 cwt
Tender: 49 tons 0 cwt

Boiler pressure
250 lb sq in

Cylinders
(O) 18½″ × 30″

Driving wheel diameter
6′ 3″

Tractive effort
28,241 lb

Valve gear
Stephenson (piston valves)

1000 *County of Middlesex*
1001 *County of Bucks*
1002 *County of Berks*
1005 *County of Devon*
1006 *County of Cornwall*
1008 *County of Cardigan*
1009 *County of Carmarthen*
1010 *County of Caernarvon*
1011 *County of Chester*
1012 *County of Denbigh*
1013 *County of Dorset*
1014 *County of Glamorgan*
1016 *County of Hants*
1019 *County of Merioneth*

1020	*County of Monmouth*	1024	*County of Pembroke*
1021	*County of Montgomery*	1025	*County of Radnor*
1023	*County of Oxford*	1027	*County of Stafford*
		1028	*County of Warwick*

TOTAL: 21

0F P. & M. 0-4-0ST

Introduced 1907. Peckett design for Powlesland & Mason (Contractor).

Weight
Locomotive: 33 tons 10 cwt

Boiler pressure
150 lb sq in NS

Cylinders
(O) 15″ × 21″

Driving wheel diameter
3′ 7″

Tractive effort
14,010 lb

Valve gear
Stephenson

1151

TOTAL: 1

0F Cardiff Rly. 0-4-0ST

Introduced 1893. Kitson design for Cardiff Railway.

Weight
Locomotive: 25 tons 10 cwt

Boiler pressure
160 lb sq in NS

Cylinders
(O) 14″ × 21″

Driving wheel diameter
3′ 2½″

Tractive effort
14,540 lb

Valve gear
Hawthorn Kitson

1338

TOTAL: 1

1F 1366 0-6-0PT

Introduced 1934. Collett development of 1361 class, with pannier tanks.

Weight
Locomotive: 35 tons 15 cwt

Boiler pressure
165 lb sq in NS

Cylinders
(O) 16″ × 20″

Driving wheel diameter
3′ 8″

Tractive effort
16,320 lb

Valve Gear
Stephenson

1367 1368 1369

TOTAL: 3

Class 1000 4-6-0 No. 1021 *County of Montgomery* [*J. R. Carter*

Class 1400 0-4-2T No. 1445 [*R. A. Panting*

Class 1500 0-6-0PT No. 1507 [*J. B. Bucknall*

1P 1400 0-4-2T

Introduced 1932. Collett design for light branch work (originally designated 4800 class). Push-and-pull fitted.

Weight
Locomotive: 41 tons 6 cwt

Boiler pressure
165 lb sq in NS

Cylinders
16½″ × 24″

Driving wheel diameter
5′ 2″

Tractive effort
13,900 lb

Valve gear
Stephenson

1409	1424	1442	1447	1453	1466	1472
1420	1432	1444	1450	1455	1471	1474
1421	1440	1445	1451	1458		

TOTAL: 19

4F 1500 0-6-0PT

Introduced 1949. Hawksworth short-wheelbase heavy shunting design.

Weight
Locomotive: 58 tons 4 cwt

Boiler pressure
200 lb sq in NS

Cylinders
(O) 17½″ × 24″

Driving wheel diameter
4′ 7½″

Tractive effort
22,515 lb

Valve gear
Walschaerts (piston valves)

1500	1503	1504	1506	1507

TOTAL: 5

2F 1600 0-6-0PT

Introduced 1949. Hawksworth light branch line and shunting design.

Weight
Locomotive: 41 tons 12 cwt

Boiler pressure
165 lb sq in NS

Cylinders
16½″ × 24″

Driving wheel diameter
4′ 1½″

Tractive effort
18,515 lb

Valve gear
Stephenson

1607	1617	1628	1639	1654	1660	1665
1608	1619	1630	1641	1655	1661	1666
1611	1621	1631	1643	1656	1662	1667
1612	1622	1632	1648	1657	1663	1668
1613	1623	1636	1650	1658	1664	1669
1614	1627	1638	1651			

TOTAL: 39

3MT 2251 0-6-0

Introduced 1930. Collett design.

Weight
Locomotive: 43 tons 8 cwt
Tender: 36 tons 15 cwt
47 tons 6 cwt
(ex-R.O.D. tender from 3000 Class 2-8-0)

Boiler pressure
200 lb sq in

Cylinders
17½" × 24"

Driving wheel diameter
5' 2"

Tractive effort
20,155 lb

Valve gear
Stephenson

2201	2218	2231	2243	2248	2261	2286
2204	2219	2232	2244	2249	2268	2287
2210	2221	2236	2245	2251	2273	2289
2211	2222	2241	2246	2253	2277	2291
2214	2224	2242	2247	2257	2283	2298
2217						

Class continued with 3200

8F 2800 2-8-0

Introduced 1903. Churchward design, earlier locomotives subsequently fitted with new boiler and superheater.
* Introduced 1938. Collett locomotives with side-window cab and detail alterations.

Weight
Locomotive: 75 tons 10 cwt
76 tons 5 cwt*
Tender: 40 tons 0 cwt

Boiler pressure
225 lb sq in

Cylinders
(O) 18½" × 30"

Driving wheel diameter
4' 7½"

Tractive effort
35,380 lb

Valve gear
Stephenson (piston valves)

2807	2845	2859	2871	2879	2888*	2894*
2818	2851	2861	2872	2882	2889*	2895*
2822	2852	2862	2873	2884*	2890*	2896*
2836	2854	2865	2874	2885*	2891*	2897*
2839	2856	2866	2875	2886*	2892*	2898*
2841	2857	2867	2876	2887*	2893*	2899*
2842	2858					

Class continued with 3800

Class 2800 2-8-0 No. 2852 [M. Pope

Class 2251 0-6-0 No. 3210 [B. Stephenson

Class 9400 0-6-0PT No. 3401 [G. T. Storer

3MT 2251 0-6-0

Class continued from 2298

3200	3204	3208	3212	3214	3216	3218
3201	3205	3209	3213	3215	3217	3219
3203	3206	3210				

TOTAL: 53

4F 9400 0-6-0PT

Introduced 1947. Hawksworth taper boiler design for heavy shunting.
* Introduced 1949. Locomotives with non-superheated boiler.

Weight
Locomotive: 55 tons 7 cwt

Boiler pressure
200 lb sq in SS

Cylinders
$17\frac{1}{2}'' \times 24''$

Driving wheel diameter
$4'\ 7\frac{1}{2}''$

Tractive effort
22,515 lb

Valve gear
Stephenson

3400*	3401*	3402*	3403*	3405*	3406*	3409*

Class continued with 8400

3F 5700 0-6-0PT

* Introduced 1929. Collett design for shunting and light goods work developed from 2021 class.
† Introduced 1930. Locomotives with steam brake and no A.W.S. fittings, for shunting only.
‡ Introduced 1933. Locomotives with condensing apparatus for working over L.T. Metropolitan line.
§ Introduced 1933. Locomotives with detail alterations, modified cab (except 8700) and increased weight.
¶ Introduced 1948. Steam brake locomotives with increased weight.

Weight
Locomotive: 47 tons 10 cwt*†
50 tons 15 cwt‡
49 tons 0 cwt§¶

Boiler pressure
200 lb sq in NS

Cylinders
$17\frac{1}{2}'' \times 24''$

Driving wheel diameter
$4'\ 7\frac{1}{2}''$

Tractive effort
25,515 lb

Valve gear
Stephenson

3600§	3607§	3615§	3620§	3627§	3634§	3644§
3601§	3608§	3616§	3621§	3628§	3635§	3646§
3603§	3610§	3617§	3622§	3629§	3639§	3647§
3604§	3612§	3618§	3625§	3631§	3642§	3648§
3605§	3613§	3619§	3626§	3633§	3643§	3650§

3651§	3677§	3696§	3716§	3738§	3759§	3779§
3652§	3678§	3698§	3717§	3739§	3761§	3781§
3653§	3679§	3699§	3719§	3742§	3762§	3782§
3654§	3680§	3700§	3720§	3744§	3763§	3784§
3658§	3681§	3701§	3721§	3745§	3764§	3786§
3659§	3682§	3702§	3725§	3746§	3765§	3787§
3660§	3683§	3705§	3727§	3747§	3766§	3788§
3661§	3685§	3706§	3728§	3748§	3767§	3789§
3662§	3686§	3707§	3729§	3749§	3768§	3790§
3664§	3687§	3708§	3730§	3751§	3770§	3791§
3665§	3689§	3709§	3731§	3752§	3771§	3792§
3668§	3690§	3710§	3733§	3753§	3772§	3794§
3669§	3691§	3711§	3734§	3754§	3775§	3795§
3671§	3692§	3712§	3735§	3756§	3776§	3796§
3672§	3693§	3714§	3736§	3757§	3777§	3797§
3673§	3695§	3715§	3737§	3758§	3778§	3798§
3675§						

Class continued with 4600

8F 2800 2-8-0

Class continued from 2899

3800*	3810*	3820*	3831*	3840*	3849*	3858*
3801*	3811*	3821*	3832*	3841*	3850*	3859*
3802*	3812*	3822*	3833*	3842*	3851*	3860*
3803*	3813*	3823*	3834*	3843*	3852*	3861*
3804*	3814*	3824*	3835*	3844*	3853*	3862*
3805*	3815*	3825*	3836*	3845*	3854*	3863*
3806*	3816*	3826*	3837*	3846*	3855*	3864*
3807*	3817*	3828*	3838*	3847*	3856*	3865*
3808*	3818*	3829*	3839*	3848*	3857*	3866*
3809*	3819*	3830*				

TOTAL: 110

7P 4073 4-6-0

"Castle"

Introduced 1923. Collett design, developed from "Star" (5085–92 converted from "Star").
† Introduced 1946. Fitted with 3-row superheater.
‡ Introduced 1947. Fitted with 4-row superheater.
• Introduced 1956. Fitted with double chimney.

Weight
Locomotive: 79 tons 17 cwt
Tender: 46 tons 14 cwt

Boiler pressure
225 lb sq in

Cylinders
Four, 16″ × 26″

Driving wheel diameter
6′ 8½″

Tractive effort
31,625 lb

Valve gear
Inside Walschaerts (rocking shafts and piston valves)

4074‡* *Caldicot Castle*
4076 *Carmarthen Castle*
4079 *Pendennis Castle*
4080‡* *Powderham Castle*
4081 *Warwick Castle*
4082 *Windsor Castle*
4087‡* *Cardigan Castle*
4088‡* *Dartmouth Castle*
4089 *Donnington Castle*
4090‡* *Dorchester Castle*
4093‡* *Dunster Castle*
4096 *Highclere Castle*
4098 *Kidwelly Castle*

Class continued with 5000

4MT 5101 2-6-2T

Introduced 1929. Modified design for new construction, with detail alterations and increased weight, of Collett rebuild of Churchward 3100 class (introduced 1903 and subsequently fitted with superheater).

Weight
Locomotive: 78 tons 9 cwt

Boiler pressure
200 lb sq in

Cylinders
(O) 18″ × 30″

Driving wheel diameter
5′ 8″

Tractive effort
24,300 lb

Valve gear
Stephenson (piston valves)

4100	4111	4125	4136	4149	4159	4172
4101	4113	4127	4137	4150	4160	4173
4103	4114	4128	4140	4151	4161	4174
4104	4115	4130	4141	4153	4165	4175
4105	4119	4131	4142	4154	4166	4176
4107	4120	4132	4143	4155	4167	4177
4108	4121	4133	4144	4156	4168	4178
4109	4122	4134	4147	4157	4169	4179
4110	4124	4135	4148	4158	4171	

Class continued with 5101

Class 5700 0-6-0PT No. 3681 [*J. White*

Class 5101 2-6-2T No. 4166 [*J. White*

Class 4200 2-8-0T No. 4257 [*G. Wheeler*

7F 4200 2-8-0T

Introduced 1910. Churchward design.

Weight
Locomotive: 81 tons 12 cwt

Boiler pressure
200 lb sq in

Cylinders
(O) 18½″ × 30″

Driving wheel diameter
4′ 7½″

Tractive effort
31,450 lb

Valve gear
Stephenson (piston valves)

4213	4237	4251	4258	4271	4280	4292
4214	4238	4252	4259	4272	4282	4294
4222	4241	4253	4262	4273	4283	4295
4225	4242	4254	4263	4275	4284	4296
4227	4243	4255	4264	4277	4285	4297
4228	4247	4256	4265	4278	4286	4298
4232	4248	4257	4268	4279	4290	4299
4233						

Class continued with 5200

4MT 4500 2-6-2T

Introduced 1906. Churchward design for light branches, developed from 4400 class with larger wheels, earlier locomotives subsequently fitted with superheater.

Weight
Locomotive: 57 tons 0 cwt

Boiler pressure
200 lb sq in

Cylinders
(O) 17″ × 24″

Driving wheel diameter
4′ 7½″

Tractive effort
21,250 lb

Valve gear
Stephenson (piston valves)

4507	4555	4564	4569	4570	4574

TOTAL: 6

4MT 4575 2-6-2T

Introduced 1927. Development of Churchward 4500 class with detail alterations and increased weight.
* Introduced 1953. Push-and-pull fitted.

Weight
Locomotive: 61 tons 0 cwt

Boiler pressure
200 lb sq in

Cylinders
(O) 17″ × 24″

Driving wheel diameter
4′ 7½″

Tractive effort
21,250 lb

Valve gear
Stephenson (piston valves)

4591	4593

Class continued with 5508

3F 5700 0-6-0PT

Class continued from 3798

4600§	4615§	4629§	4644§	4659§	4672§	4687§
4602§	4616§	4630§	4645§	4660§	4673§	4688§
4603§	4617§	4631§	4646§	4661§	4674§	4689§
4604§	4618§	4633§	4648§	4662§	4675§	4690§
4606§	4619§	4634§	4649§	4663§	4676§	4691§
4607§	4620§	4635§	4650§	4664§	4677§	4692§
4608§	4621§	4636§	4651§	4665§	4678§	4693§
4609§	4622§	4637§	4652§	4666§	4679§	4694§
4610§	4623§	4638§	4653§	4667§	4680§	4695§
4611§	4624§	4639§	4654§	4668§	4681§	4696§
4612§	4626§	4640§	4655§	4669§	4682§	4697§
4613§	4627§	4642§	4657§	4670§	4683§	4698§
4614§	4628§	4643§	4658§	4671§	4684§	4699§

Class continued with 5749

7F 4700 2-8-0

Introduced 1919. Churchward mixed traffic design (4700 built with smaller boiler and later rebuilt).

Weight
Locomotive: 82 tons 0 cwt
Tender: 46 tons 14 cwt

Boiler pressure
225 lb sq in

Cylinders
(O) 19″ × 30″

Driving wheel diameter
5′ 8″

Tractive effort
30,460 lb

Valve gear
Stephenson (piston valves)

4701	4703	4704	4705	4706	4707

TOTAL: 6

5MT 4900 4-6-0

"Hall"

Introduced 1928. Modified design of Collett rebuild with 6′ 0″ driving wheels of "Saint" (built 1907) for new construction, with higher-pitched boiler, modified footplating and detail differences.

Weight
Locomotive: 75 tons 0 cwt
Tender: 46 tons 14 cwt

Boiler pressure
225 lb sq in

Cylinders
(O) 18½″ × 30″

Driving wheel diameter
6′ 0″

Tractive effort
27,275 lb

Valve gear
Stephenson (piston valves)

Left:
Class 4575 2-6-2T
No. 4593
[*R. J. Henly*

Centre:
Class 4700 2-8-0
No. 4706
[*A. E. Newman*

Bottom:
Class 4900 4-6-0
No. 4933 *Himley Hall*
[*C. P. Boocock*

4902 *Aldenham Hall*
4903 *Astley Hall*
4904 *Binnegar Hall*
4905 *Barton Hall*
4907 *Broughton Hall*
4908 *Broome Hall*
4910 *Blaisdon Hall*
4914 *Cranmore Hall*
4915 *Condover Hall*
4916 *Crumlin Hall*
4918 *Dartington Hall*
4919 *Donnington Hall*
4920 *Dumbleton Hall*
4922 *Enville Hall*
4923 *Evenley Hall*
4924 *Eydon Hall*
4927 *Farnborough Hall*
4928 *Gatacre Hall*
4929 *Goytrey Hall*
4930 *Hagley Hall*
4932 *Hatherton Hall*
4933 *Himley Hall*
4935 *Ketley Hall*
4936 *Kinlet Hall*
4939 *Littleton Hall*
4942 *Maindy Hall*
4943 *Marrington Hall*
4946 *Moseley Hall*
4949 *Packwood Hall*
4950 *Patshull Hall*
4951 *Pendeford Hall*
4953 *Pitchford Hall*
4954 *Plaish Hall*
4955 *Plaspower Hall*
4956 *Plowden Hall*
4958 *Priory Hall*
4959 *Purley Hall*
4962 *Ragley Hall*
4964 *Rodwell Hall*
4966 *Shakenhurst Hall*
4970 *Sketty Hall*
4972 *Saint Brides Hall*
4975 *Umberslade Hall*
4976 *Warfield Hall*
4978 *Westwood Hall*
4979 *Wootton Hall*
4980 *Wrottesley Hall*
4981 *Abberley Hall*
4983 *Albert Hall*
4985 *Allesley Hall*
4988 *Bulwell Hall*
4989 *Cherwell Hall*
4991 *Cobham Hall*
4992 *Crosby Hall*
4993 *Dalton Hall*
4994 *Downton Hall*
4996 *Eden Hall*
4998 *Eyton Hall*

Class continued with 5900

7P 4073 4-6-0

"Castle"

Class continued from 4098

5000† *Launceston Castle*
5001* *Llandovery Castle*
5002 *Ludlow Castle*
5014 *Goodrich Castle*
5015 *Kingswear Castle*
5018 *St. Mawes Castle*
5020 *Tremanton Castle*
5022* *Wigmore Castle*
5023 *Brecon Castle*
5025 *Chirk Castle*
5026‡* *Criccieth Castle*
5027* *Farleigh Castle*
5029 *Nunney Castle*
5031* *Totnes Castle*

5037† *Monmouth Castle*
5038 *Morlais Castle*
5039 *Rhuddlan Castle*
5040 *Stokesay Castle*
5041 *Tiverton Castle*
5042 *Winchester Castle*
5043‡* *Earl of Mount Edgcumbe*
5049‡* *Earl of Plymouth*
5050† *Earl of St. Germans*
5051 *Earl Bathurst*
5054 *Earl of Ducie*
5055 *Earl of Eldon*
5056* *Earl of Powis*
5057‡* *Earl Waldegrave*
5058 *Earl of Clancarty*
5060* *Earl of Berkeley*
5063† *Earl Baldwin*
5065† *Newport Castle*
5070 *Sir Daniel Gooch*
5071‡* *Spitfire*
5073‡* *Blenheim*
5074†* *Hampden*
5076 *Gladiator*
5078†* *Beaufort*
5080 *Defiant*
5081† *Lockheed Hudson*
5085 *Evesham Abbey*
5087 *Tintern Abbey*
5089 *Westminster Abbey*
5091 *Cleeve Abbey*
5092* *Tresco Abbey*
5093† *Upton Castle*
5096† *Bridgwater Castle*
5097†* *Sarum Castle*
5098†* *Clifford Castle*
5099† *Compton Castle*

Class continued with 7000

4MT 5101 2-6-2T

Class continued from 4179

5101 5153 5164 5184 5191 5192 5199
5152 5154

TOTAL: 71

7F 4200 2-8-0T

Class continued from 4299

5200 5201 5202 5203

TOTAL: 54

8F 5205 2-8-0T

Introduced 1923. Development of Churchward 4200 class, with enlarged cylinders and detail alterations.

Weight
Locomotive: 82 tons 2 cwt

Boiler pressure
200 lb sq in

Cylinders
(O) 19″ × 30″

Driving wheel diameter
4′ 7½″

Tractive effort
33,170 lb

Valve gear
Stephenson

5205	5215	5224	5232	5240	5248	5256
5206	5216	5225	5233	5241	5249	5257
5208	5217	5226	5234	5242	5250	5259
5209	5218	5227	5235	5243	5251	5260
5210	5220	5228	5236	5244	5252	5261
5211	5221	5229	5237	5245	5253	5262
5213	5222	5230	5238	5246	5254	5263
5214	5223	5231	5239	5247	5255	5264

TOTAL: 56

4MT 4300 2-6-0

Introduced 1911. Churchward design.
* Introduced 1925. Locomotives with detail alterations affecting weight.
† Introduced 1932. Locomotives with side-window cab and detail alterations.

Weight
Locomotive: 62 tons 0 cwt
64 tons 0 cwt*
65 tons 6 cwt†
Tender: 40 tons 0 cwt

Boiler pressure
200 lb sq in

Cylinders
(O) 18½″ × 30″

Driving wheel diameter
4′ 7½″

Tractive effort
25,670 lb

Valve gear
Stephenson (piston valves)

5306 5322 5330 5336 5369 5380

Class continued with 6304

1P 5400 0-6-0PT

Introduced 1931. Collett design for light passenger work, push-and-pull fitted.

Weight
Locomotive: 46 tons 12 cwt

Boiler pressure
165 lb sq in NS

Cylinders
16½″ × 24″

Driving wheel diameter
5′ 2″

Tractive effort
14,780 lb

Valve gear
Stephenson

5410 5416 5420

TOTAL: 3

4MT 4575 2-6-2T

Class continued from 4593

5508	5531	5548	5555*	5564	5569	5571
5518	5545*	5554	5563	5568*	5570	5573

TOTAL: 16

5MT 5600 0-6-2T

Introduced 1924. Collett design for service in Welsh valleys.
* Introduced 1927. Locomotives with detail alterations.

Weight
Locomotive: 68 tons 12 cwt
69 tons 7 cwt*

Boiler pressure
200 lb sq in

Cylinders
18" × 26"

Driving wheel diameter
4′ 7½″

Tractive effort
25,800 lb

Valve gear
Stephenson (piston valves)

5601	5614	5627	5644	5660	5675	5687
5602	5615	5628	5645	5662	5676	5688
5603	5616	5629	5647	5665	5677	5689
5605	5618	5632	5648	5666	5678	5690
5606	5619	5633	5649	5667	5679	5691
5607	5620	5634	5650	5668	5680	5692
5608	5621	5635	5651	5669	5681	5693
5609	5622	5637	5654	5670	5683	5694
5610	5623	5638	5655	5671	5684	5696
5611	5624	5640	5656	5672	5685	5697
5612	5625	5641	5658	5673	5686	5699
5613	5626	5643	5659	5674		

Class continued with 6602

3F 5700 0-6-0PT

Class continued from 4699

5749* 5775* 5787*

Class continued with 6714

5MT 4900 4-6-0

"Hall"

Class continued from 4998

5900 *Hinderton Hall*
5901 *Hazel Hall*
5903 *Keele Hall*
5904 *Kelham Hall*

Above:
Class 4073 4-6-0
No. 5089
Westminster Abbey
[H. Wheeler

Right:
Class 6100 2-6-2T
No. 6117
[R. J. Henly

Below:
Class 4300 2-6-0
No. 6373
[H. Wheeler

5905	*Knowsley Hall*	5958	*Knolton Hall*
5908	*Moreton Hall*	5961	*Toynbee Hall*
5914	*Ripon Hall*	5962	*Wantage Hall*
5919	*Worsley Hall*	5963	*Wimpole Hall*
5922	*Caxton Hall*	5967	*Bickmarsh Hall*
5923	*Colston Hall*	5970	*Hengrave Hall*
5924	*Dinton Hall*	5971	*Merevale Hall*
5927	*Guild Hall*	5972	*Olton Hall*
5929	*Hanham Hall*	5974	*Wallsworth Hall*
5932	*Haydon Hall*	5975	*Winslow Hall*
5933	*Kingsway Hall*	5976	*Ashwicke Hall*
5934	*Kneller Hall*	5977	*Beckford Hall*
5936	*Oakley Hall*	5978	*Bodinnick Hall*
5937	*Stanford Hall*	5979	*Cruckton Hall*
5938	*Stanley Hall*	5983	*Henley Hall*
5939	*Tangley Hall*	5984	*Linden Hall*
5942	*Doldowlod Hall*	5985	*Mostyn Hall*
5943	*Elmdon Hall*	5986	*Arbury Hall*
5944	*Ickenham Hall*	5987	*Brocket Hall*
5945	*Leckhampton Hall*	5988	*Bostock Hall*
5948	*Siddington Hall*	5990	*Dorford Hall*
5951	*Clyffe Hall*	5991	*Gresham Hall*
5952	*Cogan Hall*	5992	*Horton Hall*
5954	*Faendre Hall*	5993	*Kirby Hall*
5955	*Garth Hall*	5994	*Roydon Hall*
5956	*Horsley Hall*	5995	*Wick Hall*
5957	*Hutton Hall*	5998	*Trevor Hall*

Class continued with **6900**

4MT 6100 2-6-2T

Introduced 1931. Development of Collett 5101 class. Locomotives for London suburban area with increased boiler pressure.

Weight
Locomotive: 78 tons 9 cwt

Boiler pressure
225 lb sq in

Cylinders
(O) 18″ × 30″

Driving wheel diameter
5′ 8″

Tractive effort
27,340 lb

Valve gear
Stephenson (piston valves)

6103	6114	6125	6134	6142	6150	6160
6106	6115	6126	6135	6143	6151	6161
6107	6116	6128	6136	6144	6154	6163
6108	6117	6129	6137	6145	6155	6164
6110	6118	6130	6138	6147	6156	6165
6111	6119	6131	6139	6148	6158	6167
6112	6122	6132	6140	6149	6159	6169
6113	6124	6133	6141			

TOTAL: 53

4MT 4300 2-6-0

Class continued from 5380

6304	6326	6345	6356	6367	6373	6381
6309	6327	6346	6357	6368	6375	6384
6314	6335	6347	6361	6369	6378	6385
6317	6337	6349	6363	6370	6379	6394
6319	6338	6350	6364	6372	6380	6395
6320	6344	6353	6365			

Class continued with 7303

2P 6400 0-6-0PT

Introduced 1932. Collett design for light passenger work, variation of 5400 class with smaller wheels, push-and-pull fitted.

Weight
Locomotive: 45 tons 12 cwt

Boiler pressure
180 lb sq in NS

Cylinders
$16\frac{1}{2}'' \times 24''$

Driving wheel diameter
$4' \, 7\frac{1}{2}''$

Tractive effort
18,010 lb

Valve gear
Stephenson

6400	6412	6419	6424	6431	6434	6437
6403	6416	6421	6430	6433	6435	

TOTAL: 13

5MT 5600 0-6-2T

Class continued from 5699

6602*	6615*	6632*	6649*	6662*	6675*	6688*
6603*	6618*	6633*	6650*	6663*	6676*	6689*
6604*	6619*	6634*	6651*	6664*	6677*	6690*
6605*	6620*	6635*	6652*	6665*	6678*	6691*
6606*	6621*	6636*	6653*	6666*	6679*	6692*
6607*	6622*	6637*	6654*	6667*	6680*	6693*
6608*	6623*	6638*	6655*	6668*	6681*	6694*
6609*	6624*	6639*	6656*	6670*	6682*	6695*
6610*	6625*	6642*	6657*	6671*	6683*	6696*
6611*	6626*	6643*	6658*	6672*	6684*	6697*
6612*	6627*	6644*	6659*	6673*	6685*	6698*
6613*	6628*	6646*	6660*	6674*	6686*	6699*
6614*	6631*	6648*	6661*			

TOTAL: 170

3F 5700 0-6-0PT

Class continued from 5787

6714†	6741†	6760¶	6763¶	6765¶	6769¶	6777¶
6724†	6742†	6762¶	6764¶	6768¶	6772¶	

Class continued with 7780

5MT 6800 4-6-0

"Grange"

Introduced 1936. Collett design, variation of "Hall" with smaller wheels, incorporating certain parts of withdrawn 4300 2-6-0 locomotives.

Weight
Locomotive: 74 tons 0 cwt
Tender: 40 tons 0 cwt

Boiler pressure
225 lb sq in

Cylinders
(O) $18\frac{1}{2}'' \times 30''$

Driving wheel diameter
5′ 8″

Tractive effort
28,875 lb

Valve gear
Stephenson (piston valves)

6800 *Arlington Grange*
6803 *Bucklebury Grange*
6804 *Brockington Grange*
6806 *Blackwell Grange*
6807 *Birchwood Grange*
6808 *Beenham Grange*
6809 *Burghclere Grange*
6810 *Blakemere Grange*
6811 *Cranbourne Grange*
6812 *Chesford Grange*
6813 *Eastbury Grange*
6814 *Enborne Grange*
6815 *Frilford Grange*
6816 *Frankton Grange*
6817 *Gwenddwr Grange*
6818 *Hardwick Grange*
6819 *Highnam Grange*
6820 *Kingstone Grange*
6821 *Leaton Grange*
6822 *Manton Grange*
6823 *Oakley Grange*
6824 *Ashley Grange*
6825 *Llanvair Grange*
6826 *Nannerth Grange*
6827 *Llanfrechfa Grange*
6828 *Trellech Grange*
6829 *Burmington Grange*
6830 *Buckenhill Grange*
6831 *Bearley Grange*
6832 *Brockton Grange*
6833 *Calcot Grange*
6834 *Dummer Grange*
6835 *Eastham Grange*
6836 *Estevarney Grange*
6837 *Forthampton Grange*
6838 *Goodmoor Grange*
6839 *Hewell Grange*
6840 *Hazeley Grange*
6841 *Marlas Grange*
6842 *Nunhold Grange*
6843 *Poulton Grange*
6844 *Penhydd Grange*
6845 *Paviland Grange*
6846 *Ruckley Grange*
6847 *Tidmarsh Grange*
6848 *Toddington Grange*

Class 5600 0-6-2T No. 6624 [J. White

Class 6800 4-6-0 No. 6807 *Birchwood Grange* [B. Stephenson

Class 6959 4-6-0 No. 6993 *Arthog Hall*

6849 *Walton Grange*
6850 *Cleeve Grange*
6851 *Hurst Grange*
6852 *Headbourne Grange*
6853 *Morehampton Grange*
6854 *Roundhill Grange*
6855 *Saighton Grange*
6856 *Stowe Grange*
6857 *Tudor Grange*
6858 *Woolston Grange*
6859 *Yiewsley Grange*
6860 *Aberporth Grange*
6861 *Crynant Grange*
6862 *Derwent Grange*
6863 *Dolhywel Grange*
6864 *Dymock Grange*
6866 *Morfa Grange*
6867 *Peterston Grange*
6868 *Penrhos Grange*
6869 *Resolven Grange*
6870 *Bodicote Grange*
6871 *Bourton Grange*
6872 *Crawley Grange*
6873 *Caradoc Grange*
6874 *Haughton Grange*
6875 *Hindford Grange*
6876 *Kingsland Grange*
6877 *Llanfair Grange*
6878 *Longford Grange*
6879 *Overton Grange*

TOTAL: 76

5MT 4900 4-6-0

"Hall"

Class continued from 5998

6900 *Abney Hall*
6901 *Arley Hall*
6903 *Belmont Hall*
6904 *Charfield Hall*
6905 *Claughton Hall*
6906 *Chicheley Hall*
6907 *Davenham Hall*
6908 *Downham Hall*
6909 *Frewin Hall*
6910 *Gossington Hall*
6911 *Holker Hall*
6912 *Helmster Hall*
6913 *Levens Hall*
6914 *Langton Hall*
6915 *Mursley Hall*
6916 *Misterton Hall*
6917 *Oldlands Hall*
6918 *Sandon Hall*
6919 *Tylney Hall*
6920 *Barningham Hall*
6921 *Borwick Hall*
6922 *Burton Hall*
6923 *Croxteth Hall*
6924 *Grantley Hall*
6925 *Hackness Hall*
6926 *Holkham Hall*
6927 *Lilford Hall*
6928 *Underley Hall*
6929 *Whorlton Hall*
6930 *Aldersey Hall*
6931 *Aldborough Hall*
6932 *Burwarton Hall*
6933 *Birtles Hall*
6934 *Beachamwell Hall*
6935 *Browsholme Hall*
6936 *Breccles Hall*
6937 *Conyngham Hall*
6938 *Corndean Hall*
6939 *Calveley Hall*
6940 *Didlington Hall*
6941 *Fillongley Hall*
6942 *Eshton Hall*
6943 *Farnley Hall*
6944 *Fledborough Hall*
6945 *Glasfryn Hall*
6946 *Heatherden Hall*

6947 *Helmingham Hall*
6948 *Holbrooke Hall*
6950 *Kingthorpe Hall*
6951 *Impney Hall*
6952 *Kimberley Hall*
6953 *Leighton Hall*
6954 *Lotherton Hall*
6955 *Lydcott Hall*
6956 *Mottram Hall*
6957 *Norcliffe Hall*
6958 *Oxburgh Hall*

TOTAL: 173

5MT 6959 4-6-0

"Modified Hall"

Introduced 1944. Hawksworth development of "Hall", with larger superheater, "one-piece" main frames and plate-framed bogie.

Weight
Locomotive: 75 tons 16 cwt
Tender: 46 tons 14 cwt

Boiler pressure
225 lb sq in

Cylinders
(O) $18\frac{1}{2}'' \times 30''$

Driving wheel diameter
6′ 0″

Tractive effort
27,275 lb

Valve gear
Stephenson (piston valves)

6959 *Peatling Hall*
6960 *Raveningham Hall*
6961 *Stedham Hall*
6962 *Soughton Hall*
6963 *Throwley Hall*
6964 *Thornbridge Hall*
6965 *Thirlestaine Hall*
6966 *Witchingham Hall*
6967 *Willesley Hall*
6968 *Woodcock Hall*
6969 *Wraysbury Hall*
6970 *Whaddon Hall*
6971 *Athelhampton Hall*
6972 *Beningbrough Hall*
6973 *Bricklehampton Hall*
6974 *Bryngwyn Hall*
6975 *Capesthorne Hall*
6976 *Graythwaite Hall*
6977 *Grundisburgh Hall*
6978 *Haroldstone Hall*
6979 *Helperly Hall*
6980 *Llanrumney Hall*
6981 *Marbury Hall*
6982 *Melmerby Hall*
6983 *Otterington Hall*
6984 *Owsden Hall*
6985 *Parwick Hall*
6986 *Rydal Hall*
6987 *Shervington Hall*
6988 *Swithland Hall*
6989 *Wightwick Hall*
6990 *Witherslack Hall*
6991 *Acton Burnell Hall*
6992 *Arborfield Hall*
6993 *Arthog Hall*
6994 *Baggrave Hall*
6995 *Benthall Hall*
6996 *Blackwell Hall*
6997 *Bryn-Ivor Hall*
6998 *Burton Agnes Hall*
6999 *Capel Dewi Hall*

Class continued with **7900**

7P 4073 4-6-0

"Castle"

Class continued from 5099

7000† *Viscount Portal*
7001†**Sir James Milne*
7002†**Devizes Castle*
7003†**Elmley Castle*
7004‡**Eastnor Castle*
7005† *Sir Edward Elgar*
7006†**Lydford Castle*
7007†**Great Western*
7008†**Swansea Castle*
7009† *Athelney Castle*
7010†**Avondale Castle*
7011† *Banbury Castle*
7012† *Barry Castle*
7013‡**Bristol Castle*
7014†**Caerhays Castle*
7015†**Carn Brea Castle*
7017† *G. J. Churchward*
7018‡**Drysllwyn Castle*
7019‡**Fowey Castle*
7020†**Gloucester Castle*
7021†**Haverfordwest Castle*
7022‡**Hereford Castle*
7023†**Penrice Castle*
7024‡**Powis Castle*
7025† *Sudeley Castle*
7026† *Tenby Castle*
7027† *Thornbury Castle*
7028†**Cadbury Castle*
7029‡**Clun Castle*
7030‡**Cranbrook Castle*
7031† *Cromwell's Castle*
7032†**Denbigh Castle*
7033†**Hartlebury Castle*
7034‡**Ince Castle*
7035†**Ogmore Castle*
7036‡**Taunton Castle*
7037† *Swindon*

TOTAL: 100

8F 7200 2-8-2T

Introduced 1934. Collett rebuild, with extended bunker and trailing wheels, of Churchward 4200 class 2-8-0T.

Weight
92 tons 2 cwt

Boiler pressure
200 lb sq in

Cylinders
(O) 19″ × 30″

Driving wheel diameter
4′ 7½″

Tractive effort
33,170 lb

Valve gear
Stephenson (piston valves)

7200	7208	7216	7225	7232	7239	7247
7201	7209	7217	7226	7233	7240	7248
7202	7210	7218	7227	7234	7242	7249
7203	7211	7219	7228	7235	7243	7250
7204	7212	7220	7229	7236	7244	7251
7205	7213	7221	7230	7237	7245	7252
7206	7214	7222	7231	7238	7246	7253
7207	7215	7223				

TOTAL: 52

Class 4073 4-6-0 No. 7002 *Devizes Castle* (fitted with double chimney) [*H. Wheeler*

Class 7200 2-8-2T No. 7216 [*N. E. Preedy*

Class 7400 0-6-0PT No. 7413 [*A. W. Martin*

4MT 4300 2-6-0

Class continued from 6395

7303*	7308	7314	7318	7325†	7332†	7337†
7304*	7310	7315	7319	7326†	7333†	7339†
7306	7312	7317	7320	7327†	7335†	7340†
7307						

TOTAL: 67

2F 7400 0-6-0PT

Introduced 1936. Development of Collett 6400 class. Non push-and-pull fitted locomotives.

Weight
Locomotive: 45 tons 9 cwt

Boiler pressure
180 lb sq in NS

Cylinders
16½″ × 24″

Driving wheel diameter
4′ 7½″

Tractive effort
18,010 lb

Valve gear
Stephenson

7403	7412	7423	7430	7436	7442	7446
7404	7413	7424	7431	7437	7443	7448
7405	7414	7426	7432	7439	7444	7449
7407	7418	7427	7435	7441	7445	

TOTAL: 27

3F 5700 0-6-0PT

Class continued from 6777

7780* 7782*

Class continued with 8701

5MT 7800 4-6-0

"Manor"

Introduced 1938. Collett design for secondary lines, incorporating certain parts of withdrawn 4300 2-6-0 locomotives.

Weight
Locomotive: 68 tons 18 cwt
Tender: 40 tons 0 cwt

Boiler pressure
225 lb sq in

Cylinders
(O) 18″ × 30″

Driving wheel diameter
5′ 8″

Tractive effort
27,340 lb

Valve gear
Stephenson (piston valves)

7800 *Torquay Manor*
7801 *Anthony Manor*
7802 *Bradley Manor*
7803 *Barcote Manor*
7804 *Baydon Manor*
7805 *Broome Manor*
7806 *Cockington Manor*
7807 *Compton Manor*
7808 *Cookham Manor*
7809 *Childrey Manor*
7810 *Draycott Manor*
7811 *Dunley Manor*
7812 *Erlestoke Manor*
7813 *Freshford Manor*
7814 *Fringford Manor*
7815 *Fritwell Manor*
7816 *Frilsham Manor*
7817 *Garsington Manor*
7818 *Granville Manor*
7819 *Hinton Manor*
7820 *Dinmore Manor*
7821 *Ditcheat Manor*
7822 *Foxcote Manor*
7823 *Hook Norton Manor*
7824 *Iford Manor*
7825 *Lechlade Manor*
7826 *Longworth Manor*
7827 *Lydham Manor*
7828 *Odney Manor*
7829 *Ramsbury Manor*

TOTAL: 30

5MT 6959 4-6-0

"Modified Hall"

Class continued from 6999

7900 *Saint Peter's Hall*
7901 *Dodington Hall*
7902 *Eaton Mascot Hall*
7903 *Foremarke Hall*
7904 *Fountains Hall*
7905 *Fowey Hall*
7906 *Fron Hall*
7907 *Hart Hall*
7908 *Henshall Hall*
7909 *Heveningham Hall*
7910 *Hown Hall*
7911 *Lady Margaret Hall*
7912 *Little Linford Hall*
7913 *Little Wyrley Hall*
7914 *Lleweni Hall*
7915 *Mere Hall*
7916 *Mobberley Hall*
7917 *North Aston Hall*
7918 *Rhose Wood Hall*
7919 *Runter Hall*
7920 *Coney Hall*
7921 *Edstone Hall*
7922 *Salford Hall*
7923 *Speke Hall*
7924 *Thornycroft Hall*
7925 *Westol Hall*
7926 *Willey Hall*
7927 *Willington Hall*
7928 *Wolf Hall*
7929 *Wyke Hall*

TOTAL: 71

Class 5700 0-6-0PT No. 7780 [R. Puntis

Class 7800 4-6-0 No. 7825 *Lechlade Manor* [H. Wheeler

Class 5700 0-6-0PT No. 9710 (fitted with condensing apparatus) [J. Hodge

4MT 8100 2-6-2T

Introduced 1938. Collett rebuild, with higher pressure and smaller wheels, of Churchward locomotives in 5100 class.

Weight
Locomotive: 76 tons 11 cwt

Boiler pressure
225 lb sq in

Cylinders
(O) 18″ × 30″

Driving wheel diameter
5′ 6″

Tractive effort
28,165 lb

Valve gear
Stephenson (piston valves)

8102 8103 8104 8106 8109

TOTAL: 5

4F 9400 0-6-0PT

Class continued from 3409

8400*	8415*	8433*	8458*	8471*	8480*	8491*
8401*	8418*	8436*	8459*	8472*	8481*	8493*
8402*	8420*	8437*	8461*	8474*	8484*	8495*
8403*	8425*	8444*	8464*	8475*	8486*	8496*
8405*	8426*	8446*	8465*	8478*	8487*	8497*
8409*	8430*	8452*	8466*	8479*	8488*	8498*
8414*	8431*	8456*	8469*			

Class continued with 9401

3F 5700 0-6-0PT

Class continued from 7782

8701*	8714*	8723*	8743*	8752§	8768§	8791§
8702*	8716*	8728*	8745*	8759§	8783§	8793§
8707*	8717*	8732*	8747*	8766§	8785§	8794§
8710*	8718*	8738*	8749*	8767§	8786§	8795§
8712*	8720*	8739*				

Class continued with 9600

4F 9400 0-6-0PT

Class continued from 8498

9401	9412*	9422*	9431*	9444*	9456*	9470*
9404	9413*	9423*	9435*	9446*	9457*	9471*
9405	9415*	9425*	9437*	9450*	9461*	9472*
9406	9418*	9426*	9440*	9452*	9463*	9473*
9408	9419*	9429*	9441*	9453*	9464*	9475*
9411*	9420*	9430*	9442*	9455*	9466*	9477*

9479*	9482*	9484*	9488*	9490*	9494*	9498*
9480*	9483*	9485*	9489*	9493*	9495*	

TOTAL: 108

3F 5700 0-6-0PT

Class continued from 8795

9600§	9621§	9641§	9661§	9681§	9742§	9776§
9601§	9622§	9642§	9662§	9682§	9743§	9777§
9602§	9623§	9644§	9663§	9700‡	9744§	9778§
9603§	9624§	9645§	9664§	9704‡	9746§	9779§
9605§	9625§	9646§	9665§	9706‡	9747§	9780§
9606§	9626§	9647§	9666§	9707‡	9748§	9782§
9607§	9628§	9648§	9667§	9710‡	9752§	9784§
9608§	9629§	9649§	9668§	9711§	9753§	9786§
9609§	9630§	9650§	9669§	9713§	9754§	9787§
9610§	9631§	9651§	9670§	9715§	9755§	9788§
9611§	9632§	9652§	9671§	9716§	9760§	9789§
9612§	9633§	9653§	9672§	9724§	9763§	9790§
9613§	9634§	9654§	9674§	9726§	9764§	9791§
9614§	9635§	9655§	9675§	9729§	9766§	9792§
9615§	9636§	9656§	9676§	9730§	9768§	9793§
9616§	9637§	9657§	9677§	9731§	9769§	9794§
9617§	9638§	9658§	9678§	9732§	9770§	9796§
9618§	9639§	9659§	9679§	9733§	9773§	9798§
9619§	9640§	9660§	9680§	9734§	9774§	9799§
9620§						

TOTAL: 422

LOCOMOTIVE SUPERINTENDENTS AND CHIEF MECHANICAL ENGINEERS

Sir Daniel Gooch	1837–1864
Joseph Armstrong	1854–1864* 1864–1877
George Armstrong (*Bro. of J. Armstrong*) ...	1864–1896*
William Dean	1877–1902
G. J. Churchward	1902–1921
Charles B. Collett	1922–1941
F. W. Hawksworth	1941–1949

* In charge of standard gauge locomotives at Stafford Road Works, Wolverhampton, with wide powers in design and construction.

POWER AND WEIGHT CLASSIFICATION

Since 1920 Western Region locomotives have been classified for power and weight by a letter on a coloured disc on the cab side. The letter represents the power of the locomotive and is approximately proportional to the tractive effort as under:

Power class	*Tractive effort lb.*	*Power class*	*Tractive effort lb.*
E	33,001–38,000	B	18,501–20,500
D	25,001–33,000	A	16,500–18,500
C	20,501–25,000	Ungrouped	Below 16,500

The colour of the circle represents the routes over which the engine may work. Red engines are limited to the main lines and lines capable of carrying the heaviest locomotives; blue engines are allowed over additional routes, yellow engines over nearly the whole system and uncoloured engines are more or less unrestricted.

Class	*Power Class*	*Route Restriction Colour*
4-6-0		
1000	D	Red
4073	D	Red
4900	D	Red
6800	D	Red
6959	D	Red
7800	D	Blue
2-8-0		
2800	E	Blue
4700	D	Red
2-6-0		
4300	D	Blue
0-6-0		
2251	B	Yellow
2-8-2T		
7200	E	Red
2-8-0T		
4200	E	Red

Class	*Power Class*	*Route Restriction Colour*
2-6-2T		
4500	C	Yellow
5101	D	Blue
6100	D	Blue
8100	D	Blue
0-6-2T		
5600	D	Red
0-6-0T		
1366	—	—
1500	C	Red
1600	A	—
5400	—	Yellow
5700	C	Yellow
9700–10	C	Blue
6400	A	Yellow
7400	A	Yellow
9400	C	Red
0-4-2T		
1400	—	—
0-4-0T		
1151	—	—
1338	—	—

Ex-S.R. STEAM LOCOMOTIVES
Nos. 30021-35030
and Isle of Wight Locos 14-36

The numbers of locomotives in service have been checked in S.R. to January 30, 1963, and W.R. to January 12, 1963.

NOTE: Certain Southern classes are not numbered in a continuous numerical sequence. For the sake of clarity therefore, some locomotives are shown out of numerical order.

2P M7 0-4-4T

Introduced 1897. Drummond L.S.W. M7 design. Some locomotives originally Drummond X14 design, with increased front overhang, steam reverser and detail alterations, now classified M7 (30254 originally M7).
* Introduced 1925. Fitted for push-and-pull working.

Weight
Locomotive: 60 tons 4 cwt
62 tons 0 cwt*

Boiler pressure
175 lb sq in NS

Cylinders
18½" × 26"

Driving wheel diameter
5' 7"

Tractive effort
19,755 lb

Valve gear
Stephenson

30021*	30032	30048*	30057*	30111*	30241	30328*
30024	30034	30052*	30105*	30112	30249	30379*
30025	30035	30053*	30107*	30127	30251	30480*
30029*	30036	30055*	30108*	30129*	30254	30667*
30031*	30039	30056*	30110*	30133*	30320	30670

TOTAL: 35

3F USA 0-6-0T

Introduced 1942. U.S. Army Transportation Corps design, purchased by S.R. 1946, and fitted with modified cab and bunker and other detail alterations.

Weight
Locomotive: 46 tons 10 cwt

Boiler pressure
210 lb sq in NS

Cylinders
(O) 16½" × 24"

Driving wheel diameter
4' 6"

Tractive effort
21,600 lb

Valve gear
Walschaerts (piston valves)

30064	30068	30069	30071	30072	30073	30074
30067						

See also Departmental Locomotives

TOTAL: 11

Class USA 0-6-0T No. 30067 [*J. C. Haydon*

Class M7 0-4-4T No. 30105 (fitted with push-pull apparatus) [*P. J. Hughes*

Class M7 0-4-4T No. 30251 [*L. W. P. Reeves*

1F B4 0-4-0T

Introduced 1891. Adams L.S.W. design for dock shunting.

Weight
Locomotive: 33 tons 9 cwt

Boiler pressure
140 lb sq in NS

Cylinders
(O) 16″ × 22″

Driving wheel diameter
3′ 9¾″

Tractive effort
14,650 lb

Valve gear
Stephenson

30089 30096 30102

TOTAL: 3

6F S15 4-6-0

Introduced 1920. Urie L.S.W. design, development of N15 for mixed traffic work.
* Introduced 1927. Maunsell design, with higher boiler pressure, smaller grate, modified footplating and other detail differences. 30833–7 with 6-wheel tenders for Central Section.
† Introduced 1936. Later locomotives with detail differences and reduced weight.

Weight
Locomotive: 79 tons 16 cwt
80 tons 14 cwt*
79 tons 5 cwt†

Boiler pressure
180 lb sq in
200 lb sq in*†

Cylinders
(O) 21″ × 28″
(O) 20½″ × 28″*†

Driving wheel diameter
5′ 7″

Tractive effort
28,200 lb
29,855 lb*†

Valve gear
Walschaerts (piston valves)

30496	30503	30511	30824*	30831*	30837*	30843†
30497	30506	30512	30825*	30832*	30838†	30844†
30498	30507	30513	30827*	30833*	30839†	30845†
30499	30508	30514	30828*	30834*	30840†	30846†
30500	30509	30515	30829*	30835*	30841†	30847†
30501	30510	30823*	30830*	30836*	30842†	

TOTAL: 41

4F Q 0-6-0

Introduced 1938. Maunsell design, later fitted with multiple-jet blastpipe and large-diameter chimney.
* Subsequently fitted with single chimney.

Right:
Class B4 0-4-0T No. 30096
[*L. Nicolson*

Centre:
Class Q 0-6-0 No. 30531
[*P. J. Hughes*

Bottom:
Class Q 0-6-0 No. 30543 (fitted with B.R. chimney)
[*R. S. Greenwood*

Class S15 4-6-0 No. 30503 [P. H. Groom

Class S15 4-6-0 No. 30829 (with detail differences) [P J. Cupper

Class S15 4-6-0 No. 30843 (further development with detail alterations and modified tender design) [M. G. Martin

Weight
Locomotive: 49 tons 10 cwt

Boiler pressure
200 lb sq in

Cylinders
19″ × 26″

Driving wheel diameter
5′ 1″

Tractive effort
26,160 lb

Valve gear
Stephenson (piston valves)

30530*	30533	30538*	30542	30544	30546	30548
30531	30535	30541	30543*	30545*	30547*	30549*
30532	30536*					

TOTAL: 16

1P H 0-4-4T

Introduced 1904. Wainwright S.E.C. design. Fitted since 1949 for push-and-pull working.

Weight
Locomotive: 54 tons 8 cwt

Boiler pressure
160 lb sq in NS

Cylinders
18″ × 26″

Driving wheel diameter
5′ 6″

Tractive effort
17,360 lb

Valve gear
Stephenson

31005	31263	31518	31543	31544	31551

TOTAL: 6

4P5F N 2-6-0

Introduced 1917. Maunsell S.E.C. mixed traffic design.

Weight
Locomotive: 61 tons 4 cwt

Boiler pressure
200 lb sq in

Cylinders
(O) 19″ × 28″

Driving wheel diameter
5′ 6″

Tractive effort
26,035 lb

Valve gear
Walschaerts (piston valves)

31400	31413	31820	31832	31843	31854	31865
31401	31810	31821	31833	31844	31855	31866
31402	31811	31823	31834	31845	31856	31867
31403	31812	31824	31835	31846	31857	31868
31404	31813	31825	31836	31847	31858	31869
31405	31814	31826	31837	31848	31859	31870
31406	31815	31827	31838	31849	31860	31871
31407	31816	31828	31839	31850	31861	31872
31408	31817	31829	31840	31851	31862	31873
31410	31818	31830	31841	31852	31863	31874
31411	31819	31831	31842	31853	31864	31875
31412						

TOTAL: 78

4P3F U 2-6-0

Introduced 1928. Rebuild of Maunsell S.E.C. Class K ("River") 2-6-4T (introduced 1917).
* Introduced 1928. Locomotives built as Class U, with smaller splashers and detail alterations.

Weight
Locomotive: 63 tons
62 tons 6 cwt*

Boiler pressure
200 lb sq in

Cylinders
(O) 19″ × 28″

Driving wheel diameter
6′ 0″

Tractive effort
23,865 lb

Valve gear
Walschaerts (piston valves)

31611* 31618* 31625* 31633* 31790 31797 31804
31612* 31619* 31626* 31634* 31791 31798 31805
31613* 31620* 31627* 31635* 31792 31799 31806
31614* 31621* 31628* 31636* 31793 31800 31807
31615* 31622* 31629* 31637* 31794 31801 31808
31616* 31623* 31631* 31638* 31795 31802 31809
31617* 31624* 31632* 31639* 31796 31803

TOTAL: 48

4P3F U1 2-6-0

Introduced 1928. 3-cylinder development of Maunsell Class U (prototype 31890, originally built 1925 as 2-6-4T and subsequently rebuilt).

Weight
Locomotive: 65 tons 6 cwt

Boiler pressure
200 lb sq in

Cylinders
Three, 16″ × 28″

Driving wheel diameter
6′ 0″

Tractive effort
25,385 lb

Valve gear
Walschaerts (piston valves)

31890 31891 31901 31910

TOTAL: 4

6F W 2-6-4T

Introduced 1931. Maunsell design, developed from Class N1 2-6-0.

Weight
Locomotive: 90 tons 14 cwt

Boiler pressure
200 lb sq in

Cylinders
Three, $16\frac{1}{2}$″ × 28″

Driving wheel diameter
5′ 6″

Tractive effort
29,450 lb

Valve gear
Walschaerts (piston valves)

31911 31914 31916 31918 31920 31922 31924
31912 31915 31917 31919 31921 31923 31925
31913

TOTAL: 15

Class U 2-6-0 No. 31802 [*L. King*

Class N 2-6-0 No. 31831 [*J. Davenport*

Class U1 2-6-0 No. 31891 [*P. J. Cupper*

Left:
Class H 0-4-4T
No. 31005
[D. L. Perciv

Centre:
Class W 2-6-4T
No. 31922
[L. Els

Bottom:
Class E2 0-6-0T
No. 32109
[L. Ki

3F E2 0-6-0T

Introduced 1913. L. B. Billinton L.B.S.C. design.
* Introduced 1915. Later locomotive with tanks extended further forward.

Weight
Locomotive: 52 tons 15 cwt
53 tons 10 cwt*

Boiler pressure
170 lb sq in NS

Cylinders
$17\frac{1}{2}'' \times 26''$

Driving wheel diameter
4′ 6″

Tractive effort
21,305 lb

Valve gear
Stephenson

32104 32109*

TOTAL: 2

2MT E4 0-6-2T

Introduced 1897. R. J. Billinton L.B.S.C. design, development of E3 with larger wheels, reboilered with Marsh boiler and extended smokebox, cylinder diameter reduced from 18″ by S.R.

Weight
Locomotive: 57 tons 10 cwt

Boiler pressure
170 lb sq in NS

Cylinders
$17\frac{1}{2}'' \times 26''$

Driving wheel diameter
5′ 0″

Tractive effort
19,175 lb

Valve gear
Stephenson

32474 32479 32503

TOTAL: 3

0P A1X 0-6-0T

Introduced 1911. Rebuild of Stroudley L.B.S.C. "Terrier" A1 with Marsh boiler and extended smokebox.
* Locomotive with increased cylinder diameter.

Weight
Locomotive: 28 tons 5 cwt

Boiler pressure
150 lb sq in NS

Cylinders
12″ × 20″
$14\frac{3}{16}'' \times 20''$*

Driving wheel diameter
4′ 0″

Tractive effort
7,650 lb
10,695 lb*

Valve gear
Stephenson

32635 32640 32650 32661 32662 32670 32678
32636* 32646

See also Departmental Locomotives

TOTAL: 10

5F Q1 0-6-0

Introduced 1942. Bulleid "Austerity" design.

Weight
Locomotive: 51 tons 5 cwt

Boiler pressure
230 lb sq in

Cylinders
19″ × 26″

Driving wheel diameter
5′ 1″

Tractive effort
30,080 lb

Valve gear
Stephenson (piston valves)

33001	33007	33013	33019	33025	33031	33036
33002	33008	33014	33020	33026	33032	33037
33003	33009	33015	33021	33027	33033	33038
33004	33010	33016	33022	33028	33034	33039
33005	33011	33017	33023	33029	33035	33040
33006	33012	33018	33024	33030		

TOTAL: 40

7P5F, 7P6F* WC & BB 4-6-2

† Introduced 1945. Bulleid "West Country" class, with Bulleid valve gear.

‡ Introduced 1946. Bulleid "Battle of Britain" class, with Bulleid valve gear.

* Introduced 1957. Rebuilt with Walschaerts valve gear, modified details and air-smoothed casing removed.

§ Introduced 1962. Fitted with Giesl oblong ejector.

Weight
Locomotive: 86 tons†‡
90 tons 1 cwt*

Boiler pressure
250 lb sq in

Cylinders
Three, $16\frac{3}{8}$″ × 24″

Driving wheel diameter
6′ 2″

Tractive effort
27,715 lb

Valve gear
Bulleid (piston valves)†‡
Walschaerts (piston valves)*

34001†*_Exeter_
34002† _Salisbury_
34003†*_Plymouth_
34004†*_Yeovil_
34005†*_Barnstaple_
34006† _Bude_
34007† _Wadebridge_
34008†*_Padstow_
34009†*_Lyme Regis_
34010†*_Sidmouth_
34011† _Tavistock_
34012†*_Launceston_
34013†*_Okehampton_
34014†*_Budleigh Salterton_
34015† _Exmouth_
34016†*_Bodmin_
34017†*_Ilfracombe_
34018†*_Axminster_
34019† _Bideford_
34020† _Seaton_
34021†*_Dartmoor_
34022†*_Exmoor_
34023† _Blackmore Vale_
34024†*_Tamar Valley_

Right:
Class E4 0-6-2T
No. 32503
[*Alan Williams*

Centre:
Class A1X 0-6-0T
No. 32635 (in Brighton Works livery)
[*R. K. Evans*

Bottom:
Class A1X 0-6-0T
No. 32646
[*L. W. P. Reeves*

Rebuilt Class WC 4-6-2 No. 34005 *Barnstaple* [*B. Stephenson*

Class BB 4-6-2 No. 34064 *Fighter Command* (fitted with Giesl oblong ejector) [*B. Stephenson*

Class MN 4-6-2 No. 35022 *Holland America Line* [*M. Pope*

34025†**Whimple*
34026†**Yes Tor*
34027†**Taw Valley*
34028†**Eddystone*
34029†**Lundy*
34030† *Watersmeet*
34031†**Torrington*
34032†**Camelford*
34033† *Chard*
34034†**Honiton*
34035† *Shaftesbury*
34036†**Westward Ho*
34037†**Clovelly*
34038† *Lynton*
34039†**Boscastle*
34040†**Crewkerne*
34041† *Wilton*
34042†**Dorchester*
34043† *Combe Martin.*
34044†**Woolacombe*
34045†**Ottery St. Mary*
34046†**Braunton*
34047†**Callington*
34048†**Crediton*
34049‡ *Anti-Aircraft Command*
34050‡**Royal Observer Corps*
34051‡ *Winston Churchill*
34052‡**Lord Dowding*
34053‡**Sir Keith Park*
34054‡ *Lord Beaverbrook*
34055‡ *Fighter Pilot*
34056‡**Croydon*
34057‡ *Biggin Hill*
34058‡**Sir Frederick Pile*
34059‡**Sir Archibald Sinclair*
34060‡*25 *Squadron*
34061‡ 73 *Squadron*
34062‡*17 *Squadron*
34063‡ 229 *Squadron*
34064‡§*Fighter Command*
34065‡ *Hurricane*
34066‡ *Spitfire*
34067‡ *Tangmere*
34068‡ *Kenley*
34069‡ *Hawkinge*
34070‡ *Manston*
34071‡*601 *Squadron*
34072‡ 257 *Squadron*
34073‡ 249 *Squadron*
34074‡ 46 *Squadron*
34075‡ 264 *Squadron*
34076‡ 41 *Squadron*
34077‡*603 *Squadron*
34078‡ 222 *Squadron*
34079‡ 141 *Squadron*
34080‡ 74 *Squadron*
34081‡ 92 *Squadron*
34082‡*615 *Squadron*
34083‡ 605 *Squadron*
34084‡ 253 *Squadron*
34085‡*501 *Squadron*
34086‡ 219 *Squadron*
34087‡*145 *Squadron*
34088‡*213 *Squadron*
34089‡*602 *Squadron*
34090‡**Sir Eustace Missenden, Southern Railway*
34091† *Weymouth*
34092† *City of Wells*
34093†**Saunton*
34094† *Mortehoe*
34095†**Brentor*
34096†**Trevone*
34097†**Holsworthy*
34098†**Templecombe*
34099† *Lynmouth*
34100†**Appledore*
34101†**Hartland*
34102† *Lapford*
34103† *Calstock*
34104†**Bere Alston*
34105† *Swanage*
34106† *Lydford*
34107† *Blandford Forum*
34108†**Wincanton*
34109‡**Sir Trafford Leigh-Mallory*
34110‡ 66 *Squadron*

TOTAL: 110

8P MN 4-6-2

Introduced 1941. Bulleid design originally with 280 lb. pressure, multiple-jet blastpipe and Bulleid valve gear. Rebuilt since 1956 with Walschaerts valve gear and modified details; air-smoothed casing removed.

Weight
Locomotive: 97 tons 18 cwt

Boiler pressure
250 lb sq in

Cylinders
Three, 18″ × 24″

Driving wheel diameter
6′ 2″

Tractive effort
33,495 lb

Valve gear
Walschaerts (piston valves)

35001 *Channel Packet*
35002 *Union Castle*
35003 *Royal Mail*
35004 *Cunard White Star*
35005 *Canadian Pacific*
35006 *Peninsular & Oriental S.N. Co.*
35007 *Aberdeen Commonwealth*
35008 *Orient Line*
35009 *Shaw Savill*
35010 *Blue Star*
35011 *General Steam Navigation*
35012 *United States Lines*
35013 *Blue Funnel*
35014 *Nederland Line*
35015 *Rotterdam Lloyd*
35016 *Elders Fyffes*
35017 *Belgian Marine*
35018 *British India Line*
35019 *French Line CGT*
35020 *Bibby Line*
35021 *New Zealand Line*
35022 *Holland-America Line*
35023 *Holland-Afrika Line*
35024 *East Asiatic Company*
35025 *Brocklebank Line*
35026 *Lamport & Holt Line*
35027 *Port Line*
35028 *Clan Line*
35029 *Ellerman Lines*
35030 *Elder Dempster Lines*

TOTAL: 30

ISLE OF WIGHT LOCOMOTIVES

0P O2 0-4-4T

Introduced 1889. Adams L.S.W. design. Fitted with Westinghouse brake for I.O.W. in 1923. Bunkers enlarged from 1932.

Weight
Locomotive: 48 tons 8 cwt

Boiler pressure
160 lb sq in NS

Cylinders
$17\frac{1}{2}$″ × 24″

Driving wheel diameter
4′ 10″

Tractive effort
17,235 lb

Valve gear
Stephenson

Class Q1 0-6-0 No. 33011 [*Alan Williams*

Class O2 0-4-4T No. 30 *Shorwell* [*K. R. Pirt*

Class T9 4-4-0 No. 120 (restored to L.S.W.R. livery) [*C. F. Verrall*

14	*Fishbourne*	27	*Merstone*
16	*Ventnor*	28	*Ashey*
17	*Seaview*	29	*Alverstone*
18	*Ningwood*	30	*Shorwell*
20	*Shanklin*	31	*Chale*
21	*Sandown*	32	*Bonchurch*
22	*Brading*	33	*Bembridge*
24	*Calbourne*	35	*Freshwater*
26	*Whitwell*	36	*Carisbrooke*

TOTAL: 18

PRESERVED LOCOMOTIVE IN WORKING ORDER

3P T9 4-4-0

Introduced 1899. Drummond L.S.W. design, fitted with superheater and larger cylinders by Urie from 1922. Withdrawn 1962 as B.R. No. 30120, and restored to pre-grouping condition. Later returned to service for special use.

Weight
Locomotive: 51 tons 18 cwt

Boiler pressure
175 lb sq in

Cylinders
19″ × 26″

Driving wheel diameter
6′ 7″

Tractive effort
17,675 lb

Valve gear
Stephenson

120

DEPARTMENTAL LOCOMOTIVES

Former running number in brackets

3F USA 0-6-0T

For details see 30064-74

DS233 (30061) DS234 (30062) DS235 (30066)

0P A1X 0-6-0T

For details see 32635-78

DS681(659)

2F G6 0-6-0T

Introduced 1894. Adams L.S.W. design, later additions by Drummond, but with Adams type boiler.

Weight
47 tons 13 cwt

Boiler pressure
160 lb sq in NS

Cylinders
$17\frac{1}{2}'' \times 24''$

Driving Wheels
4′ 10″

Tractive effort
17,235 lb

Valve gear
Stephenson

DS682 (30238)

TOTAL: 1

2F C 0-6-0

Introduced 1900. Wainwright S.E.C. design.

Weight
Locomotive: 43 tons 16 cwt

Boiler pressure
160 lb sq in NS

Cylinders
$18\frac{1}{2}'' \times 26''$

Driving wheel diameter
5′ 2″

Tractive effort
19,520 lb

Valve gear
Stephenson

(although now in Departmental stock, these locomotives still retain their former running numbers)

31271 31280 31592

TOTAL: 3

LOCOMOTIVE SUPERINTENDENTS AND CHIEF MECHANICAL ENGINEERS

LONDON & SOUTH WESTERN RAILWAY

J. Woods	1835–1841
J. V. Gooch	1841–1850
J. Beattie...	1850–1871
W. G. Beattie	1871–1878
W. Adams	1878–1895
D. Drummond	1895–1912
R. W. Urie	1912–1922

LONDON, BRIGHTON AND SOUTH COAST RAILWAY

—. Statham	?–1845
J. Gray	1845–1847
S. Kirtley	1847
J. C. Craven	1847–1869
W. Stroudley	1870–1889
R. J. Billinton	1890–1904
D. Earle Marsh	1905–1911
L. B. Billinton	1911–1922

SOUTH EASTERN RAILWAY

B. Cubitt..	1842–1845
J. Cudworth	1845–1876
A. M. Watkin	1876
R. Mansell	1877–1878
J. Stirling	1878–1898

LONDON, CHATHAM & DOVER RAILWAY

W. Cubitt	1853–1860
W. Martley	1860–1874
W. Kirtley	1874–1898

SOUTH EASTERN & CHATHAM RAILWAY

H. S. Wainwright	1899–1913
R. E. L. Maunsell	1913–1922

SOUTHERN RAILWAY

R. E. L. Maunsell	1923–1937
O. V. Bulleid	1937–1949

EX-L.M.S. STEAM LOCOMOTIVES
Nos. 41200-58182

The numbers of locomotives in service have been checked in L.M.R. to December 29, 1962, E. & N.E.R. to January 12, 1963, Sc.R. to January 19, 1963, S.R. to January 7, 1963, and W.R. to January 12, 1963.

2MT — 2-6-2T

Introduced 1946. Ivatt L.M.S. taper boiler design.

Weight
63 tons 5 cwt

Boiler pressure
200 lb sq in

Cylinders
(O) 16" × 24"
(O) 16½" × 24"*

Driving wheel diameter
5' 0"

Tractive effort
17,410 lb
18,510 lb*

Valve gear
Walschaerts (piston valves)

41200	41216	41232	41253	41284	41300*	41315*
41201	41217	41233	41260	41285	41301*	41316*
41202	41218	41234	41261	41286	41302*	41317*
41203	41219	41237	41262	41287	41303*	41318*
41204	41220	41238	41264	41289	41304*	41319*
41205	41221	41239	41268	41290*	41305*	41320*
41206	41222	41240	41270	41291*	41306*	41321*
41207	41223	41241	41272	41292*	41307*	41322*
41208	41224	41242	41273	41293*	41308*	41323*
41209	41225	41243	41274	41294*	41309*	41324*
41210	41226	41244	41275	41295*	41310*	41325*
41211	41227	41245	41276	41296*	41311*	41326*
41212	41228	41248	41279	41297*	41312*	41327*
41213	41229	41249	41281	41298*	41313*	41328*
41214	41230	41250	41282	41299*	41314*	41329*
41215	41231	41251	41283			

TOTAL: 109

OF — 0-4-0T

Introduced 1907. Deeley Midland design.

Weight
32 tons 16 cwt

Boiler pressure
160 lb sq in NS

Cylinders
(O) 15" × 22"

Driving wheel diameter
3' 9¾"

Tractive effort
14,635 lb

Valve gear
Walschaerts

41528 41531 41533 41535 41537

TOTAL: 5

Ivatt Class 2MT 2-6-2T No. 41266 [*J. K. Morton*

Class 0F 0-4-0T No. 41537 [*P. J. C. Skelton*

1F 0-6-0T

Introduced 1878. Johnson Midland design. Rebuilt with Belpaire firebox.

Weight
39 tons 11 cwt

Boiler pressure
140 lb sq in NS

Cylinders
17″ × 24″

Driving wheel diameter
4′ 7″

Tractive effort
15,005 lb

Valve gear
Stephenson

41708	41734	41763	41804	41835	41844	41875
41712	41739					

TOTAL: 9

4MT 2-6-4T

Introduced 1945. Fairburn development of Stanier design with shorter wheelbase and detail alterations.

Weight
85 tons 5 cwt

Boiler pressure
200 lb sq in·

Cylinders
(O) 19⅝″ × 26″

Driving wheel diameter
5′ 9″

Tractive effort
24,670 lb

Valve gear
Walschaerts (piston valves)

42050	42073	42099	42125	42151	42179	42206
42051	42074	42100	42126	42152	42180	42208
42052	42075	42101	42127	42153	42181	42209
42053	42076	42102	42128	42154	42182	42210
42054	42077	42103	42129	42155	42183	42212
42055	42078	42104	42131	42156	42184	42213
42056	42079	42105	42132	42157	42185	42214
42057	42080	42106	42133	42158	42186	42216
42058	42081	42107	42134	42159	42187	42218
42059	42082	42108	42135	42160	42188	42221
42060	42083	42109	42136	42161	42189	42222
42061	42084	42110	42137	42163	42190	42224
42062	42085	42112	42138	42165	42192	42225
42063	42086	42113	42139	42166	42194	42226
42064	42087	42114	42140	42167	42195	42228
42065	42089	42115	42141	42168	42196	42229
42066	42090	42116	42142	42169	42197	42230
42067	42091	42118	42143	42170	42198	42231
42068	42092	42119	42145	42171	42199	42232
42069	42093	42120	42147	42174	42200	42233
42070	42095	42121	42148	42176	42201	42234
42071	42096	42123	42149	42177	42202	42235
42072	42098	42124	42150	42178	42204	42236

Class 1F 0-6-0T No. 41712 [G. W. *Mcrrison*

Fowler Class 4MT 2-6-4T No. 42343 [*D. L. Percival*

42238	42246	42259	42267	42277	42284	42292
42239	42247	42260	42269	42278	42285	42293
42240	42249	42261	42270	42279	42286	42294
42241	42250	42262	42271	42280	42287	42295
42242	42251	42263	42273	42281	42288	42296
42243	42252	42264	42274	42282	42289	42297
42244	42253	42265	42275	42283	42291	42299
42245	42256	42266				

Class continued with 42673

4MT 2-6-4T

Introduced 1927. Fowler L.M.S. parallel boiler design.

* Introduced 1933. Fitted with side window cab and doors.

Weight
86 tons 5 cwt

Boiler pressure
200 lb sq in

Cylinders
(O) 19″ × 26″

Driving wheel diameter
5′ 9″

Tractive effort
23,125 lb

Valve gear
Walschaerts (piston valves)

42301	42322	42339	42361	42381	42401*	42413*
42309	42327	42343	42366	42384	42405*	42414*
42310	42333	42350	42368	42389	42406*	42416*
42311	42334	42353	42369	42391	42408*	42417*
42313	42335	42355	42374	42392	42409*	42419*
42316	42337	42357	42378	42394	42410*	42421*
42317	42338	42359	42379	42400*	42411*	42424*
42319						

TOTAL: 50

4MT 2-6-4T

Introduced 1935. Stanier taper-boiler design.

Weight
87 tons 17 cwt

Boiler pressure
200 lb sq in

Cylinders
(O) $19\frac{5}{8}$″ × 26″

Driving wheel diameter
5′ 9″

Tractive effort
24,670 lb

Valve gear
Walschaerts (piston valves)

42425	42436	42445	42456	42464	42478	42487
42426	42437	42446	42458	42465	42480	42488
42430	42439	42447	42459	42466	42481	42489
42431	42440	42449	42460	42468	42482	42491
42432	42441	42451	42461	42469	42484	42492
42434	42442	42453	42462	42474	42485	42493
42435	42444	42455	42463	42477	42486	42494

Fowler Class 4MT 2-6-4T No. 42414 (with side window cab) [*A. W. Martin*

Stanier Class 4MT 2-6-4T No. 42646 [*P. H. Groom*

Fairburn Class 4MT 2-6-4T No. 42697 [*J. E. Wilkinson*

42542	42561	42582	42602	42617	42633	42654
42543	42562	42583	42603	42618	42634	42655
42546	42563	42584	42604	42619	42636	42656
42547	42564	42586	42605	42620	42639	42657
42548	42565	42587	42606	42622	42640	42659
42550	42566	42588	42607	42623	42643	42660
42551	42567	42589	42608	42625	42644	42662
42554	42569	42590	42609	42626	42645	42663
42555	42571	42592	42610	42628	42647	42664
42556	42572	42594	42611	42629	42649	42665
42557	42573	42595	42612	42630	42650	42667
42558	42574	42597	42613	42631	42651	42668
42559	42577	42598	42614	42632	42652	42670
42560	42581	42601	42616			

TOTAL : 144

4MT 2-6-4T

Class continued from 42299

42673	42680	42686	42690	42694	42696	42698
42675	42681	42688	42691	42695	42697	42699
42676	42682	42689	42693			

TOTAL: 231

5MT 2-6-0

Introduced 1926. Hughes L.M.S. design built under Fowler's direction.

Weight
Locomotive: 66 tons 0 cwt

Boiler pressure
180 lb sq in

Cylinders
(O) 21″ × 26′

Driving wheel diameter
5′ 6″

Tractive effort
26,580 lb

Valve gear
Walschaerts (piston valves)

42700	42711	42727	42738	42755	42768	42783
42701	42712	42728	42739	42756	42769	42785
42702	42715	42729	42740	42757	42770	42787
42703	42716	42730	42741	42758	42771	42788
42704	42717	42731	42746	42759	42772	42789
42705	42718	42732	42747	42760	42774	42790
42706	42719	42733	42748	42761	42776	42791
42707	42721	42734	42750	42762	42777	42792
42708	42722	42735	42751	42763	42778	42793
42709	42723	42736	42753	42765	42780	42794
42710	42725	42737	42754	42767	42782	42795

Hughes-Fowler Class 5MT 2-6-0 No. 42802 [*D. A. Anderson*

Stanier Class 5MT 2-6-0 No. 42969 [*G. W. Morrison*

Ivatt Class 4MT 2-6-0 No. 43003 [*J. B. Bucknall*

42796	42817	42843	42861	42890	42910	42928
42798	42819	42844	42863	42892	42911	42931
42799	42820	42845	42865	42894	42912	42932
42800	42821	42846	42867	42895	42913	42933
42801	42823	42848	42869	42896	42914	42934
42802	42826	42849	42870	42897	42916	42935
42803	42827	42851	42871	42898	42917	42936
42805	42828	42852	42872	42900	42919	42937
42806	42831	42853	42873	42901	42920	42938
42810	42832	42854	42878	42902	42921	42940
42812	42838	42855	42879	42904	42922	42941
42813	42839	42856	42880	42905	42923	42942
42814	42840	42858	42885	42907	42924	42943
42815	42841	42859	42886	42908	42925	42944
42816	42842	42860	42888	42909	42926	

TOTAL: 181

5MT 2-6-0

Introduced 1933. Stanier L.M.S. taper boiler design, some with safety valves mounted on the top feed.

Weight
Locomotive: 69 tons 2 cwt

Boiler pressure
225 lb sq in

Cylinders
(O) 18″ × 28″

Driving wheel diameter
5′ 6″

Tractive effort
26,290 lb

Valve gear
Walschaerts (piston valves)

42945	42951	42957	42963	42969	42975	42980
42946	42952	42958	42964	42970	42976	42981
42947	42953	42959	42965	42971	42977	42982
42948	42954	42960	42966	42972	42978	42983
42949	42955	42961	42967	42973	42979	42984
42950	42956	42962	42968	42974		

TOTAL: 40

4MT 2-6-0

Introduced 1947. Ivatt L.M.S. taper boiler design with double chimney. Later engines introduced with single chimney with which earlier engines have been rebuilt.

Weight
Locomotive: 59 tons 2 cwt

Boiler pressure
225 lb sq in

Cylinders
(O) 17½″ × 26″

Driving wheel diameter
5′ 3″

Tractive effort
24,170 lb

Valve gear
Walschaerts (piston valves)

43000	43024	43047	43070	43093	43116	43139
43001	43025	43048	43071	43094	43117	43140
43002	43026	43049	43072	43095	43118	43141
43003	43027	43050	43073	43096	43119	43142
43004	43028	43051	43074	43097	43120	43143
43005	43029	43052	43075	43098	43121	43144
43006	43030	43053	43076	43099	43122	43145
43007	43031	43054	43077	43100	43123	43146
43008	43032	43055	43078	43101	43124	43147
43009	43033	43056	43079	43102	43125	43148
43010	43034	43057	43080	43103	43126	43149
43011	43035	43058	43081	43104	43127	43150
43012	43036	43059	43082	43105	43128	43151
43013	43037	43060	43083	43106	43129	43152
43014	43038	43061	43084	43107	43130	43153
43015	43039	43062	43085	43108	43131	43154
43016	43040	43063	43086	43109	43132	43155
43017	43041	43064	43087	43110	43133	43156
43018	43042	43065	43088	43111	43134	43157
43019	43043	43066	43089	43112	43135	43158
43020	43044	43067	43090	43113	43136	43159
43021	43045	43068	43091	43114	43137	43160
43022	43046	43069	43092	43115	43138	43161
43023						

TOTAL: 162

3F 0-6-0

Introduced 1885. Johnson Midland locomotives rebuilt from 1916 by Fowler with Belpaire firebox.

Weight
Locomotive: 43 tons 17 cwt

Boiler pressure
175 lb sq in NS

Cylinders
18″ × 26″

Driving wheel diameter
5′ 3″

Tractive effort
19,890 lb

Valve gear
Stephenson

43342	43453	43521	43620	43637	43658	43669

TOTAL: 7

4F 0-6-0

Introduced 1911. Fowler superheated Midland design.

Weight
Locomotive: 48 tons 15 cwt

Boiler pressure
175 lb sq in

Cylinders
20″ × 26″

Driving wheel diameter
5′ 3″

Tractive effort
24,555 lb

Valve gear
Stephenson (piston valves)

Ex-Midland (Johnson) Class 3F 0-6-0 No. 43658 [J. C. Haydon

Ex-Midland Class 4F 0-6-0 No. 44022 [J. E. Wilkinson

Class 4F 0-6-0 No. 44475 [A. W. Martin

43845	43882	43918	43945	43960	43979	44003
43850	43885	43923	43947	43963	43981	44007
43853	43887	43924	43949	43964	43982	44009
43854	43888	43925	43950	43967	43983	44010
43855	43893	43928	43951	43968	43986	44012
43856	43903	43929	43952	43969	43987	44013
43861	43906	43931	43953	43971	43988	44015
43865	43908	43935	43954	43972	43991	44022
43870	43913	43937	43955	43975	43994	44023
43871	43915	43940	43957S	43976	43995	44025
43880	43917	43942	43958	43977	43999	44026

TOTAL: 77

4F — 0-6-0

Introduced 1924. Post-grouping development of Midland design with reduced boiler mountings.

* Introduced 1922. Locomotives built for S. & D.J. to Midland design (taken into L.M.S. stock 1930).

Weight
Locomotive: 48 tons 15 cwt

Boiler pressure
175 lb sq in

Cylinders
20″ × 26″

Driving wheel diameter
5′ 3″

Tractive effort
24,555 lb

Valve gear
Stephenson (piston valves)

44027	44051	44076	44101	44127	44160	44182
44028	44053	44078	44102	44130	44162	44183
44030	44054	44079	44106	44131	44164	44184
44034	44055	44080	44109	44132	44165	44185
44035	44056	44081	44110	44133	44167	44186
44038	44057	44083	44112	44134	44168	44188
44039	44059	44085	44113	44135	44169	44190
44040	44060	44086	44114	44137	44170	44191
44041	44061	44089	44115	44139	44171	44192
44042	44063	44091	44117	44146	44172	44195
44043	44065	44092	44118	44149	44174	44197
44044	44066	44094	44119	44150	44176	44200
44045	44068	44096	44121	44151	44177	44202
44046	44069	44097	44123	44153	44178	44203
44047	44071	44098	44124	44155	44179	44205
44048	44074	44099	44125	44156	44180	44207
44049	44075	44100	44126	44157	44181	44208

44209	44266	44333	44390	44446	44500	44558*
44210	44268	44334	44392	44447	44501	44559*
44211	44269	44335	44394	44448	44504	44560*
44212	44270	44336	44395	44449	44505	44562
44213	44271	44337	44396	44450	44512	44564
44214	44272	44339	44398	44451	44514	44565
44215	44274	44341	44399	44452	44516	44566
44218	44275	44342	44400	44454	44517	44567
44219	44276	44344	44401	44455	44519	44568
44220	44277	44345	44402	44456	44520	44569
44221	44278	44346	44403	44457	44522	44570
44222	44279	44347	44405	44458	44523	44571
44223	44280	44348	44408	44460	44524	44572
44226	44282	44349	44411	44461	44525	44574
44229	44284	44350	44413	44462	44526	44575
44231	44286	44351	44414	44463	44527	44577
44232	44287	44352	44416	44464	44528	44578
44233	44288	44353	44418	44465	44529	44580
44235	44289	44354	44419	44466	44530	44581
44236	44290	44355	44420	44467	44531	44582
44237	44292	44356	44421	44468	44532	44583
44238	44294	44358	44422	44469	44533	44584
44239	44295	44359	44424	44470	44534	44586
44240	44296	44362	44425	44472	44535	44587
44241	44297	44363S	44426	44475	44536	44588
44242	44299	44364	44428	44476	44538	44589
44243	44300	44367	44429	44478	44539	44591
44244	44301	44370	44431	44479	44540	44592
44246	44302	44373S	44432	44481	44541	44593
44247	44303	44374S	44433	44484	44542	44595
44248	44304	44376	44434	44485	44543	44596
44250	44305	44377	44436	44486	44544	44597
44252	44308	44378	44437	44489	44545	44598
44259	44309	44379	44439	44490	44548	44599
44260	44310	44380	44440	44492	44549	44601
44261	44311	44381	44441	44493	44551	44602
44262	44315	44384	44442	44494	44552	44603
44263	44321	44386	44443	44497	44554	44604
44264	44327	44387	44444	44499	44556	44605
44265	44332	44389	44445			

TOTAL: 396

5MT 4-6-0

Introduced 1934. Stanier L.M.S. taper boiler design.
Experimental locomotives:
Introduced 1947[1]. Stephenson link motion (outside), Timken roller bearings.

Introduced 1948[2]. C.protti valve gear.

Introduced 1948[3]. Caprotti valve gear, Timken roller bearings.

Introduced 1948[4]. Caprotti valve gear, Timken roller bearings, double chimney.

Introduced 1947[5]. Timken roller bearings.

Introduced 1947[6]. Timken roller bearings, double chimney.

Introduced 1949[7]. Fitted with steel firebox.

Introduced 1950[8]. Skefko roller bearings.

Introduced 1950[9]. Timken roller bearings on driving coupled axle only.

Introduced 1950[10]. Skefko roller bearings on driving coupled axle only.

Introduced 1951[11]. Caprotti valve gear, Skefko roller bearings, double chimney.

Weight
Locomotive: 72 tons 2 cwt
75 tons 6 cwt ([1], [5], [6], [8], [9], [10])
74 tons 0 cwt ([2], [3], [4], [11])
72 tons 2 cwt ([7])

Boiler pressure
225 lb sq in

Cylinders
(O) 18½″ × 28″

Driving wheel diameter
6′ 0″

Tractive effort
25,455 lb

Valve gear
Walschaerts (piston valves) except where otherwise shown

44658	44676[10]	44694[9]	44712	44730	44748[3]	44766[6]
44659	44677[10]	44695[9]	44713	44731	44749[3]	44767[1]
44660	44678[8]	44696[9]	44714	44732	44750[3]	44768
44661	44679[8]	44697[9]	44715	44733	44751[3]	44769
44662	44680[8]	44698	44716	44734	44752[3]	44770
44663	44681[8]	44699	44717	44735	44753[3]	44771
44664	44682[8]	44700	44718[7]	44736	44754[3]	44772
44665	44683[8]	44701	44719[7]	44737	44755[4]	44773
44666	44684[8]	44702	44720[7]	44738[2]	44756[4]	44774
44667	44685[8]	44703	44721[7]	44739[2]	44757[4]	44775
44668[10]	44686[11]	44704	44722[7]	44740[2]	44758[5]	44776
44669[10]	44687[11]	44705	44723[7]	44741[2]	44759[5]	44777
44670[10]	44688[9]	44706	44724[7]	44742[2]	44760[5]	44778
44671[10]	44689[9]	44707	44725[7]	44743[2]	44761[5]	44779
44672[10]	44690[9]	44708	44726[7]	44744[2]	44762[5]	44780
44673[10]	44691[9]	44709	44727[7]	44745[2]	44763[5]	44781
44674[10]	44692[9]	44710	44728	44746[2]	44764[5]	44782
44675[10]	44693[9]	44711	44729	44747[2]	44765[6]	44783

Class 5MT 4-6-0 No. 44687 (with Caprotti valve gear, Skefko roller bearings and double chimney) [*J. R. Carter*

Class 5MT 4-6-0 No. 44725 (fitted with steel firebox) [*Alan Williams*

Class 5MT 4-6-0 No. 44749 (with Caprotti valve gear and Timken roller bearings) [*J. B. Bucknall*

44784
44785
44786
44787
44788
44789
44790
44791
44792
44793
44794
44795
44796
44797
44798
44799
44800
44801
44802
44803
44804
44805
44806
44807
44808
44809
44810
44811
44812
44813
44814
44815
44816
44817
44818
44819
44820
44821
44822
44823
44824
44825
44826
44827
44828
44829
44830
44831
44832
44833
44834
44835
44836
44837
44838
44839
44840
44841
44842
44843
44844
44845
44846
44847
44848
44849
44850
44851
44852
44853
44854
44855
44856
44857
44858
44859
44860
44861
44862
44863
44864
44865
44866
44867
44868
44869
44870
44871
44872
44873
44874
44875
44876
44877
44878
44879
44880
44881
44882
44883
44884
44885
44886
44887
44888
44889
44890
44891
44892
44893
44894
44895
44896
44897
44898
44899
44900
44901
44902
44903
44904
44905
44906
44907
44908
44909
44910
44911
44912
44913
44914
44915
44916
44917
44918
44919
44920
44921
44922
44923
44924
44925
44926
44927
44928
44929
44930
44931
44932
44933
44934
44935
44936
44937
44938
44939
44940
44941
44942
44943
44944
44945
44946
44947
44948
44949
44950
44951
44952
44953
44954
44955
44956
44957
44958
44959
44960
44961
44962
44963
44964
44965
44966
44967
44968
44969
44970
44971
44972
44973
44974
44975
44976
44977
44978
44979
44980
44981
44982
44983
44984
44985
44986
44987
44988
44989
44990
44991
44992
44993
44994
44995
44996
44997
44998
44999
45000
45001
45002
45003
45004
45005
45006
45007
45008
45009
45010
45011
45012
45013
45014
45015
45016
45017
45018
45019
45020
45021
45022
45023
45024
45025
45026
45027
45028
45029
45031
45032
45033
45034
45035
45037
45038
45039
45040
45041
45042
45043
45044
45045
45046
45047
45048
45049
45050
45051
45052
45053
45054
45055
45056
45057
45058
45059
45060
45061
45062
45063
45064
45065
45066
45067
45068
45069
45070
45071
45072
45073
45074
45075
45076
45077
45078
45079
45080
45081
45082
45083
45084
45087
45088
45089
45090
45091
45092
45093
45094
45095
45096
45097
45099
45100
45101
45102
45103
45104
45105
45106
45107
45108
45109
45110
45111
45112
45113
45114
45115
45116
45117
45118
45120
45121
45122
45123
45124
45126

45127	45131	45135	45139	45143	45146	45149
45128	45132	45136	45140	45144	45147	45150
45129	45133	45137	45141	45145	45148	45153
45130	45134	45138	45142			

45154	*Lanarkshire Yeomanry*	45156	*Ayrshire Yeomanry*
45155		45158	*Glasgow Yeomanry*

45160	45205	45246	45289	45330	45372	45414
45161	45206	45247	45290	45331	45373	45415
45162	45207	45248	45291	45332	45374	45416
45163	45208	45249	45292	45333	45375	45417
45164	45209	45250	45293	45334	45376	45418
45166	45210	45251	45294	45335	45377	45419
45167	45211	45252	45295	45336	45378	45420
45168	45212	45253	45296	45337	45379	45421
45170	45213	45254	45297	45338	45380	45422
45171	45214	45255	45298	45339	45381	45423
45172	45215	45256	45299	45340	45382	45424
45173	45216	45257	45300	45341	45383	45425
45175	45217	45258	45301	45342	45384	45426
45176	45218	45259	45302	45343	45385	45427
45177	45219	45260	45303	45344	45386	45428
45178	45220	45261	45304	45345	45387	45429
45180	45221	45262	45305	45346	45388	45430
45181	45222	45263	45306	45347	45389	45431
45182	45223	45264	45307	45348	45390	45432
45183	45224	45267	45308	45349	45391	45433
45184	45225	45268	45309	45350	45392	45434
45185	45226	45269	45310	45351	45393	45435
45186	45227	45270	45311	45352	45394	45436
45187	45228	45271	45312	45353	45395	45437
45188	45229	45272	45313	45354	45396	45438
45189	45230	45273	45314	45356	45397	45439
45190	45231	45274	45315	45357	45398	45440
45191	45232	45275	45316	45358	45399	45441
45192	45233	45276	45317	45359	45400	45442
45193	45234	45277	45318	45360	45402	45443
45194	45235	45278	45319	45361	45403	45444
45195	45236	45279	45320	45362	45404	45445
45196	45237	45280	45321	45363	45405	45446
45197	45238	45281	45322	45364	45406	45447
45198	45239	45282	45323	45365	45407	45448
45199	45240	45283	45324	45366	45408	45449
45200	45241	45284	45325	45367	45409	45450
45201	45242	45285	45326	45368	45410	45451
45202	45243	45286	45327	45369	45411	45454
45203	45244	45287	45328	45370	45412	45455
45204	45245	45288	45329	45371	45413	45456

Outside Stephenson link motion fitted to Class 5MT 4-6-0 No. 44767 [*R. S. Greenwood*

Class 5MT 4-6-0 No. 45156 *Ayrshire Yeomanry* [*G. W. Morrison*

Class 7P 4-6-0 No. 45527 *Southport* [*J. K. Morton*

45457	45464	45470	45476	45482	45488	45494
45459	45465	45471	45477	45483	45489	45495
45460	45466	45472	45478	45484	45490	45496
45461	45467	45473	45479	45485	45491	45497
45462	45468	45474	45480	45486	45492	45498
45463	45469	45475	45481	45487	45493	45499

TOTAL: 820

7P "Patriot" 4-6-0

Introduced 1946. Ivatt rebuild of Fowler parallel boiler locomotives, introduced 1933, with larger taper boiler, new cylinders and double chimney. (Fowler locomotives numbered 45502–41 were officially considered as rebuilds of L.N.W. "Claughton" class, introduced 1912).

Weight
Locomotive: 82 tons 0 cwt

Boiler Pressure
250 lb sq in

Cylinders
Three, 17″ × 26″

Driving wheel diameter
6′ 9″

Tractive effort
29,570 lb

Valve gear
Walschaerts (piston valves)

45512	*Bunsen*
45521	*Rhyl*
45522	*Prestatyn*
45523	*Bangor*
45525	*Colwyn Bay*
45526	*Morecambe and Heysham*
45527	*Southport*
45528	*R.E.M.E.*
45529	*Stephenson*
45530	*Sir Frank Ree*
45531	*Sir Frederick Harrison*
45532	*Illustrious*
45534	*E. Tootal Broadhurst*
45535	*Sir Herbert Walker, K.C.B.*
45540	*Sir Robert Turnbull*
45545	*Planet*

TOTAL: 16

6P5F & 7P "Jubilee" 4-6-0

6P5F, introduced 1934. Stanier L.M.S. taper boiler development of the "Patriot" class.

† Fitted with double chimney.

* **7P,** introduced 1942. Rebuilt with larger boiler and double chimney.

Weight
Locomotive: 79 tons 11 cwt
82 tons 0 cwt*

Boiler pressure
225 lb sq in
250 lb sq in*

Cylinders
Three, 17″ × 26″

Driving wheel diameter
6′ 9″

Tractive effort
26,610 lb
29,570 lb*

Valve gear
Walschaerts (piston valves)

45552	*Silver Jubilee*	45610	*Ghana*
45553	*Canada*	45611	*Hong Kong*
45554	*Ontario*	45612	*Jamaica*
45555	*Quebec*	45613	*Kenya*
45556	*Nova Scotia*	45614	*Leeward Islands*
45557	*New Brunswick*	45617	*Mauritius*
45558	*Manitoba*	45618	*New Hebrides*
45560	*Prince Edward Island*	45620	*North Borneo*
45561	*Saskatchewan*	45622	*Nyasaland*
45562	*Alberta*	45623	*Palestine*
45563	*Australia*	45624	*St. Helena*
45564	*New South Wales*	45625	*Sarawak*
45565	*Victoria*	45626	*Seychelles*
45567	*South Australia*	45627	*Sierra Leone*
45568	*Western Australia*	45629	*Straits Settlements*
45569	*Tasmania*	45631	*Tanganyika*
45571	*South Africa*	45632	*Tonga*
45572	*Eire*	45633	*Aden*
45573	*Newfoundland*	45634	*Trinidad*
45574	*India*	45635	*Tobago*
45575	*Madras*	45638	*Zanzibar*
45577	*Bengal*	45639	*Raleigh*
45578	*United Provinces*	45640	*Frobisher*
45579	*Punjab*	45641	*Sandwich*
45580	*Burma*	45642	*Boscawen*
45581	*Bihar and Orissa*	45643	*Rodney*
45583	*Assam*	45644	*Howe*
45584	*North West Frontier*	45645	*Collingwood*
45585	*Hyderabad*	45646	*Napier*
45586	*Mysore*	45647	*Sturdee*
45588	*Kashmir*	45648	*Wemyss*
45589	*Gwalior*	45649	*Hawkins*
45590	*Travancore*	45650	*Blake*
45591	*Udaipur*	45652	*Hawke*
45592	*Indore*	45653	*Barham*
45593	*Kholapur*	45654	*Hood*
45595	*Southern Rhodesia*	45655	*Keith*
45596†	*Bahamas*	45657	*Tyrwhitt*
45597	*Barbados*	45658	*Keyes*
45598	*Basutoland*	45659	*Drake*
45599	*Bechuanaland*	45660	*Rooke*
45600	*Bermuda*	45661	*Vernon*
45601	*British Guiana*	45663	*Jervis*
45602	*British Honduras*	45664	*Nelson*
45604	*Ceylon*	45666	*Cornwallis*
45605	*Cyprus*	45667	*Jellicoe*
45606	*Falkland Islands*	45668	*Madden*
45608	*Gibraltar*	45669	*Fisher*

Class 6P5F 4-6-0 No. 45585 *Hyderabad* [*R. K. Evans*

Class 7P 4-6-0 No. 45735 *Comet* [*J. B. Bucknall*

Class 7P 4-6-0 No. 46142 *The York & Lancaster Regiment* [*J. E. Wilkinson*

45670 *Howard of Effingham*
45671 *Prince Rupert*
45672 *Anson*
45674 *Duncan*
45675 *Hardy*
45676 *Codrington*
45680 *Camperdown*
45681 *Aboukir*
45682 *Trafalgar*
45684 *Jutland*
45685 *Barfleur*
45689 *Ajax*
45690 *Leander*
45694 *Bellerophon*
45695 *Minotaur*
45696 *Arethusa*
45697 *Achilles*
45698 *Mars*
45699 *Galatea*
45700 *Amethyst*
45701 *Conqueror*
45702 *Colossus*
45703 *Thunderer*
45704 *Leviathan*
45705 *Seahorse*
45706 *Express*
45708 *Resolution*
45709 *Implacable*
45710 *Irresistible*
45712 *Victory*
45714 *Revenge*
45716 *Swiftsure*
45717 *Dauntless*
45719 *Glorious*
45721 *Impregnable*
45723 *Fearless*
45726 *Vindictive*
45730 *Ocean*
45732 *Sanspareil*
45733 *Novelty*
45734 *Meteor*
45735* *Comet*
45736* *Phoenix*
45737 *Atlas*
45738 *Samson*
45739 *Ulster*
45740 *Munster*
45741 *Leinster*
45742 *Connaught*

TOTAL: 145

7P "Royal Scot" 4-6-0

Introduced 1943. Stanier rebuild of Fowler L.M.S. locomotives (introduced 1927) with taper boiler, new cylinders and double chimney.

Weight
Locomotive: 83 tons 0 cwt

Boiler pressure
250 lb sq in

Cylinders
Three, 18″ × 26″

Driving wheel diameter
6′ 9″

Tractive effort
33,150 lb

Valve gear
Walschaerts (piston valves)

46101
46108 *Seaforth Highlander*
46110 *Grenadier Guardsman*
46111 *Royal Fusilier*
46112
46114 *Coldstream Guardsman*
46115 *Scots Guardsman*
46116 *Irish Guardsman*
46118 *Royal Welch Fusilier*
46119 *Lancashire Fusilier*
46120 *Royal Inniskilling Fusilier*
46122 *Royal Ulster Rifleman*
46125 *3rd Carabinier*
46126 *Royal Army Service Corps*

46128 *The Lovat Scouts*
46129 *The Scottish Horse*
46132 *The King's Regiment, Liverpool*
46133 *The Green Howards*
46136 *The Border Regiment*
46138 *The London Irish Rifleman*
46140 *The King's Royal Rifle Corps*
46141 *The North Staffordshire Regiment*
46142 *The York & Lancaster Regiment*
46143 *The South Staffordshire Regiment*
46144 *Honourable Artillery Company*
46148 *The Manchester Regiment*
46149 *The Middlesex Regiment*
46150 *The Life Guardsman*
46152 *The King's Dragoon Guardsman*
46155 *The Lancer*
46156 *The South Wales Borderer*
46157 *The Royal Artilleryman*
46158 *The Loyal Regiment*
46160 *Queen Victoria's Rifleman*
46162 *Queen's Westminster Rifleman*
46163 *Civil Service Rifleman*
46165 *The Ranger (12th London Regiment)*
46166 *London Rifle Brigade*
46167 *The Hertfordshire Regiment*
46168 *The Girl Guide*
46169 *The Boy Scout*

TOTAL: 41

8P "Coronation" 4-6-2

Introduced 1937. Stanier L.M.S. enlargement of "Princess Royal" class. 46220–29/35–48 originally streamlined. (Streamlined casing removed from 1946.)

* Introduced 1947. Ivatt development with roller bearings and detail alterations.

Weight
Locomotive: 105 tons 5 cwt
106 tons 8 cwt*

Boiler pressure
250 lb sq in

Cylinders
Four, $16\frac{1}{2}'' \times 28''$

Driving wheel diameter
6′ 9″

Tractive effort
40,000 lb

Valve gear
Walschaerts (rocking shafts and piston valves)

46220 *Coronation*
46221 *Queen Elizabeth*
46222 *Queen Mary*
46223 *Princess Alice*
46224 *Princess Alexandra*
46225 *Duchess of Gloucester*
46226 *Duchess of Norfolk*
46228 *Duchess of Rutland*
46229 *Duchess of Hamilton*
46230 *Duchess of Buccleuch*
46233 *Duchess of Sutherland*
46234 *Duchess of Abercorn*
46235 *City of Birmingham*
46236 *City of Bradford*

Class 8P 4-6-2 No. 46245 *City of London* [*M. Pope*

Class 8P 4-6-2 No. 46257 *City of Salford* (with detail differences) [*A. Howard Thomas*

Class 2MT 2-6-0 No. 46402 [*B. Stephenson*

46237	*City of Bristol*	46248	*City of Leeds*
46238	*City of Carlisle*	46249	*City of Sheffield*
46239	*City of Chester*	46250	*City of Lichfield*
46240	*City of Coventry*	46251	*City of Nottingham*
46241	*City of Edinburgh*	46252	*City of Leicester*
46242	*City of Glasgow*	46253	*City of St. Albans*
46243	*City of Lancaster*	46254	*City of Stoke-on-Trent*
46244	*King George VI*	46255	*City of Hereford*
46245	*City of London*	46256*	*Sir William A. Stanier, F.R.S.*
46246	*City of Manchester*	46257*	*City of Salford*
46247	*City of Liverpool*		

TOTAL: 35

2MT — 2-6-0

Introduced 1946. Ivatt L.M.S. taper boiler design.

Weight
Locomotive: 47 tons 2 cwt

Boiler pressure
200 lb sq in

Cylinders
(O) 16″ × 24″
(O) 16½″ × 24″*

Driving wheel diameter
5′ 0″

Tractive effort
17,410 lb
18,510 lb*

Valve gear
Walschaerts (piston valves)

46400	46420	46437	46455	46474*	46496*	46512*
46401	46421	46438	46456	46475*	46497*	46513*
46402	46422	46439	46457	46479*	46498*	46514*
46403	46423	46440	46458	46480*	46499*	46515*
46404	46424	46441	46459	46482*	46500*	46516*
46405	46425	46442	46460	46483*	46501*	46517*
46406	46426	46443	46461	46484*	46502*	46518*
46409	46427	46444	46462	46485*	46503*	46519*
46410	46428	46445	46463	46486*	46504*	46520*
46411	46429	46446	46464	46487*	46505*	46521*
46412	46430	46447	46465*	46488*	46506*	46522*
46413	46431	46448	46467*	46489*	46507*	46523*
46414	46432	46449	46468*	46490*	46508*	46524*
46416	46433	46450	46470*	46491*	46509*	46525*
46417	46434	46451	46472*	46492*	46510*	46526*
46418	46435	46452	46473*	46495*	46511*	46527*
46419	46436	46454				

TOTAL: 115

0F 0-4-0ST

Introduced 1932. Kitson design prepared to Stanier's requirements for L.M.S.

* Introduced 1953. Extended side tanks and coal space.

Weight
33 tons 0 cwt
34 tons 0 cwt*

Boiler pressure
160 lb sq in NS

Cylinders
(O) 15½" × 20"

Driving wheel diameter
3' 10"

Tractive effort
14,205 lb

Valve gear
Stephenson

47000 47002 47004 47006* 47007* 47008* 47009*
47001 47003 47005*

TOTAL: 10

2F 0-6-0T

Introduced 1928. Fowler L.M.S. short-wheelbase dock tanks.

Weight
43 tons 12 cwt

Boiler pressure
160 lb sq in NS

Cylinders
(O) 17" × 22"

Driving wheel diameter
3' 11"

Tractive effort
18,400 lb

Valve gear
Walschaerts

47160 47161 47164 47165 47166

TOTAL: 5

3F 0-6-0T

Introduced 1899. Johnson large Midland design, rebuilt with Belpaire firebox from 1919; fitted with condensing apparatus for London area.

* Non-condensing locomotives.

Weight
48 tons 15 cwt

Boiler pressure
160 lb sq in

Cylinders
18" × 26"

Driving wheel diameter
4' 7"

Tractive effort
20,835 lb

Valve gear
Stephenson

47201* 47207 47223 47228 47231* 47248* 47257*
47202 47211 47225 47230* 47236* 47250*

TOTAL: 13

Class 0F 0-4-0ST No. 47006 [P. H. Wells

Class 2F 0-6-0T No. 47165 [M. Howarth

3F 0-6-0T

Introduced 1924. Post-grouping development of Midland design with detail alterations.

* Introduced 1929. Locomotives built for S. & D.J. (taken into L.M.S. stock 1930).

† Push-and-pull fitted.

Weight
49 tons 10 cwt

Driving wheel diameter
4′ 7″

Boiler pressure
160 lb sq in NS

Tractive effort
20,835 lb

Cylinders
18″ × 26″

Valve gear
Stephenson

47264	47324	47385S	47447	47502	47578	47641
47266	47325	47386	47449	47503	47579	47643
47267	47326	47388	47450	47505	47581	47645
47272	47327	47389	47451	47506	47582	47646
47273	47330	47390	47452	47507	47583	47647
47276	47333	47391	47453	47511	47584	47648
47278	47336	47393	47454	47512	47587	47649
47279	47338	47395	47458	47515	47589	47651
47280	47341	47396	47459	47517	47590	47653
47281	47343	47397	47460	47518	47592S	47654
47283	47344	47399	47461	47519	47594	47655†
47284	47345	47400	47464	47520	47596	47656
47285	47349	47406	47465	47521	47597S	47657
47286	47350	47408	47467	47524	47598	47658S
47287	47354	47410	47468	47530	47599	47659
47288	47355	47412	47469	47531	47602	47660
47289	47357	47413	47471	47532	47603	47661S
47293	47359	47415	47472	47533	47606	47662
47294S	47360	47416	47476	47534	47609	47664
47295	47361	47419	47478†	47535	47611	47665
47297	47362	47423	47480†	47539	47612	47666
47298	47365	47427	47481†	47543	47614	47667
47300	47367	47428	47482	47544	47615	47668
47305	47368	47429S	47485	47547	47616	47669
47306	47371	47430	47487	47549	47618S	47671
47307	47372	47432	47490	47550S	47622	47673
47308	47373	47434	47492	47551	47623	47674
47313*	47375	47435	47493	47557	47627	47675
47314*	47377	47437	47494	47558	47628	47676
47317	47378	47439	47495	47564	47629	47677
47318S	47379	47441	47496	47565	47631	47679
47320	47380S	47442	47499	47566	47638	47680
47321	47383	47444	47500	47577	47640	47681†
47322	47384	47445	47501			

TOTAL: 235

Ex-Midland Class 3F 0-6-0T No. 47236 [*P. J. Lynch*

Class 3F 0-6-0T No. 47653 [*D. L. Percival*

Class 8F 2-8-0 No. 48621 [*P. H. Groom*

8F 2-8-0

Introduced 1935. Stanier L.M.S. taper boiler design.

Weight
Locomotive: 72 tons 2 cwt

Boiler pressure
225 lb sq in

Cylinders
(O) 18½″ × 28″

Driving wheel diameter
4′ 8½″

Tractive effort
32,440 lb

Valve gear
Walschaerts (piston valves)

48000	48067	48112	48151	48190	48249	48288
48001	48069	48113	48152	48191	48250	48289
48002	48070	48114	48153	48192	48251	48290
48003	48073	48115	48154	48193	48252	48291
48004	48074	48116	48155	48194	48253	48292
48005	48075	48117	48156	48195	48254	48293
48006	48076	48118	48157	48196	48255	48294
48007	48077	48119	48158	48197	48256	48295
48008	48078	48120	48159	48198	48257	48296
48010	48079	48121	48160	48199	48258	48297
48011	48080	48122	48161	48200	48259	48301
48012	48081	48123	48162	48201	48260	48302
48016	48082	48124	48163	48202	48261	48303
48017	48083	48125	48164	48203	48262	48304
48018	48084	48126	48165	48204	48263	48305
48020	48085	48127	48166	48205	48264	48306
48024	48088	48128	48167	48206	48265	48307
48026	48089	48129	48168	48207	48266	48308
48027	48090	48130	48169	48208	48267	48309
48029	48092	48131	48170	48209	48268	48310
48033	48093	48132	48171	48210	48269	48311
48035	48094	48133	48172	48211	48270	48312
48036	48095	48134	48173	48212	48271	48313
48037	48096	48135	48174	48213	48272	48314
48039	48097	48136	48175	48214	48273	48315
48045	48098	48137	48176	48215	48274	48316
48046	48099	48138	48177	48216	48275	48317
48050	48100	48139	48178	48217	48276	48318
48053	48101	48140	48179	48218	48277	48319
48054	48102	48141	48180	48219	48278	48320
48055	48103	48142	48181	48220	48279	48321
48056	48104	48143	48182	48221	48280	48322
48057	48105	48144	48183	48222	48281	48323
48060	48106	48145	48184	48223	48282	48324
48061	48107	48146	48185	48224	48283	48325
48062	48108	48147	48186	48225	48284	48326
48063	48109	48148	48187	48246	48285	48327
48064	48110	48149	48188	48247	48286	48328
48065	48111	48150	48189	48248	48287	48329

48330
48331
48332
48333
48334
48335
48336
48337
48338
48339
48340
48341
48342
48343
48344
48345
48346
48347
48348
48349
48350
48351
48352
48353
48354
48355
48356
48357
48358
48359
48360
48361
48362
48363
48364
48365
48366
48367
48368
48369
48370
48371
48372
48373
48374
48375
48376
48377
48378
48379
48380
48381
48382
48383
48384
48385
48386
48387
48388
48389
48390
48391
48392
48393
48394
48395
48396
48397
48398
48399
48400
48401
48402
48403
48404
48405
48406
48407
48408
48409
48410
48411
48412
48413
48414
48415
48416
48417
48418
48419
48420
48421
48422
48423
48424
48425
48426
48427
48428
48429
48430
48431
48432
48433
48434
48435
48436
48437
48438
48439
48440
48441
48442
48443
48444
48445
48446
48447
48448
48449
48450
48451
48452
48453
48454
48455
48456
48457
48458
48459
48460
48461
48462
48463
48464
48465
48466
48467
48468
48469
48470
48471
48472
48473
48474
48475
48476
48477
48478
48479
48490
48491
48492
48493
48494
48495
48500
48501
48502
48503
48504
48505
48506
48507
48508
48509
48510
48511
48512
48513
48514
48515
48516
48517
48518
48519
48520
48521
48522
48523
48524
48525
48526
48527
48528
48529
48530
48531
48532
48533
48534
48535
48536
48537
48538
48539
48540
48541
48542
48543
48544
48545
48546
48547
48548
48549
48550
48551
48552
48553
48554
48555
48556
48557
48558
48559
48600
48601
48602
48603
48604
48605
48606
48607
48608
48609
48610
48611
48612
48613
48614
48615
48617
48618
48619
48620
48621
48622
48623
48624
48625
48626
48627
48628
48629
48630
48631
48632
48633
48634
48635
48636
48637
48638
48639
48640
48641
48642
48643
48644
48645
48646
48647
48648
48649
48650
48651
48652
48653
48654
48655
48656
48657
48658
48659
48660
48661
48662
48663
48664
48665
48666
48667
48668
48669
48670
48671
48672
48673
48674
48675
48676
48677
48678
48679
48680
48681
48682
48683
48684
48685
48686
48687
48688
48689
48690
48691
48692
48693
48694
48695
48696
48697
48698
48699
48700
48701
48702
48703
48704
48705
48706
48707
48708
48709
48710
48711
48712
48713
48714
48715
48716
48717
48718
48719
48720

48721	48729	48737	48745	48752	48759	48766
48722	48730	48738	48746	48753	48760	48767
48723	48731	48739	48747	48754	48761	48768
48724	48732	48740	48748	48755	48762	48769
48725	48733	48741	48749	48756	48763	48770
48726	48734	48742	48750	48757	48764	48771
48727	48735	48743	48751	48758	48765	48772
48728	48736	48744				

TOTAL: 661

7F 0-8-0

Introduced 1936. L.N.W. G2a class. Bowen-Cooke G1 superheated design of 1912, rebuilt with G2 boiler and Belpaire firebox.

Weight
Locomotive: 62 tons 0 cwt

Boiler pressure
175 lb sq in

Cylinders
20½" × 24"

Driving wheel diameter
4' 5½"

Tractive effort
28,045 lb

Valve gear
Joy (piston valves)

48895 49173 49361

TOTAL: 3

7F 0-8-0

Introduced 1921. Development of L.N.W. G2 class. Bowen-Cooke G1 superheated design of 1912 with higher pressure boiler. Many later rebuilt with Belpaire firebox.

Weight
Locomotive: 62 tons 0 cwt

Boiler pressure
175 lb sq in

Cylinders
20½" × 24"

Driving wheel diameter
4' 5½"

Tractive effort
28,045 lb

Valve gear
Joy (piston valves)

49406 49407 49430 49446 49448 49454

TOTAL: 6

0F 0-4-0ST

Introduced 1891. Aspinall L. & Y. Class 21.

Weight
21 tons 5 cwt

Boiler pressure
160 lb sq in NS

Cylinders
(O) 13" × 18"

Driving wheel diameter
3' 0⅜"

Tractive effort
11,335 lb

Valve gear
Stephenson

51218 51232 51237 51253

TOTAL: 4

7F 2-8-0

Introduced 1914. Fowler design for S. & D.J. (All taken into L.M.S. stock, 1930.)

Weight
Locomotive: 64 tons 15 cwt

Boiler pressure
190 lb sq in

Cylinders
(O) 21″ × 28″

Driving wheel diameter
4′ 8½″

Tractive effort
35,295 lb

Valve gear
Walschaerts (piston valves)

53806	53807	53808	53809	53810

TOTAL: 5

2F 0-6-0

Introduced 1883. Drummond Caledonian "Standard Goods"; later additions by Lambie and McIntosh.

* Some rebuilt with L.M.S. boiler.

Weight
Locomotive: 41 tons 6 cwt
42 tons 4 cwt*

Boiler pressure
180 lb sq in NS

Cylinders
18″ × 26″

Driving wheel diameter
5′ 0″

Tractive effort
21,480 lb

Valve gear
Stephenson

57261	57278	57302	57326	57336	57355	57375
57269	57291	57309	57328	57348	57360	57384
57270	57296					

TOTAL: 16

3F 0-6-0

Introduced 1899. McIntosh Caledonian "812" (Nos. 57566–57607) and "652" (remainder) classes.

Weight
Locomotive: 45 tons 14 cwt

Boiler pressure
180 lb sq in NS

Cylinders
18½″ × 26″

Driving wheel diameter
5′ 0″

Tractive effort
22,690 lb

Valve gear
Stephenson

57566	57572	57590	57600	57625	57630	57634
57568	57581	57592	57607	57627		

TOTAL: 12

Above: Class 7F (L.N.W. G2) 0-8-0 No. 49430 [*J. B. Bucknall*

Right: Class 0F 0-4-0ST No. 51218 [*R. C. Riley*

Below: Ex-S. & D. Class 7F 2-8-0 No. 53810 [*Alan Williams*

Ex-Caledonian Class 2F 0-6-0 No. 57326 [P. J. Hughes

Ex-Caledonian (McIntosh) Class 3F 0-6-0 No. 57607 [D. A. Anderson

Ex-Caledonian (Pickersgill) Class 3F 0-6-0 No. 57679 [S. Creer

3F 0-6-0

Introduced 1918. Pickersgill Caledonian "294" class (superheated) and "670" class.

Weight
Locomotive: 50 tons 13 cwt

Boiler pressure
180 lb sq in

Cylinders
18½" × 26"

Driving wheel diameter
5' 0"

Tractive effort
22,690 lb

Valve gear
Stephenson (piston valves)

57652 57668 57670 57679 57688 57689 57690
57661

TOTAL: 8

2F 0-6-0

Introduced 1917. Johnson Midland 4' 11" design of 1875 rebuilt with Belpaire firebox.

Weight
Locomotive: 37 tons 12 cwt to
(Various) 40 tons 3 cwt

Boiler pressure
160 lb sq in NS

Cylinders
18" × 26"

Driving wheel diameter
4' 11"

Tractive effort
19,420 lb

Valve gear
Stephenson

58143 58148 58182

TOTAL: 3

PRESERVED LOCOMOTIVES IN WORKING ORDER

4-2-2

Introduced 1886. Neilson & Co. design for the Caledonian Railway incorporating Drummond details. Withdrawn as L.M.S. No. 14010 in 1935. Restored to Caledonian livery and returned to service for special use 1958.

Weight
Locomotive and Tender: 75 tons

Boiler pressure
150 lb sq in NS

Cylinders
18" × 26"

Driving wheel diameter
7' 0"

Tractive effort
12,785 lb

Valve gear
Stephenson

123

4-6-0

Introduced 1894. Jones Highland Goods design. Withdrawn 1934 as L.M.S. No. 17916 for preservation. Restored to original condition and returned to service for special use 1959.

Weight Locomotive: 56 tons	**Driving wheel diameter** 5′ 3″
Boiler pressure 175 lb sq in NS	**Tractive effort** 24,555 lb
Cylinders (O) 20″ × 26″	**Valve gear** Stephenson

103

DEPARTMENTAL LOCOMOTIVES

2F 0-6-0ST

Introduced 1891. Aspinall rebuild of L. & Y. Barton Wright Class 23 0-6-0. Originally introduced 1877.

Weight 43 tons 17 cwt	**Driving wheel diameter** 4′ 6″
Boiler pressure 140 lb sq in NS	**Tractive effort** 17,545 lb
Cylinders $17\frac{1}{2}$″ × 26″	**Valve gear** Stephenson

11305 11324 11368

TOTAL: 3

LOCOMOTIVE SUPERINTENDENTS AND CHIEF MECHANICAL ENGINEERS

BRITISH RAILWAYS (L.M. REGION)

H. G. Ivatt ... 1948-1951

L.M.S.

George Hughes	1923–1925
Sir Henry Fowler ...	1925–1931
E. H. J. Lemon (Sir Ernest Lemon)	1931–1932
Sir William Stanier ...	1932–1944
Charles E. Fairburn ...	1944–1945
H. G. Ivatt	1945–1947

CALEDONIAN

Robert Sinclair (First Loco. engineer)*	1847–1856
Benjamin Connor ...	1856–1876
George Brittain... ...	1876–1882
Dugald Drummond ...	1882–1890
Hugh Smellie	1890
J. Lambie	1890–1895
J. F. McIntosh	1895–1914
William Pickersgill ...	1914–1923

GLASGOW & SOUTH WESTERN

Patrick Stirling	1853–1866
James Stirling	1866–1878
Hugh Smellie	1878–1890
James Manson	1890–1912
Peter Drummond ...	1912–1918
R. H. Whitelegg ...	1918–1923

* Exclusive of previous service with constituent company.

FURNESS

R. Mason 1890–1897
W. F. Pettigrew ... 1897–1918
D. J. Rutherford ... 1918–1923

LANCASHIRE & YORKSHIRE

Sir John Hawkshaw (Consultant),* Hurst and Jenkins successively to 1868
W. Hurst 1868–1876
W. Barton Wright ... 1876–1886
John A. F. Aspinall ... 1886–1899
H. A. Hoy 1899–1904
George Hughes ... 1904–1921
The L. & Y. amalgamated with L.N.W.R. as from January 1st, 1922

LONDON & NORTH WESTERN

Francis Trevithick and J. E. McConnell, first loco. engineers, 1846, with Alexander Allan largely responsible for design at Crewe.*
John Ramsbottom ... 1857–1871
Francis William Webb... 1871–1903
George Whale 1903–1909
Charles John Bowen-Cooke ... 1909–1920
Capt. Hewitt Pearson Montague Beames ... 1920–1921
George Hughes 1922

LONDON, TILBURY & SOUTHEND

Thomas Whitelegg ... 1880–1910
Robert Harben Whitelegg 1910–1912
(L.T. & S.R. absorbed by M.R., control of locos. transferred to Derby as from August, 1912.)

MARYPORT & CARLISLE

Hugh Smellie 1870–1878
J. Campbell 1878–
William Coulthard ... * –1904
J. B. Adamson 1904–1923

HIGHLAND

William Stroudley (First loco. engineer) 1866–1869
David Jones 1869–1896
Peter Drummond ... 1896–1911
F. G. Smith 1912–1915
C. Cumming 1915–1923

MIDLAND

Matthew Kirtley (First loco. engineer) 1844–1873
Samuel Waite Johnson... 1873–1903
Richard Mountford Deeley... 1903–1909
Henry Fowler 1909–1923

SOMERSET & DORSET JOINT

Until leased by Mid. and L. & S. W. (as from 1st November, 1875) locomotives were bought from outside builders, principally George England of Hatcham Iron Works, S.E. After the above date, Derby and its various Loco. Supts. and C.M.Es. have acted for S. & D.J. aided by a resident Loco. Supt. stationed at Highbridge Works.

NORTH STAFFORDSHIRE

L. Clare 1876–1882
L. Longbottom 1882–1902
J. H. Adams 1902–1915
J. A. Hookham 1915–1923
W. Angus was Loco. Supt. at Stoke prior to 1876. No earlier records can be traced.

WIRRAL

Eric G. Barker 1892–1902
T. B. Hunter 1903–1923
Barker of the Wirral Railway is noteworthy for originating the 4-4-4 tank type in this country (1896).

NORTH LONDON

(Worked by L. & N.W. by agreement dated December, 1908.)
William Adams 1853–1873
J. C. Park 1873–1893
Henry J. Pryce 1893–1908

* Date of actual entry into office not known.

Ex-L.N.E.R. STEAM LOCOMOTIVES
Nos. 60001-69028

The numbers of locomotives in service have been checked in E. & N.E.R. to January 12, 1963, L.M.R. to December 29, 1962, and Sc.R. to January 19, 1963.

8P6F — A4 — 4-6-2

Introduced 1935. Gresley streamlined design with corridor tender (except those marked †). All fitted with double chimney.
* Inside cylinder reduced to 17″.

Weight
Locomotive: 102 tons 19 cwt
Tender: 64 tons 19 cwt
60 tons 7 cwt†

Boiler pressure
250 lb sq in

Cylinders
Three, 18½″ × 26″
Two, 18½″ × 26″ One, 17″ × 26″*

Driving wheel diameter
6′ 8″

Tractive effort
35,455 lb
33,616 lb*

Valve gear
Walschaerts (with derived motion and piston valves)

60001† *Sir Ronald Matthews*
60002† *Sir Murrough Wilson*
60004 *William Whitelaw*
60005† *Sir Charles Newton*
60006† *Sir Ralph Wedgwood*
60007 *Sir Nigel Gresley*
60008† *Dwight D. Eisenhower*
60009 *Union of South Africa*
60010 *Dominion of Canada*
60011 *Empire of India*
60012* *Commonwealth of Australia*
60013 *Dominion of New Zealand*
60015 *Quicksilver*
60016† *Silver King*
60017 *Silver Fox*
60018† *Sparrow Hawk*
60019† *Bittern*
60020*† *Guillemot*
60021 *Wild Swan*
60022 *Mallard*
60023† *Golden Eagle*
60024 *Kingfisher*
60025 *Falcon*
60026† *Miles Beevor*
60027 *Merlin*
60029 *Woodcock*
60031 *Golden Plover*
60032 *Gannet*
60034 *Lord Faringdon*

TOTAL: 29

7P6F — A3 — 4-6-2

Introduced 1927. Development of Gresley G.N. 180 lb Pacific (introduced 1922, L.N.E.R. A1, later A10) with 220 lb pressure (60044–83, 60103–12 rebuilt from A10). Some have G.N.-type tender with coal rails, remainder L.N.E.R. pattern*. All fitted with double chimney.

Class A4 4-6-2 No. 60032 *Gannet* [*D. C. Benber*

Class A3 4-6-2 No. 60066 *Merry Hampton* (with G.N. tender and German-type smoke deflectors) [*B. Stephenson*

Class A3 4-6-2 No. 60103 *Flying Scotsman* (with L.N.E.R. tender and German-type smoke deflectors) [*G. Wheeler*

Weight
Locomotive: 96 tons 5 cwt
Tender: 56 tons 6 cwt
57 tons 18 cwt*

Boiler pressure
220 lb sq in

Cylinders
Three, 19″ × 26″

Driving wheel diameter
6′ 8″

Tractive effort
32,910 lb

Valve gear
Walschaerts (with derived motion and piston valves)

60036 *Colombo*
60037 *Hyperion*
60038* *Firdaussi*
60039* *Sandwich*
60040 *Cameronian*
60041 *Salmon Trout*
60042 *Singapore*
60043 *Brown Jack*
60044 *Melton*
60045 *Lemberg*
60046* *Diamond Jubilee*
60047 *Donovan*
60048* *Doncaster*
60050 *Persimmon*
60051* *Blink Bonny*
60052 *Prince Palatine*
60053* *Sansovino*
60054 *Prince of Wales*
60056 *Centenary*
60057 *Ormonde*
60058* *Blair Athol*
60060* *The Tetrarch*
60061 *Pretty Polly*
60062 *Minoru*
60063 *Isinglass*
60065 *Knight of Thistle*
60066 *Merry Hampton*
60070* *Gladiateur*
60071 *Tranquil*
60073 *St. Gatien*
60074 *Harvester*
60075 *St. Frusquin*
60077* *The White Knight*
60080 *Dick Turpin*
60082 *Neil Gow*
60083 *Sir Hugo*
60084* *Trigo*
60085 *Manna*
60086* *Gainsborough*
60087* *Blenheim*
60088 *Book Law*
60089 *Felstead*
60090 *Grand Parade*
60091* *Captain Cuttle*
60092* *Fairway*
60094 *Colorado*
60096 *Papyrus*
60097 *Humorist*
60098* *Spion Kop*
60099* *Call Boy*
60100* *Spearmint*
60101* *Cicero*
60103* *Flying Scotsman*
60105 *Victor Wild*
60106 *Flying Fox*
60107 *Royal Lancer*
60108 *Gay Crusader*
60110 *Robert the Devil*
60112 *St. Simon*

TOTAL: 59

8P6F A1 4-6-2

Introduced 1948. Peppercorn development of Thompson Class A1/1 (Class A1/1 was rebuild of Gresley A10 No. 4470, B.R. No. 60113).

* Fitted with roller bearings.

All fitted with double chimney.

Class A1 4-6-2 No. 60119 *Patrick Stirling* [*N. E. Preedy*

Class A2/3 4-6-2 No. 60500 *Edward Thompson* [*P. H. Wells*

Class A2 4-6-2 No. 60528 *Tudor Minstrel* [*H. Wheeler*

Weight
Locomotive: 104 tons 2 cwt
Tender: 60 tons 7 cwt

Boiler Pressure
250 lb sq in

Cylinders
Three, 19″ × 26″

Driving wheel diameter
6′ 8″

Tractive effort
37,400 lb

Valve gear
Walschaerts (piston valves)

60114 *W. P. Allen*
60116 *Hal o' the Wynd*
60117 *Bois Roussel*
60118 *Archibald Sturrock*
60119 *Patrick Stirling*
60120 *Kittiwake*
60121 *Silurian*
60124 *Kenilworth*
60125 *Scottish Union*
60126 *Sir Vincent Raven*
60127 *Wilson Worsdell*
60128 *Bongrace*
60129 *Guy Mannering*
60130 *Kestrel*
60131 *Osprey*
60132 *Marmion*
60133 *Pommern*
60134 *Foxhunter*
60136 *Alcazar*
60138 *Boswell*
60139 *Sea Eagle*
60140 *Balmoral*
60141 *Abbotsford*
60142 *Edward Fletcher*
60143 *Sir Walter Scott*
60144 *King's Courier*
60145 *Saint Mungo*
60146 *Peregrine*
60147 *North Eastern*
60148 *Aboyeur*
60149 *Amadis*
60150 *Willbrook*
60151 *Midlothian*
60152 *Holyrood*
60154* *Bon Accord*
60155* *Borderer*
60156* *Great Central*
60157* *Great Eastern*
60158 *Aberdonian*
60159 *Bonnie Dundee*
60160 *Auld Reekie*
60161 *North British*
60162 *Saint Johnstoun*

TOTAL: 43

8P7F A2 4-6-2

A2/3, introduced 1946. Development of Thompson Class A2/2. Fitted with double chimney.

* **A2,** introduced 1947. Peppercorn development of Class A2/2 with shorter wheelbase.

† **A2,** rebuilt with double chimney and multiple valve regulator.

Weight
Locomotive: 101 tons 10 cwt
101 tons 0 cwt*†
Tender: 60 tons 7 cwt

Boiler Pressure
250 lb sq in

Cylinders
Three, 19″ × 26″

Driving wheel diameter
6′ 2″

Tractive effort
40,430 lb

Valve gear
Walschaerts (piston valves)

Class A2 4-6-2 No. 60532 *Blue Peter* (with double chimney and multiple valve regulator) [*H. Wheeler*

Class V2 2-6-2 No. 60902 (with double chimney) [*J. C. Haydon*

Class V2 2-6-2 No. 60967 [*D. J. Dippie*

60500	*Edward Thompson*	60525*	*A. H. Peppercorn*
60512	*Steady Aim*	60527*	*Sun Chariot*
60513	*Dante*	60528*	*Tudor Minstrel*
60520	*Owen Tudor*	60530*	*Sayajirao*
60522	*Straight Deal*	60532†	*Blue Peter*
60523	*Sun Castle*	60533†	*Happy Knight*
60524	*Herringbone*	60535*	*Hornet's Beauty*

TOTAL: 14

7P6F V2 2-6-2

Introduced 1936. Gresley design.
* Fitted with double chimney.

Weight
Locomotive: 93 tons 2 cwt
Tender: 52 tons

Boiler pressure
220 lb sq in

Cylinders
Three, $18\frac{1}{2}'' \times 26''$

Driving wheel diameter
6′ 2″

Tractive effort
33,730 lb

Valve gear
Walschaerts (with derived motion and piston valves)

60802 60804 60806
60803 60805 60808

60809 *The Snapper, The East Yorkshire Regiment, The Duke of York's Own*

60810 60814 60817* 60822 60825 60830 60833
60812 60816 60818 60824 60828 60831 60834
60813

60835 *The Green Howard, Alexandra, Princess of Wales's Own Yorkshire Regiment*

60836 60838 60843 60846
60837 60841 60844

60847 *St. Peter's School York A.D. 627*

60852 60855 60858* 60861 60864 60868 60870
60853 60856 60859 60862* 60865 60869 60871
60854

60872 *King's Own Yorkshire Light Infantry*

60876	60884	60892	60901	60910	60922	60932
60877	60885	60895	60902*	60912	60923	60935
60880*	60886	60897	60903*	60913	60924	60939
60881*	60887	60898	60904	60916	60925	60940
60882	60889	60899	60905	60919	60929	60941
60883	60891	60900	60906	60921	60931	60942

Class B1 4-6-0 No. 61095 (with self-weighing tender) [D. J. Dippie

Class B1 4-6-0 No. 61348 [D. Smith

Class B16/2 4-6-0 No. 61437 [W. A. Richards

60944	60946	60950	60954	60957	60961	60963*
60945	60948	60952	60955	60959	60962	

60964 *The Durham Light Infantry*

60966	60968	60970	60973	60975	60981	60982
60967	60969	60972	60974	60976		

TOTAL: 115

5MT B1 4-6-0

Introduced 1942. Thompson design.

Weight
Locomotive: 71 tons 3 cwt
Tender: 52 tons

Boiler pressure
225 lb sq in

Cylinders
(O) 20″ × 26″

Driving wheel diameter
6′ 2″

Tractive effort
26,880 lb

Valve gear
Walschaerts (piston valves)

61001 *Eland*
61002 *Impala*
61003 *Gazelle*
61004 *Oryx*
61006 *Blackbuck*
61007 *Klipspringer*
61008 *Kudu*
61010 *Wildebeeste*
61012 *Puku*
61013 *Topi*
61014 *Oribi*
61016 *Inyala*
61017 *Bushbuck*
61018 *Gnu*
61019 *Nilghai*
61021 *Reitbok*
61022 *Sassaby*
61023 *Hirola*
61024 *Addax*
61026 *Ourebi*
61029 *Chamois*
61030 *Nyala*
61031 *Reedbuck*
61032 *Stembok*
61033 *Dibatag*
61034 *Chiru*
61035 *Pronghorn*
61037 *Jairou*
61038 *Blacktail*
61039 *Steinbok*
61040 *Roedeer*

61041	61068	61088	61105	61125	61144	61162
61042	61069	61089	61107	61126	61145	61165
61044	61070	61090	61109	61127	61146	61167
61049	61071	61092	61110	61129	61147	61168
61050	61072	61093	61113	61131	61148	61169
61051	61073	61094	61115	61132	61152	61172
61053	61074	61095	61116	61133	61153	61173
61055	61075	61097	61117	61134	61155	61174
61056	61076	61098	61118	61135	61156	61175
61058	61080	61099	61119	61138	61157	61176
61059	61081	61101	61120	61140	61158	61177
61061	61083	61102	61121	61141	61159	61178
61062	61084	61103	61122	61142	61160	61179
61065	61087	61104	61123	61143	61161	61180

61181 61185 61188

61189 *Sir William Gray*

61190	61195	61198	61204	61207	61210	61213
61191	61196	61199	61205	61208	61212	61214
61194	61197					

61215 *William Henton Carver*

61216 61218 61219 61220

61221 *Sir Alexander Erskine-Hill*

61223	61225	61229	61233
61224	61227	61232	

61237	*Geoffrey H. Kitson*	61245	*Murray of Elibank*
61238	*Leslie Runciman*	61248	*Geoffrey Gibbs*
61240	*Harry Hinchcliffe*	61249	*FitzHerbert Wright*
61242	*Alexander Reith Gray*	61250	*A. Harold Bibby*
61243	*Sir Harold Mitchell*	61251	*Oliver Bury*
61244	*Strang Steel*		

61252	61276	61305	61325	61345	61365	61390
61255	61277	61306	61326	61346	61367	61392
61256	61278	61307	61327	61347	61369	61393
61257	61279	61308	61328	61348	61370	61394
61258	61281	61309	61329	61349	61372	61396
61259	61285	61310	61330	61350	61374	61397
61261	61288	61312	61331	61351	61375	61398
61262	61289	61313	61334	61353	61378	61399
61263	61291	61314	61336	61354	61382	61400
61264	61292	61315	61337	61355	61383	61401
61268	61293	61318	61338	61356	61384	61402
61269	61294	61319	61340	61357	61385	61403
61270	61299	61320	61341	61358	61386	61404
61272	61300	61321	61342	61359	61387	61406
61273	61302	61322	61343	61360	61388	61407
61274	61303	61323	61344	61361	61389	61409
61275	61304	61324				

TOTAL: 288

5MT B16 4-6-0

* **B16/2,** introduced 1937. Gresley rebuild of Raven N.E. B16/1 with Walschaerts valve gear and derived motion for inside cylinder.
† **B16/3,** introduced 1944. Thompson rebuild of Raven N.E. B16/1 with individual sets of Walschaerts valve gear for each cylinder.

Class B16/3 4-6-0 No. 61448 [A. Swain

Class K1 2-6-0 No. 62037 [P. J. Hughes

Class Q6 0-8-0 No. 63410 [A. W. Martin

Weight
Locomotive: 79 tons 4 cwt*
78 tons 19 cwt†
Tender: 46 tons 12 cwt

Boiler pressure
180 lb sq in

Cylinders
Three, 18½″ × 26″

Driving wheel diameter
5′ 8″

Tractive effort
30,030 lb

Valve gear
Walschaerts (piston valves)

61418†	61435*	61444†	61453†	61457*	61464†	61472†
61420†	61437*	61448†	61454†	61461†	61467†	61475*
61421*	61438*	61449†	61455*	61463†	61468†	61476†
61434†						

TOTAL: 22

5P6F K1 2-6-0

Introduced 1949. Peppercorn development of Thompson K1/1 (rebuilt from Gresley K4) with increased length.

Weight
Locomotive: 66 tons 17 cwt
Tender: 44 tons 4 cwt

Boiler pressure
225 lb sq in

Cylinders
(O) 20″ × 26″

Driving wheel diameter
5′ 2″

Tractive effort
32,080 lb

Valve gear
Walschaerts (piston valves)

62001	62011	62021	62032	62043	62053	62062
62002	62012	62022	62033	62044	62054	62063
62003	62013	62023	62035	62045	62055	62064
62004	62014	62024	62036	62046	62056	62065
62005	62015	62025	62037	62047	62057	62066
62006	62016	62026	62038	62048	62058	62067
62007	62017	62027	62039	62049	62059	62068
62008	62018	62028	62040	62050	62060	62069
62009	62019	62029	62041	62051	62061	62070
62010	62020	62030	62042			

TOTAL: 67

6F Q6 0-8-0

Introduced 1913. Raven N.E. design.
* Some locomotives are fitted with tender from withdrawn B15 locomotives.

Weight
Locomotive: 65 tons 18 cwt
Tender: 44 tons 2 cwt
44 tons 0 cwt*

Boiler pressure
180 lb sq in

Cylinders
(O) 20″ × 26″

Driving wheel diameter
4′ 7¼″

Tractive effort
28,800 lb

Valve gear
Stephenson (piston valves)

63340	63357	63375	63392	63409	63426	63443
63341	63358	63376	63393	63410	63427	63444
63342	63359	63377	63394	63411	63428	63445
63343	63360	63378	63395	63412	63429	63446
63344	63361	63379	63396	63413	63430	63447
63345	63362	63380	63397	63414	63431	63448
63346	63363	63381	63398	63415	63432	63449
63347	63364	63382	63399	63416	63433	63450
63348	63365	63383	63400	63417	63434	63451
63349	63366	63384	63401	63418	63435	63452
63350	63367	63385	63402	63419	63436	63453
63351	63368	63386	63403	63420	63437	63454
63352	63369	63387	63404	63421	63438	63455
63353	63370	63388	63405	63422	63439	63456
63354	63371	63389	63406	63423	63440	63458
63355	63373	63390	63407	63424	63441	63459
63356	63374	63391	63408	63425	63442	

TOTAL: 118

8F (O1) 7F (O4) — O1 & O4 — 2-8-0

O4/1, introduced 1911. Robinson G.C. design with small boiler, Belpaire firebox, steam and vacuum brakes and water scoop.

***O4/3**, introduced 1917. R.O.D. locomotives with steam brake only and no scoop.

†**O4/6**, introduced 1924. Rebuilt from O5 retaining higher cab.

‡**O4/7**, introduced 1939. Rebuilt with shortened O2-type boiler, retaining G.C. smokebox.

§**O4/8**, introduced 1944. Rebuilt with 100A (B1) boiler, retaining original cylinders.

(O4/4 were rebuilds with O2 boilers, since rebuilt again; O5 was a G.C. development of O4 with larger boiler and Belpaire firebox.)

Weight
Locomotive: 73 tons 4 cwt
73 tons 4 cwt*†
73 tons 17 cwt‡
72 tons 10 cwt§
Tender: 48 tons 6 cwt (with scoop)
47 tons 6 cwt (without scoop)

Boiler Pressure
180 lb sq in

Cylinders
(O) 21″ × 26″.

Driving wheel diameter
4′ 8″

Tractive effort
31,325 lb

Valve gear
Stephenson (piston valves)

Class O4/8 2-8-0 No. 63688 [K. R. Pirt

Class O1 2-8-0 No. 63773 [P. J. Sharpe

Class O4/7 2-8-0 No. 63824 [P. J. Hughes

¶**O1,** introduced 1944. Thompson rebuild with 100A boiler, Walschaerts valve gear and new cylinders.

Weight
Locomotive: 73 tons 6 cwt
Tender as O4

Boiler pressure
225 lb sq in

Cylinders
(O) 20″ × 26″

Driving wheel diameter
4′ 8″

Tractive effort
35,520 lb

Valve gear
Walschaerts (piston valves)

63571¶	63622	63675§	63722	63768¶	63818§	63872¶
63576	63628§	63678¶	63725¶	63770‡	63819§	63873§
63577	63630¶	63679§	63726§	63772‡	63822§	63877§
63585	63632	63683§	63727	63773¶	63824‡	63878§
63586	63636§	63684	63728§	63774*	63827§	63879¶
63589¶	63639§	63685*	63730§	63780¶	63828§	63880‡
63590¶	63644§	63687¶	63731§	63781§	63829§	63882§
63592¶	63645§	63688§	63732§	63784¶	63836§	63884§
63593	63646¶	63691§	63734§	63785§	63840§	63887¶
63594¶	63647§	63692	63736	63786¶	63841§	63890¶
63596¶	63650¶	63697§	63738§	63788§	63842*	63893§
63601	63651§	63701*	63739§	63791§	63843‡	63897§
63604§	63652¶	63702*	63741§	63793§	63846*	63898§
63606§	63653§	63703§	63742§	63795¶	63850§	63899§
63607	63661‡	63704§	63744*	63800§	63852§	63902†
63611	63663¶	63705§	63746¶	63801§	63853§	63906†
63612§	63665*	63706§	63750§	63802§	63858§	63907†
63613§	63670¶	63707	63754§	63803¶	63859*	63908†
63615‡	63671	63715§	63763§	63807§	63861§	63913†
63618	63672§	63717§	63764*	63813*	63863¶	63914§
63619¶	63674§	63720§	63765§	63816§	63868¶	

TOTAL: O1, 30; O4, 116

8F O2 2-8-0

O2/1, introduced 1921. Development of experimental Gresley G.N. 3-cylinder locomotive (L.N.E.R. 3921). Subsequently rebuilt with side-window cab, and reduced boiler mountings.

* **O2/2,** introduced 1924. Development of O2/1 with detail differences.

† **O2/3,** introduced 1932. Development of O2/2 with side-window cab and reduced boiler mountings.

‡ **O2/4,** introduced 1943. Rebuilt with 100A (B1) boiler and smokebox extended backwards (some retaining G.N. tender).

Class O4/3 2-8-0 No. 63859 [*J. B. Bucknall*

Class O4/6 2-8-0 No. 63913 [*B. E. Morrison*

Class 02/4 2-8-0 No. 63925 [*P. J. Hughes*

Weight
Locomotive: 75 tons 16 cwt
75 tons 16 cwt*
78 tons 13 cwt†
74 tons 2 cwt‡

Tender: 43 tons 2 cwt (G.N. type)
52 tons (L.N.E.R. type)

Boiler pressure
180 lb sq in

Cylinders
Three, $18\frac{1}{2}'' \times 26''$

Driving wheel diameter
4′ 8″

Tractive effort
36,740 lb

Valve gear
Walschaerts (with derived motion and piston valves)

63924‡	63932‡	63940*	63949‡	63968‡	63976‡	63983‡
63925‡	63935‡	63941*	63956†	63969†	63977†	63984†
63926‡	63936*	63942*	63960‡	63972†	63978†	63985†
63927	63937*	63943*	63962†	63973†	63980†	63986†
63928‡	63938‡	63945‡	63963†	63974†	63981†	63987†
63931‡	63939*	63946*	63964‡	63975†		

TOTAL: 40

5F J37 0-6-0

Introduced 1914. Reid N.B. design. Superheated development of J35.

Weight
Locomotive: 54 tons 14 cwt
Tender: 40 tons 19 cwt

Boiler pressure
180 lb sq in

Cylinders
$19\frac{1}{2}'' \times 26''$

Driving wheel diameter
5′ 0″

Tractive effort
25,210 lb

Valve gear
Stephenson (piston valves)

64537	64555	64570	64583	64597	64611	64624
64541	64557	64571	64585	64599	64613	64625
64546	64558	64572	64586	64600	64614	64626
64547	64559	64573	64587	64602	64616	64627
64548	64561	64575	64588	64603	64618	64629
64549	64562	64576	64589	64605	64619	64632
64550	64563	64577	64591	64606	64620	64633
64551	64564	64579	64592	64608	64621	64634
64552	64568	64580	64593	64610	64623	64636
64554	64569	64582	64595			

TOTAL: 67

34002
SALISBURY
34002

Above: Class 7P 4-

Previous page: Class

Next page: Class

25 *3rd Carabinier*

No. 34002 *Salisbury*

60017 *Silver Fox*

[*From paintings by V. Welch*

SILVER FOX
60017
60017

2F J36 0-6-0

Introduced 1888. Holmes N.B. design.

Weight
Locomotive: 41 tons 19 cwt
Tender: 33 tons 9 cwt

Boiler pressure
165 lb sq in NS

Cylinders
18¼″ × 26″

Driving wheel diameter
5′ 0″

Tractive effort
19,690 lb

Valve Gear
Stephenson

65214	
65222	*Somme*
65224	*Mons*
65234	
65243	*Maude*
65251	
65253	*Joffre*
65261	

65265	65273	65282	65287	65290	65307
65267	65277	65285	65288	65297	65309

65311 *Haig*

65319	65325	65329	65335	65341	65346
65323	65327	65331	65338	65345	

TOTAL: 32

5F J27 0-6-0

Introduced 1906. W. Worsdell N.E. design developed from J26.
* Introduced 1921. Raven locomotives. Superheated, with piston valves.
† Introduced 1943. Piston valves, but superheater removed.

Weight
Locomotive: 47 tons 0 cwt NS
49 tons 10 cwt
Tender: 36 tons 19 cwt

Boiler pressure
180 lb sq in SS

Cylinders
18½″ × 26″

Driving wheel diameter
4′ 7¼″

Tractive effort
24,640 lb

Valve gear
Stephenson

65788	65808	65822	65841	65855	65871*	65883*
65789	65809	65823	65842	65857	65872†	65884†
65790	65810	65825	65844	65858	65873†	65885†
65791	65811	65828	65845	65859	65874†	65887*
65792	65812	65830	65846	65860†	65875†	65888†
65794	65813	65831	65849	65861†	65876†	65889†
65795	65814	65832	65850	65862†	65878†	65890*
65796	65815	65833	65851	65864†	65879†	65891†
65801	65817	65834	65852	65865†	65880*	65892†
65802	65819	65835	65853	65869†	65881†	65893†
65804	65820	65838	65854	65870†	65882†	65894*
65805	65821					

TOTAL: 79

Class O2/2 2-8-0 No. 63937 [K. R. Pirt

Class O2/3 2-8-0 No. 63978 [P. J. Sharpe

Class J37 0-6-0 No. 64571 [P. Ransome-Wallis

6F J38 0-6-0

Introduced 1926. Gresley design. Predecessor of J39, with smaller wheels, boiler 6″ longer than J39 and smokebox 6″ shorter.
* Rebuilt with J39 boiler.

Weight
Locomotive: 58 tons 19 cwt
Tender: 44 tons 4 cwt

Boiler pressure
180 lb sq in

Cylinders
20″ × 26″

Driving wheel diameter
4′ 8″

Tractive effort
28,415 lb

Valve gear
Stephenson (piston valves)

65900	65905	65910	65915	65920	65926*	65931
65901	65906*	65911	65916	65921	65927*	65932
65902	65907	65912	65917*	65922	65929	65933
65903*	65908*	65913	65918*	65924	65930	65934
65904	65909	65914	65919	65925		

TOTAL: 33

4MT V3 2-6-2T

Introduced 1939. Gresley design. Development of V1, introduced 1930, with higher pressure (locomotives numbered below 67682 rebuilt from V1).

Weight
86 tons 16 cwt

Boiler pressure
200 lb sq in

Cylinders
Three, 16″ × 26″

Driving wheel diameter
5′ 8″

Tractive effort
24,960 lb

Valve gear
Walschaerts (with derived motion and piston valves)

67620	67638	67645	67652	67658	67682	67686
67628	67640	67646	67653	67662	67683	67690
67635	67642	67647	67654	67663	67684	67691
67636	67643	67651	67656	67678		

TOTAL: 26

4F J94 0-6-0ST

Introduced 1943. Riddles Ministry of Supply design, purchased by L.N.E.R., 1946.

Weight
48 tons 5 cwt

Boiler pressure
170 lb sq in NS

Cylinders
18″ × 26″

Driving wheel diameter
4′ 3″

Tractive effort
23,870 lb

Valve gear
Stephenson

Class J36 0-6-0 No. 65222 *Somme* [*W. S. Sellar*

Class J27 0-6-0 No. 65822 [*J. K. Morton*

Class J38 0-6-0 No. 65932 [*R. J. Buckley*

68006	68015	68025	68038	68045	68053	68067
68008	68016	68029	68039	68046	68054	68068
68010	68019	68031	68040	68047	68059	68070
68011	68020	68032	68041	68049	68060	68071
68012	68021	68035	68042	68050	68061	68078
68013	68023	68036	68043	68051	68062	68079
68014	68024	68037				

TOTAL: 45

2F J72 0-6-0T

Introduced 1898. W. Worsdell N.E. design.

Weight
38 tons 12 cwt

Boiler pressure
140 lb sq in NS

Cylinders
17″ × 24″

Driving wheel diameter
4′ $1\frac{1}{4}$″

Tractive effort
16,760 lb

Valve gear
Stephenson

68723 68736

Class continued with 69001

4F J50 0-6-0T

* **J50/2,** introduced 1922. Gresley G.N. design (68904–17 rebuilt from smaller J51, built 1915–22).
† **J50/3,** introduced 1926. Post-grouping development with detail differences.
‡ **J50/1,** introduced 1929. Rebuilt from smaller J51, built 1913–14.
§ **J50/4,** introduced 1937. Development of J50/3 with larger bunker.

Weight
57 tons*
56 tons 6 cwt‡
58 tons 3 cwt†§

Boiler pressure
175 lb sq in NS

Cylinders
$18\frac{1}{2}$″ × 26″

Driving wheel diameter
4′ 8″

Tractive effort
23,635 lb

Valve gear
Stephenson

68892‡	68908*	68925*	68935*	68965†	68984§
68904*	68922*	68934*	68937*	68977†	68988§

See also Departmental Locomotives

TOTAL: 19

Top: Class V3 2-6-
No. 67636
[*W. S. Sell*

Centre: Class J
0-6-0ST No. 68013
[*C. P. Booco*

Left: Class J50/2
0-6-0T No. 68904
[*P. J. Sharpe*

2F J72 0-6-0T

Class continued from 68736

69001 69005 69009 69016 69020 69023 69025
69003 69006 69011 69019 69021 69024 69028
69004 69008

TOTAL: 18

PRESERVED LOCOMOTIVE IN WORKING ORDER

1P D40 4-4-0

Introduced 1920. Heywood G.N. of S. superheated development of Pickersgill 1899 design. Withdrawn 1958 as B.R. No. 62277 and restored to original condition, being returned to service for special use in 1959.

Weight
Locomotive: 48 tons 13 cwt
Tender: 37 tons 8 cwt

Boiler pressure
165 lb sq in

Cylinders
18″ × 26″

Driving wheel diameter
6′ 1″

Tractive effort
16,185 lb

Valve gear
Stephenson

49 *Gordon Highlander*

DEPARTMENTAL LOCOMOTIVES

Former running number in brackets

4F J50 0-6-0T

For details see 68892-68988

10*(68911) 12*(68917) 14†(68961) 15†(68971) 16†(68976)
11*(68914) 13*(68928)

Class J50/4 0-6-0T No. 68984 [G. W. Morrison

Class J72 0-6-0T No. 69021 [B. K. B. Green

Class J66 0-6-0T Departmental No. 32 [L. Sandler

Unclass. Y3 0-4-0T

Introduced 1927.
Sentinel Wagon Works design. Two-speed Geared Sentinel locomotives.

Sprocket gear ratio
15 : 19

Weight
Locomotive: 20 tons 16 cwt

Boiler pressure
275 lb sq in

Cylinders
6¾″ × 9″

Driving wheel diameter
2′ 6″

Tractive effort
Low gear: 15,960 lb
High gear: 5,960 lb

Valve gear
Poppet

7 (68166) 40 (68173) 41 (68177) **TOTAL: 3**

2F J66 0-6-0T

Introduced 1886. J. Holden G.E. design.

Weight
Locomotive: 40 tons 6 cwt

Boiler pressure
160 lb sq in NS

Cylinders
16½″ × 22″

Driving wheel diameter
4′ 0″

Tractive effort
16,970 lb

Valve Gear
Stephenson

32 (68370) **TOTAL: 1**

2F J69 0-6-0T

J69/1, introduced 1902. Development of Holden J67 with 180 lb pressure, larger tanks and larger firebox (some rebuilt from J67).
* **J69/2,** introduced 1950. J67/1 rebuilt with 180 lb boiler and larger firebox.

Weight
40 tons 9 cwt

Boiler pressure
180 lb sq in NS

Cylinders
16½″ × 22″

Driving wheel diameter
4′ 0″

Tractive effort
19,090 lb

Valve gear
Stephenson

44* (68498) 45 (68543) **TOTAL: 2**

Unclass. Y1/1 0-4-0T

Introduced 1925.
Sentinel Wagon Works design. Single-speed Geared Sentinel locomotive.

Sprocket gear ratio
11 : 25

Weight
Locomotive: 20 tons 17 cwt

Boiler pressure
275 lb sq in

Cylinders
6¾″ × 9″

Driving wheel diameter
2′ 6″

Tractive effort
7,260 lb

Valve gear
Poppet

39 (68131) **TOTAL: 1**

Unclass. Y4 0-4-0T

Introduced 1913. Hill G.E. design.

Weight
Locomotive: 38 tons 1 cwt

Boiler pressure
180 lb sq in NS

Cylinders
(O) 17″ × 20″

Driving wheel diameter
3′ 10″

Tractive effort
19,225 lb

Valve gear
Walschaerts

33 (68129) **TOTAL: 1**

ROUTE AVAILABILITY OF LOCOMOTIVES

R.A. No.	*Ex-L.N.E.R.*	*Ex-L.M.S.R.*	*B.R.*
1	Y1, Y3.	2MT (2-6-2T).	
2	J72.	2MT (2-6-0).	
3	J36, J66, J69.	2F (0-6-0), 1F (0-6-0T).	2MT (2-6-0), 2MT (2-6-2T).
4		3F (0-6-0 Mid.), 4MT (2-6-0), 4MT (2-6-4T T.B.).	3MT (2-6-0), 4MT (2-6-0), 3MT (2-6-2T)
5	B1, J27, J94.	4F (0-6-0), 3F (0-6-0T), 4MT (2-6-4T P.B.).	4MT (2-6-4T).
6	K1, O1, O2, O4, WD8, Q6, J50, Y4.	8F (2-8-0 Std.), 7F(0-8-0 L.N.W.).	
7	V3.	5MT (4-6-0),5MT(2-6-0).	4MT(4-6-0), 5MT (4-6-0).
8	B16, J37, J38.	6P (4-6-0 "Jubilee").	6MT (4-6-2), 7MT (4-6-2).
9	A1, A2, A3, A4, V2.	7P (4-6-0 Rebuilt "Jubilee"), 7P (4-6-0 Rebuilt "Patriot"), 7P (4-6-0 "Royal Scot").	9F (2-10-0).

LOCOMOTIVE SUPERINTENDENTS AND CHIEF MECHANICAL ENGINEERS

BRITISH RAILWAYS (E. & N.E. REGIONS)

A. H. Peppercorn .. 1948–1949 *(post abolished)*

L.N.E.R.

Sir Nigel Gresley .. 1923–1941
E. Thompson 1941–1946
A. H. Peppercorn .. 1946–1947

GREAT NORTHERN

A. Sturrock	1850–1866
P. Stirling	1866–1895
H. A. Ivatt	1896–1911
H. N. Gresley	1911–1922

NORTH EASTERN

E. Fletcher	1854–1883
A. McDonnell*	1883–1884
T. W. Worsdell	1885–1890
W. Worsdell	1890–1910
Sir Vincent Raven ..	1910–1922

GREAT EASTERN

R. Sinclair	1862–1866
S. W. Johnson	1866–1873
W. Adams	1873–1878
M. Bromley	1878–1881
T. W. Worsdell	1881–1885
J. Holden	1885–1907
S. D. Holden	1908–1912
A. J. Hill	1912–1922

LANCASHIRE, DERYSHIRE AND EAST COAST

R. A. Thom	1902–1907

MANCHESTER, SHEFFIELD AND LINCOLNSHIRE

Richard Peacock ..	–1854
W. G. Craig	1854–1859
Charles Sacré	1859–1886
T. Parker	1886–1893
H. Pollitt	1893–1897

GREAT CENTRAL

H. Pollitt	1897–1900
J. G. Robinson	1900–1922

HULL AND BARNSLEY

M. Stirling	1885–1922

MIDLAND AND GREAT NORTHERN JOINT

W. Marriott	1884–1924

NORTH BRITISH

T. Wheatley†	1867–1874
D. Drummond	1875–1882
M. Holmes	1882–1903
W. P. Reid	1903–1919
W. Chalmers	1919–1922

GREAT NORTH OF SCOTLAND

D. K. Clark	1853–1855
J. F. Ruthven	1855–1857
W. Cowan	1857–1883
J. Manson	1883–1890
J. Johnson	1890–1894
W. Pickersgill	1894–1914
T. E. Heywood	1914–1922

* Between McDonnell and T. W. Worsdell there was an interval during which the office was covered by a Locomotive Committee.

† Previous to whom the records are indeterminate.

B.R. STEAM LOCOMOTIVES
Nos. 70000-92250

7P6F — 4-6-2

Introduced 1951. Designed at Derby.

Weight
Locomotive: 94 tons 4 cwt

Boiler pressure
250 lb sq in

Cylinders
(O) 20″ × 28″

Driving wheel diameter
6′ 2″

Tractive effort
32,150 lb

Valve gear
Walschaerts (piston valves)

70000 *Britannia*
70001 *Lord Hurcomb*
70002 *Geoffrey Chaucer*
70003 *John Bunyan*
70004 *William Shakespeare*
70005 *John Milton*
70006 *Robert Burns*
70007 *Coeur-de-Lion*
70008 *Black Prince*
70009 *Alfred the Great*
70010 *Owen Glendower*
70011 *Hotspur*
70012 *John of Gaunt*
70013 *Oliver Cromwell*
70014 *Iron Duke*
70015 *Apollo*
70016 *Ariel*
70017 *Arrow*
70018 *Flying Dutchman*
70019 *Lightning*
70020 *Mercury*
70021 *Morning Star*
70022 *Tornado*
70023 *Venus*
70024 *Vulcan*
70025 *Western Star*
70026 *Polar Star*
70027 *Rising Star*
70028 *Royal Star*
70029 *Shooting Star*
70030 *William Wordsworth*
70031 *Byron*
70032 *Tennyson*
70033 *Charles Dickens*
70034 *Thomas Hardy*
70035 *Rudyard Kipling*
70036 *Boadicea*
70037 *Hereward the Wake*
70038 *Robin Hood*
70039 *Sir Christopher Wren*
70040 *Clive of India*
70041 *Sir John Moore*
70042 *Lord Roberts*
70043 *Lord Kitchener*
70044 *Earl Haig*
70045 *Lord Rowallan*
70046 *Anzac*
70047
70048 *The Territorial Army 1908-1958*
70049 *Solway Firth*
70050 *Firth of Clyde*
70051 *Firth of Forth*
70052 *Firth of Tay*
70053 *Moray Firth*
70054 *Dornoch Firth*

TOTAL: 55

Standard Class 7P6F 4-6-2 No. 70031 *Byron* [*J. R. Carter*

Standard Class 6P5F 4-6-2 No. 72006 *Clan Mackenzie* [*Alan Williams*

Standard Class 3MT 2-6-0 No. 77008 [*P. Ransome-Wallis*

6P5F 4-6-2

Introduced 1952. Designed at Derby.

Weight
Locomotive: 86 tons 19 cwt

Boiler pressure
225 lb. sq in

Cylinders
(O) $19\frac{1}{2}'' \times 28''$

Driving wheel diameter
6′ 2″

Tractive effort
27,520 lb

Valve gear
Walschaerts (piston valves)

72005 *Clan Macgregor*
72006 *Clan Mackenzie*
72007 *Clan Mackintosh*
72008 *Clan Macleod*
72009 *Clan Stewart*

TOTAL: 5

5MT 4-6-0

Introduced 1951. Designed at Doncaster.
* Introduced 1956. Fitted with Caprotti valve gear.

Weight
Locomotive: 76 tons 4 cwt

Boiler Pressure
225 lb sq in

Cylinders
(O) 19″ × 28″

Driving wheel diameter
6′ 2″

Tractive effort
26,120 lb

Valve gear
Walschaerts (piston valves)

73000	73012	73024	73036	73047	73058	73069
73001	73013	73025	73037	73048	73059	73070
73002	73014	73026	73038	73049	73060	73071
73003	73015	73027	73039	73050	73061	73072
73004	73016	73028	73040	73051	73062	73073
73005	73017	73029	73041	73052	73063	73074
73006	73018	73030	73042	73053	73064	73075
73007	73019	73031	73043	73054	73065	73076
73008	73020	73032	73044	73055	73066	73077
73009	73021	73033	73045	73056	73067	73078
73010	73022	73034	73046	73057	73068	73079
73011	73023	73035				

73080 *Merlin*
73081 *Excalibur*
73082 *Camelot*
73083 *Pendragon*
73084 *Tintagel*
73085 *Melisande*
73086 *The Green Knight*
73087 *Linette*
73088 *Joyous Gard*
73089 *Maid of Astolat*

73090	73093	73096	73099	73102	73105	73108
73091	73094	73097	73100	73103	73106	73109
73092	73095	73098	73101	73104	73107	

73110 *The Red Knight*
73111 *King Uther*
73112 *Morgan le Fay*
73113 *Lyonnesse*
73114 *Etarre*
73115 *King Pellinore*
73116 *Iseult*
73117 *Vivien*
73118 *King Leodegrance*
73119 *Elaine*

Standard Class 5MT 4-6-0 No. 73054 [*Alan Williams*

Standard Class 4MT 4-6-0 No. 75073 (fitted with double chimney) [*Alan Williams*

Standard Class 4MT 2-6-0 No. 76063 [*J. Scrace*

73120	73128*	73136*	73144*	73151*	73158*	73165*
73121	73129*	73137*	73145*	73152*	73159*	73166*
73122	73130*	73138*	73146*	73153*	73160*	73167*
73123	73131*	73139*	73147*	73154*	73161*	73168
73124	73132*	73140*	73148*	73155*	73162*	73169
73125*	73133*	73141*	73149*	73156*	73163*	73170
73126*	73134*	73142*	73150*	73157*	73164*	73171
73127*	73135*	73143*				

TOTAL: 172

4MT 4-6-0

Introduced 1951. Designed at Brighton.
* Introduced 1957. Fitted with double chimney.

Weight
Locomotive: 69 tons

Boiler Pressure
225 lb sq in

Cylinders
(O) 18″ × 28″

Driving wheel diameter
5′ 8″

Tractive effort
25,100 lb

Valve gear
Walschaerts (piston valves)

75000	75012	75024	75036	75047	75058	75069*
75001	75013	75025	75037	75048	75059	75070*
75002	75014	75026*	75038	75049	75060	75071*
75003*	75015	75027	75039	75050	75061	75072*
75004	75016	75028	75040	75051	75062	75073*
75005*	75017	75029*	75041	75052	75063	75074*
75006*	75018	75030	75042	75053	75064	75075*
75007	75019	75031	75043	75054	75065*	75076*
75008*	75020*	75032	75044	75055	75066*	75077*
75009	75021	75033	75045	75056	75067*	75078*
75010	75022	75034	75046	75057	75068*	75079*
75011	75023	75035				

TOTAL: 80

4MT 2-6-0

Introduced 1953. Designed at Doncaster.

Weight
Locomotive: 59 tons 2 cwt

Boiler pressure
225 lb sq in

Cylinders
(O) $17\frac{1}{2}$″ × 26″

Driving wheel diameter
5′ 3″

Tractive effort
24,170 lb

Valve gear
Walschaerts (piston valves)

76000	76005	76010	76015	76020	76025	76030
76001	76006	76011	76016	76021	76026	76031
76002	76007	76012	76017	76022	76027	76032
76003	76008	76013	76018	76023	76028	76033
76004	76009	76014	76019	76024	76029	76034

76035	76047	76059	76071	76082	76093	76104
76036	76048	76060	76072	76083	76094	76105
76037	76049	76061	76073	76084	76095	76106
76038	76050	76062	76074	76085	76096	76107
76039	76051	76063	76075	76086	76097	76108
76040	76052	76064	76076	76087	76098	76109
76041	76053	76065	76077	76088	76099	76110
76042	76054	76066	76078	76089	76100	76111
76043	76055	76067	76079	76090	76101	76112
76044	76056	76068	76080	76091	76102	76113
76045	76057	76069	76081	76092	76103	76114
76046	76058	76070				

TOTAL: 115

3MT 2-6-0

Introduced 1954. Designed at Swindon.

Weight
Locomotive: 57 tons 9 cwt

Boiler Pressure
200 lb sq in

Cylinders
(O) $17\frac{1}{2}'' \times 26''$

Driving wheel diameter
5′ 3″

Tractive effort
21,490 lb

Valve gear
Walschaerts (Piston valves)

77000	77003	77006	77009	77012	77015	77018
77001	77004	77007	77010	77013	77016	77019
77002	77005	77008	77011	77014	77017	

TOTAL: 20

2MT 2-6-0

Introduced 1953. Designed at Derby.

Weight
Locomotive: 49 tons 5 cwt

Boiler Pressure
200 lb sq in

Cylinders
(O) $16\frac{1}{2}'' \times 24''$

Driving wheel diameter
5′ 0″

Tractive effort
18,515 lb

Valve gear
Walschaerts (piston valves)

78000	78010	78020	78029	78038	78047	78056
78001	78011	78021	78030	78039	78048	78057
78002	78012	78022	78031	78040	78049	78058
78003	78013	78023	78032	78041	78050	78059
78004	78014	78024	78033	78042	78051	78060
78005	78015	78025	78034	78043	78052	78061
78006	78016	78026	78035	78044	78053	78062
78007	78017	78027	78036	78045	78054	78063
78008	78018	78028	78037	78046	78055	78064
78009	78019					

TOTAL: 65

4MT 2-6-4T

Introduced 1951. Designed at Brighton.

Weight
Locomotive: 88 tons 10 cwt

Boiler pressure
225 lb sq in

Cylinders
(O) 18″ × 28″

Driving wheel diameter
5′ 8″

Tractive effort
25,100 lb

Valve gear
Walschaerts (piston valves)

80000	80022	80044	80066	80088	80111	80133
80001	80023	80045	80067	80089	80112	80134
80002	80024	80046	80068	80090	80113	80135
80003	80025	80047	80069	80091	80114	80136
80004	80026	80048	80070	80092	80115	80137
80005	80027	80049	80071	80093	80116	80138
80006	80028	80050	80072	80094	80117	80139
80007	80029	80051	80073	80095	80118	80140
80008	80030	80052	80074	80096	80119	80141
80009	80031	80053	80075	80097	80120	80142
80010	80032	80054	80076	80098	80121	80143
80011	80033	80055	80077	80099	80122	80144
80012	80034	80056	80078	80100	80123	80145
80013	80035	80057	80079	80101	80124	80146
80014	80036	80058	80080	80102	80125	80147
80015	80037	80059	80081	80104	80126	80148
80016	80038	80060	80082	80105	80127	80149
80017	80039	80061	80083	80106	80128	80150
80018	80040	80062	80084	80107	80129	80151
80019	80041	80063	80085	80108	80130	80152
80020	80042	80064	80086	80109	80131	80153
80021	80043	80065	80087	80110	80132	80154

TOTAL: 154

3MT 2-6-2T

Introduced 1952. Designed at Swindon.

Weight
Locomotive: 73 tons 10 cwt

Boiler Pressure
200 lb sq in

Cylinders
(O) 17½″ × 26″

Driving wheel diameter
5′ 3″

Tractive effort
21,490 lb

Valve gear
Walschaerts (piston valves)

Above:
Standard Class 4MT 2-6-4T No. 80031
[P. J. Cupper

Right:
Standard Class 3MT 2-6-2T No. 82011
[D. L. Percival

Below:
Standard Class 9F 2-10-0 No. 92239
[Alan Williams

82000	82007	82014	82021	82027	82033	82039
82001	82008	82015	82022	82028	82034	82040
82002	82009	82016	82023	82029	82035	82041
82003	82010	82017	82024	82030	82036	82042
82004	82011	82018	82025	82031	82037	82043
82005	82012	82019	82026	82032	82038	82044
82006	82013	82020				

TOTAL: 45

2MT 2-6-2T

Introduced 1953. Designed at Derby.

Weight
Locomotive: 63 tons 5 cwt

Boiler pressure
200 lb sq in

Cylinders
(O) 16½″ × 24″

Driving wheel diameter
5′ 0″

Tractive effort
18,515 lb

Valve gear
Walschaerts (piston valves)

84000	84005	84010	84014	84018	84022	84026
84001	84006	84011	84015	84019	84023	84027
84002	84007	84012	84016	84020	84024	84028
84003	84008	84013	84017	84021	84025	84029
84004	84009					

TOTAL: 30

8F WD 2-8-0

Introduced 1943. Riddles Ministry of Supply "Austerity" locomotives purchased by British Railways, 1948.

Weight
Locomotive: 70 tons 5 cwt
Tender: 55 tons 10 cwt

Boiler Pressure
225 lb sq in

Cylinders
(O) 19″ × 28″

Driving wheel diameter
4′ 8½″

Tractive effort
34,215 lb

Valve gear
Walschaerts (piston valves)

90000	90007	90014	90024	90032	90040	90047
90001	90008	90015	90025	90033	90041	90048
90002	90009	90016	90026	90035	90042	90049
90003	90010	90017	90027	90036	90043	90050
90004	90011	90018	90029	90037	90044	90051
90005	90012	90019	90030	90038	90045	90052
90006	90013	90020	90031	90039	90046	90053

90054
90055
90056
90057
90058
90059
90061
90063
90064
90065
90066
90067
90068
90069
90070
90071
90072
90073
90074
90075
90076
90077
90078
90079
90080
90081
90082
90084
90085
90086
90088
90089
90090
90091
90092
90094
90095
90096
90097
90098
90099
90100
90101
90102
90103
90104
90107
90108
90109
90110
90111
90112
90113
90114
90115
90116
90117
90118
90119
90120
90121
90122
90123
90124
90125
90126
90127
90129
90130
90131
90132
90133
90135
90136
90138
90139
90140
90141
90142
90143
90144
90145
90146
90147
90148
90149
90151
90152
90153
90154
90155
90156
90157
90158
90159
90160
90161
90162
90164
90165
90166
90168
90169
90170
90171
90172
90173
90175
90176
90177
90178
90179
90180
90181
90182
90183
90184
90185
90186
90187
90188
90189
90190
90192
90193
90194
90195
90197
90199
90200
90201
90202
90203
90204
90205
90206
90207
90208
90209
90210
90211
90212
90213
90214
90215
90216
90217
90218
90219
90220
90221
90222
90223
90224
90225
90226
90227
90228
90229
90230
90231
90232
90233
90234
90235
90236
90237
90238
90239
90240
90241
90242
90243
90245
90246
90248
90249
90250
90251
90252
90254
90255
90257
90258
90259
90260
90261
90262
90263
90264
90265
90266
90267
90268
90269
90271
90272
90273
90274
90275
90276
90277
90279
90280
90281
90282
90283
90284
90285
90289
90290
90291
90292
90293
90294
90295
90296
90297
90299
90300
90301
90302
90304
90305
90306
90309
90310
90311
90312
90313
90314
90315
90316
90317
90318
90319
90321
90322
90323
90324
90325
90326
90327
90328
90329
90330
90331
90332
90333
90334
90335
90336
90337
90338
90339
90340
90341
90342
90343
90344
90345
90346
90347
90348
90349
90350
90351
90352
90353
90354
90357
90358
90359
90360
90361
90362
90363
90364
90365
90366
90367
90368
90369
90370
90371
90372
90373
90374
90375
90377
90378
90379
90380
90381
90382
90383
90384
90385
90386
90388
90389
90390
90392
90393
90394
90395
90396
90397
90398
90399
90400
90401
90402
90403
90404
90405
90406
90407
90408
90409
90410
90411
90412
90413
90415
90416
90417
90418
90419
90420
90421
90422
90423
90424
90426
90427

Standard Class 2MT 2-6-2T No. 84020 [J. Scrace

Class WD 2-8-0 No. 90040 [D. L. Percival

Class 9F 2-10-0 No. 92029 (fitted with Crosti boiler) [P. Kingston

90428	90469	90514	90558	90602	90649	90692
90429	90470	90515	90560	90604	90650	90694
90430	90471	90516	90561	90605	90651	90695
90432	90472	90517	90563	90606	90652	90696
90433	90474	90518	90564	90609	90654	90697
90434	90475	90519	90566	90610	90655	90698
90435	90476	90520	90567	90611	90656	90699
90437	90477	90521	90568	90612	90658	90700
90438	90478	90522	90569	90613	90659	90702
90439	90479	90524	90570	90614	90660	90703
90440	90480	90525	90571	90615	90661	90704
90441	90481	90527	90572	90617	90662	90705
90442	90482	90528	90573	90618	90663	90706
90443	90483	90529	90574	90619	90664	90707
90444	90484	90530	90576	90620	90666	90708
90445	90485	90531	90577	90621	90667	90709
90446	90486	90533	90578	90622	90668	90710
90447	90487	90534	90579	90623	90669	90711
90448	90488	90535	90580	90624	90670	90712
90449	90489	90536	90581	90625	90671	90713
90450	90490	90537	90582	90626	90672	90714
90451	90491	90538	90583	90627	90673	90715
90452	90492	90539	90584	90628	90674	90716
90453	90493	90540	90585	90629	90675	90717
90454	90496	90541	90586	90631	90676	90718
90456	90497	90542	90587	90632	90677	90719
90457	90498	90543	90588	90633	90678	90720
90458	90499	90544	90589	90635	90679	90721
90459	90500	90545	90590	90636	90680	90722
90460	90501	90546	90592	90639	90681	90723
90461	90502	90547	90593	90640	90682	90724
90462	90503	90548	90595	90641	90683	90725
90463	90504	90551	90596	90642	90684	90727
90464	90506	90552	90597	90643	90685	90728
90465	90507	90553	90598	90644	90686	90729
90466	90509	90555	90599	90645	90687	90730
90467	90510	90556	90600	90646	90688	90731
90468	90511	90557	90601	90647	90689	

TOTAL: 649

9F 2-10-0

Introduced 1954. Designed at Brighton.
* Introduced 1955. Fitted with Crosti boiler. Crosti pre-heater now sealed off for orthodox working.
† Introduced 1957. Fitted with double chimney.
‡ Introduced 1958. Fitted with Mechanical Stoker and double chimney.

§ Introduced 1960. Fitted with Giesl oblong ejector.

Weight Locomotive: 86 tons 14 cwt 90 tons 4 cwt*	**Driving wheel diameter** 5′ 0″
Boiler pressure 250 lb sq in	**Tractive effort** 39,670 lb
Cylinders (O) 20″ × 28″	**Valve gear** Walschaerts (piston valves)

92000†	92032	92064	92096	92127	92158	92189†
92001	92033	92065	92097	92128	92159	92190†
92002	92034	92066	92098	92129	92160	92191†
92003	92035	92067	92099	92130	92161	92192†
92004	92036	92068	92100	92131	92162	92193†
92005	92037	92069	92101	92132	92163	92194†
92006	92038	92070	92102	92133	92164	92195†
92007	92039	92071	92103	92134	92165‡	92196†
92008	92040	92072	92104	92135	92166‡	92197†
92009	92041	92073	92105	92136	92167‡	92198†
92010	92042	92074	92106	92137	92168	92199†
92011	92043	92075	92107	92138	92169	92200†
92012	92044	92076	92108	92139	92170	92201†
92013	92045	92077	92109	92140	92171	92202†
92014	92046	92078	92110	92141	92172	92203†
92015	92047	92079†	92111	92142	92173	92204†
92016	92048	92080	92112	92143	92174	92205†
92017	92049	92081	92113	92144	92175	92206†
92018	92050	92082	92114	92145	92176	92207†
92019	92051	92083	92115	92146	92177	92208†
92020*	92052	92084	92116	92147	92178†	92209†
92021*	92053	92085	92117	92148	92179	92210†
92022*	92054	92086	92118	92149	92180	92211†
92023*	92055	92087	92119	92150	92181	92212†
92024*	92056	92088	92120	92151	92182	92213†
92025*	92057	92089	92121	92152	92183†	92214†
92026*	92058	92090	92122	92153	92184†	92215†
92027*	92059	92091	92123	92154	92185†	92216†
92028*	92060	92092	92124	92155	92186†	92217†
92029*	92061	92093	92125	92156	92187†	92218†
92030	92062	92094	92126	92157	92188†	92219†
92031	92063	92095				

92220† *Evening Star* 92221† 92222†

92223†	92227†	92231†	92235†	92239†	92243†	92247†
92224†	92228†	92232†	92236†	92240†	92244†	92248†
92225†	92229†	92233†	92237†	92241†	92245†	92249†
92226†	92230†	92234†	92238†	92242†	92246†	92250§

TOTAL: 251

BRITISH RAILWAYS STANDARD TENDERS

N.B.—*These pairings are not permanent and are liable to alteration with changed operating conditions.*

Type	Capacity		Weight in full W.O.		Locos. to which Allocated
	Water galls.	Coal tons	tons	cwt.	
BR1 ...	4,250	7	49	3	70000–24/30–44 72000–9 73000–49
BR1A ...	5,000	7	52	10	70025–9
BR1B ...	4,725	7	50	5	92020–9/60–6/97–9 73080–9 73100–9/20–34/45–71 75065–79 76053–69
BR1C ...	4,725	9	53	5	92015–9/45–59/77–86 92100–39/50–64 73065–79/90–9 73135–44
BR1D ...	4,725	9	54	10	70045–54
BR1F ...	5,625	7	55	5	92010–4/30–44/67–76 92087–96 92140–9/68–92202 73110–9
BR1G ...	5,000	7	52	10	92000–9 73050–2 92203–50
BR1H ...	4,250	7	49	3	73053–64
BR1K ...	4,325	9	52	7	92165–7
BR2 ...	3,500	6	42	3	75000–49 76000–44
BR2A ...	3,500	6	42	3	75050–64 76045–52/70–76114 77000–19
BR3 ...	3,000	4	36	17	78000–64

B.R. DIESEL LOCOMOTIVES

BRITISH RAILWAYS diesel locomotives are listed in this publication in numerical order and classified by make. In 1957 the then British Transport Commission announced a new numbering system for all diesel locomotives, involving the use of the prefix "D" for all such locomotives, followed by a number which would not only identify the locomotive, but would also indicate its power range; at the same time, the power of main-line locomotives was to be indicated by Type numbers in the following ranges:—

Type of Locomotive	*Horsepower*
1	800–1,000
2	1,000–1,365
3	1,500–1,750
4	2,000–2,750
5	3,000+

Subsequently new batches of locomotives have been delivered and numbered outside the original groups for the type so that it is not always possible to ascertain the power of a locomotive solely by its number. Locomotives built before nationalisation, or after nationalisation to company designs, are numbered in a separate series commencing at 10000 without a prefix "D". Early British Railways diesel shunters were numbered in this series but have since been renumbered into the "D" series.

The heading to each class shows the type designation, the principal manufacturer and the wheel arrangement.

Diesel (and electric) locomotive wheel arrangements are described by a development of the Continental notation. This calculates by axles and not by wheels, and uses letters instead of numerals to denote driving axles ("A" = 1, "B" = 2, "C" = 3, etc.) and numerals only for non-powered axles. An indication of the grouping of axles is given, but powered and non-powered axles may be found in the same group. Thus British Railways' diesel-electric locomotive No. D5500 is described as an A1A-A1A, indicating that it is mounted on two six-wheel bogies, each of which has a non-powered axle in the centre and a motored axle at either end. Groups of axles are separated by a hyphen if they are quite independent of each other, but by a "plus" sign in cases where powered bogies are linked by an articulated joint to take certain stresses. If all axles on a bogie or frame unit are individually powered, a suffix letter "o" is added to the descriptive letter.

The sub-headings give brief technical details of each type. Reference marks are shown in the details and against the locomotives concerned (if known) where equipment varies from the main batch.

COUPLING OF DIESEL LOCOMOTIVES

Although several diesel locomotives may be coupled together and driven by one man in the leading cab, for various reasons it is not possible for all types of diesel units to work together. In order to distinguish locomotives that can run together, all have painted above each buffer a colour code symbol. This is repeated as a miniature symbol on the plug socket covers. Only units bearing the same symbol may run in multiple and be controlled from the leading cab.

Type of locomotive	*Coupling symbol*
All diesel-electric locomotives with electro-pneumatic control.	Blue star ★
All diesel-electric locomotives with electro-magnetic control.	Red circle ●
Diesel-hydraulic locomotives Nos. D600-4, D6300-5.	Orange square □
Diesel-hydraulic locomotives Nos. D803-70, D6306-57 (Nos. D800-2 cannot work in multiple).	White diamond ◇
Diesel-hydraulic locomotives Nos. D7000-7100.	Yellow triangle △
Ex-L.M.S. diesel-electric locomotives Nos. 10000/1.	Red diamond ♦
Ex-S.R. diesel-electric locomotives Nos. 10201/2.	Red/white square ■
Ex-S.R. diesel-electric locomotive No. 10203.	Blue star ★

DIESEL LOCOMOTIVES

The lists of numbers include all locomotives on order at the time of going to press. For details of delivery, see the Motive Power Change list each month in Modern Railways.

Type 4 British Railways 1Co-Co1

"Peak" ★

Introduced
1959

Engine
*Sulzer 12-cyl 12LDA28-A twin-bank pressure charged of 2,300 b.h.p. at 750 r.p.m.
Sulzer 12LDA28-B, with inter-cooling of 2,500 b.h.p. at 750 r.p.m. (‡2,750 b.h.p. at 800 r.p.m.)

Weight
138 tons 2 cwt

Maximum tractive effort
70,000 lb

Total b.h.p.
2,300*
2,500

Transmission
Electric. Six Crompton Parkinson 305 h.p. axle-hung nose-suspended traction motors
†Six Brush traction motors

Driving wheel diameter
3′ 9″

D1* *Scafell Pike*
D2 *Helvellyn*
D3* *Skiddaw*
D4* *Great Gable*
D5* *Cross Fell*
D6* *Whernside*
D7* *Ingleborough*
D8* *Penyghent*
D9* *Snowdon*
D10* *Tryfan*

D11	D18	D25	D32	D38	D44	D50
D12	D19	D26	D33	D39	D45	D51
D13	D20	D27	D34	D40	D46	D52
D14	D21	D28	D35	D41	D47	D53
D15	D22	D29	D36	D42	D48	D54
D16	D23	D30	D37	D43	D49	D55
D17	D24	D31				

D56 *The Bedfordshire and Hertfordshire Regiment (T.A.)*

D57‡	D64	D70	D76	D82	D88	D94
D58	D65	D71	D77	D83	D89	D95
D59	D66	D72	D78	D84	D90	D96
D60	D67	D73	D79	D85	D91	D97
D61	D68	D74	D80	D86	D92	D98
D62	D69	D75	D81	D87	D93	D99
D63						

D100 *Sherwood Forester*

D101 D110 D119 D128 D137 D146† D155†
D102 D111 D120 D129 D138† D147† D156†
D103 D112 D121 D130 D139† D148† D157†
D104 D113 D122 D131 D140† D149† D158†
D105 D114 D123 D132 D141† D150† D159†
D106 D115 D124 D133 D142† D151† D160†
D107 D116 D125 D134 D143† D152† D161†
D108 D117 D126 D135 D144† D153† D162†
D109 D118 D127 D136 D145† D154†

D163† *Leicestershire and Derbyshire Yeomanry*

D164† D169† D174† D178† D182† D186† D190†
D165† D170† D175† D179† D183† D187† D191†
D166† D171† D176† D180† D184† D188† D192†
D167† D172† D177† D181† D185† D189† D193†
D168† D173†

Type 4 English Electric 1Co-Co1

Introduced
1958

Engine
English Electric 16-cyl 16SVT Mk. II of 2,000 b.h.p. at 850 r.p.m.

Weight
133 tons 0 cwt

Maximum tractive effort
52,000 lb

Total b.h.p. ★
2,000

Transmission
Electric. Six English Electric nose-suspended traction motors

Driving wheel diameter
3′ 9″

D200 D202 D204 D206 D207 D208 D209
D201 D203 D205

D210 *Empress of Britain*
D211 *Mauretania*
D212 *Aureol*
D213 *Andania*
D214 *Antonia*
D215 *Aquitania*
D216 *Campania*
D217 *Carinthia*
D218 *Carmania*
D219 *Caronia*
D220 *Franconia*
D221 *Ivernia*
D222 *Laconia*
D223 *Lancastria*
D224 *Lucania*
D225 *Lusitania*
D226
D227 *Parthia*
D228 *Samaria*
D229 *Saxonia*
D230 *Scythia*
D231 *Sylvania*
D232 *Empress of Canada*
D233 *Empress of England*
D234 *Accra*
D235 *Apapa*
D236

British Railways Type 4 2,500 b.h.p. diesel-electric 1Co-Co1 No. D155 [*D. L. Percival*

English Electric Type 4 2,000 b.h.p. diesel-electric 1Co-Co1 No. D375 [*Alan Williams*

North British Type 4 2,000 b.h.p. diesel-hydraulic A1A-A1A No. D602 *Bulldog* [*M. Pope*

D237	D261	D285	D308	D331	D354	D377
D238	D262	D286	D309	D332	D355	D378
D239	D263	D287	D310	D333	D356	D379
D240	D264	D288	D311	D334	D357	D380
D241	D265	D289	D312	D335	D358	D381
D242	D266	D290	D313	D336	D359	D382
D243	D267	D291	D314	D337	D360	D383
D244	D268	D292	D315	D338	D361	D384
D245	D269	D293	D316	D339	D362	D385
D246	D270	D294	D317	D340	D363	D386
D247	D271	D295	D318	D341	D364	D387
D248	D272	D296	D319	D342	D365	D388
D249	D273	D297	D320	D343	D366	D389
D250	D274	D298	D321	D344	D367	D390
D251	D275	D299	D322	D345	D368	D391
D252	D276	D300	D323	D346	D369	D392
D253	D277	D301	D324	D347	D370	D393
D254	D278	D302	D325	D348	D371	D394
D255	D279	D303	D326	D349	D372	D395
D256	D280	D304	D327	D350	D373	D396
D257	D281	D305	D328	D351	D374	D397
D258	D282	D306	D329	D352	D375	D398
D259	D283	D307	D330	D353	D376	D399
D260	D284					

Type 4 North British A1A-A1A

"Warship" □

Introduced
1958

Engines
Two N.B.L./M.A.N. 12-cyl L12V 18/21S of 1,000 b.h.p.

Weight
117 tons 8 cwt

Maximum tractive effort
50,000 lb

Total b.h.p.
2,000

Transmission
Hydraulic. Two Hardy Spicer cardan shafts to Voith-North British type L306r hydraulic transmissions each containing three torque converters

Driving wheel diameter
3′ 7″

D600 *Active*
D601 *Ark Royal*
D602 *Bulldog*
D603 *Conquest*
D604 *Cossack*

Type 4 British Railways B-B
"Warship" ◇

Introduced
1958

Engines
Two Bristol Siddeley-Maybach MD 650 V-type of 1,152 b.h.p. at 1,530 r.p.m. (*1,056 b.h.p. at 1,400 r.p.m.) † Two Paxman 12-cyl high-speed 12 YJXL of 1,200 b.h.p. at 1,500 r.p.m.

Weight
78 tons 0 cwt

Maximum tractive effort
52,400 lb

Total b.h.p.
2,000*
2,200
2,400†

Transmission
Hydraulic. Two Mekydro type K104 hydraulic transmissions containing permanently filled single torque converter and four-speed automatic gearbox

Driving wheel diameter
3′ 3½″

* These locomotives may not be coupled in multiple.

D800* *Sir Brian Robertson*
D801* *Vanguard*
D802* *Formidable*
D803 *Albion*
D804 *Avenger*
D805 *Benbow*
D806 *Cambrian*
D807 *Caradoc*
D808 *Centaur*
D809 *Champion*
D810 *Cockade*
D811 *Daring*
D812 *Royal Naval Reserve 1859-1959*
D813 *Diadem*
D814 *Dragon*
D815 *Druid*
D816 *Eclipse*
D817 *Foxhound*
D818 *Glory*
D819 *Goliath*
D820 *Grenville*
D821 *Greyhound*
D822 *Hercules*
D823 *Hermes*
D824 *Highflyer*
D825 *Intrepid*
D826 *Jupiter*
D827 *Kelly*
D828 *Magnificent*
D829 *Magpie*
D830† *Majestic*
D831 *Monarch*
D832 *Onslaught*

Type 4 North British B-B
"Warship" ◇

Introduced
1960

Engines
Two N.B.L./M.A.N. 12-cyl L12V18/21BS of 1,100 b.h.p.

Weight
79 tons 10 cwt

Maximum tractive effort
53,400 lb

Total b.h.p.
2,200

Transmission
Hydraulic. Voith

Driving wheel diameter
3′ 3½″

D833 *Panther*
D834 *Pathfinder*
D835 *Pegasus*
D836 *Powerful*
D837 *Ramillies*
D838 *Rapid*
D839 *Relentless*
D840 *Resistance*
D841 *Roebuck*
D842 *Royal Oak*
D843 *Sharpshooter*
D844 *Spartan*
D845 *Sprightly*
D846 *Steadfast*
D847 *Strongbow*
D848 *Sultan*
D849 *Superb*
D850 *Swift*
D851 *Temeraire*
D852 *Tenacious*
D853 *Thruster*
D854 *Tiger*
D855 *Triumph*
D856 *Trojan*
D857 *Undaunted*
D858 *Valorous*
D859 *Vanquisher*
D860 *Victorious*
D861 *Vigilant*
D862 *Viking*
D863 *Warrior*
D864 *Zambesi*
D865 *Zealous*

Type 4 British Railways B-B

Class continued from D832 ◇

D866 *Zebra*
D867 *Zenith*
D868 *Zephyr*
D869 *Zest*
D870 *Zulu*

Type 4 British Railways C-C

"Western"

Introduced
1961

Engines
Two Maybach MD655 V-type of 1,440 h.p. at 1,500 r.p.m.

Weight
108 tons 0 cwt

Maximum tractive effort
72,600 lb

Total b.h.p.
2,700

Transmission
Hydraulic. Voith

Driving wheel diameter
3′ 7″

D1000 *Western Enterprise*
D1001 *Western Pathfinder*
D1002 *Western Explorer*
D1003 *Western Pioneer*
D1004 *Western Crusader*
D1005 *Western Venturer*
D1006 *Western Stalwart*
D1007 *Western Talisman*
D1008 *Western Harrier*
D1009 *Western Invader*
D1010 *Western Campaigner*
D1011 *Western Thunderer*
D1012 *Western Firebrand*
D1013 *Western Ranger*
D1014 *Western Leviathan*
D1015 *Western Champion*
D1016 *Western Gladiator*
D1017 *Western Warrior*

North British Type 4 2,200 b.h.p. diesel-hydraulic B-B No. D839 *Relentless* [*A. Swain*

British Railways Type 4 2,700 b.h.p. diesel-hydraulic C-C No. D1002 *Western Explorer* [*M. Pope*

Brush Type 4 2,750 b.h.p. diesel-electric Co-Co No. D1500 [*Hawker Siddeley*

D1018	*Western Buccaneer*	D1046	*Western Marquess*
D1019	*Western Challenger*	D1047	*Western Lord*
D1020	*Western Hero*	D1048	*Western Lady*
D1021	*Western Cavalier*	D1049	*Western Monarch*
D1022	*Western Sentinel*	D1050	*Western Ruler*
D1023	*Western Fusilier*	D1051	*Western Ambassador*
D1024	*Western Huntsman*	D1052	*Western Viceroy*
D1025	*Western Guardsman*	D1053	*Western Patriarch*
D1026	*Western Centurion*	D1054	*Western Governor*
D1027	*Western Lancer*	D1055	*Western Advocate*
D1028	*Western Hussar*	D1056	*Western Sultan*
D1029	*Western Legionnaire*	D1057	*Western Chieftain*
D1030	*Western Musketeer*	D1058	*Western Nobleman*
D1031	*Western Rifleman*	D1059	*Western Empire*
D1032	*Western Marksman*	D1060	*Western Dominion*
D1033	*Western Trooper*	D1061	*Western Envoy*
D1034	*Western Dragoon*	D1062	*Western Courier*
D1035	*Western Yeoman*	D1063	*Western Monitor*
D1036	*Western Emperor*	D1064	*Western Regent*
D1037	*Western Empress*	D1065	*Western Consort*
D1038	*Western Sovereign*	D1066	*Western Prefect*
D1039	*Western King*	D1067	*Western Druid*
D1040	*Western Queen*	D1068	*Western Reliance*
D1041	*Western Prince*	D1069	*Western Vanguard*
D1042	*Western Princess*	D1070	*Western Gauntlet*
D1043	*Western Duke*	D1071	*Western Renown*
D1044	*Western Duchess*	D1072	*Western Glory*
D1045	*Western Viscount*	D1073	*Western Bulwark*

Type 4 Brush Co-Co

Introduced
1962

Engine
Sulzer 12-cyl 12LDA28-C twin-bank, pressure-charged, of 2,750 b.h.p. at 800 r.p.m.

Weight
114 tons 0 cwt

Maximum tractive effort
55,000 lb

Total b.h.p.
2,750

Transmission
Electric. Six axle-hung, nose-suspended Brush traction motors

Driving wheel diameter
3′ 9″

D1500	D1508	D1515	D1522	D1529	D1536	D1543
D1501	D1509	D1516	D1523	D1530	D1537	D1544
D1502	D1510	D1517	D1524	D1531	D1538	D1545
D1503	D1511	D1518	D1525	D1532	D1539	D1546
D1504	D1512	D1519	D1526	D1533	D1540	D1547
D1505	D1513	D1520	D1527	D1534	D1541	D1548
D1506	D1514	D1521	D1528	D1535	D1542	D1549
D1507						

Shunter British Railways 0-6-0

Introduced
1957

Engine
Gardner 8L3 of 204 b.h.p. at 1,200 r.p.m.

Weight
30 tons 16 cwt

Maximum tractive effort
15,650 lb

Total b.h.p.
204

Transmission
Mechanical. Vulcan-Sinclair type 23 fluid coupling. Wilson-Drewry C.A.5 type five-speed epicyclic gearbox. Type RF 11 spiral bevel reverse and final drive unit

Driving wheel diameter
3′ 7″

D2000	D2029	D2058	D2087	D2116	D2144	D2172
D2001	D2030	D2059	D2088	D2117	D2145	D2173
D2002	D2031	D2060	D2089	D2118	D2146	D2174
D2003	D2032	D2061	D2090	D2119	D2147	D2175
D2004	D2033	D2062	D2091	D2120	D2148	D2176
D2005	D2034	D2063	D2092	D2121	D2149	D2177
D2006	D2035	D2064	D2093	D2122	D2150	D2178
D2007	D2036	D2065	D2094	D2123	D2151	D2179
D2008	D2037	D2066	D2095	D2124	D2152	D2180
D2009	D2038	D2067	D2096	D2125	D2153	D2181
D2010	D2039	D2068	D2097	D2126	D2154	D2182
D2011	D2040	D2069	D2098	D2127	D2155	D2183
D2012	D2041	D2070	D2099	D2128	D2156	D2184
D2013	D2042	D2071	D2100	D2129	D2157	D2185
D2014	D2043	D2072	D2101	D2130	D2158	D2186
D2015	D2044	D2073	D2102	D2131	D2159	D2187
D2016	D2045	D2074	D2103	D2132	D2160	D2188
D2017	D2046	D2075	D2104	D2133	D2161	D2189
D2018	D2047	D2076	D2105	D2134	D2162	D2190
D2019	D2048	D2077	D2106	D2135	D2163	D2191
D2020	D2049	D2078	D2107	D2136	D2164	D2192
D2021	D2050	D2079	D2108	D2137	D2165	D2193
D2022	D2051	D2080	D2109	D2138	D2166	D2194
D2023	D2052	D2081	D2110	D2139	D2167	D2195
D2024	D2053	D2082	D2111	D2140	D2168	D2196
D2025	D2054	D2083	D2112	D2141	D2169	D2197
D2026	D2055	D2084	D2113	D2142	D2170	D2198
D2027	D2056	D2085	D2114	D2143	D2171	D2199
D2028	D2057	D2086	D2115			

Class continued with D2372

British Railways 204 b.h.p. diesel-mechanical 0-6-0 No. D2085 [*L. Elsey*

Drewry 204 b.h.p. diesel-mechanical 0-6-0 No. 11112 (since renumbered D2211) [*R. E. Vincent*

Drewry 204 b.h.p. diesel-mechanical 0-6-0 No. D2228 (with 3ft 6in wheels) [*R. K. Evans*

Shunter Drewry 0-6-0

Introduced
1952

Engine
Gardner 8L3 of 204 b.h.p. at 1,200 r.p.m.

Weight
29 tons 15 cwt

Maximum tractive effort
16,850 lb

Total b.h.p.
204

Transmission
Mechanical. Vulcan-Sinclair type 23 fluid coupling. Wilson-Drewry C.A.5 type five-speed epicyclic gearbox. Type RF 11 spiral bevel reverse and final drive unit

Driving wheel diameter
3′ 3″

D2200	D2203	D2205	D2207	D2209	D2211	D2213
D2201	D2204	D2206	D2208	D2210	D2212	D2214
D2202						

Shunter Drewry 0-6-0

Introduced
1955

Engine
Gardner 8L3 of 204 b.h.p. at 1,200 r.p.m.

Weight
29 tons 15 cwt

Maximum tractive effort
15,650 lb

Total b.h.p.
204

Transmission
Mechanical. Vulcan-Sinclair type 23 fluid coupling. Wilson-Drewry C.A.5 type five-speed epicyclic gearbox. Type RF 11 spiral bevel reverse and final drive unit

Driving wheel diameter
3′ 6″

D2215	D2224	D2233	D2242	D2250	D2258*	D2266
D2216	D2225	D2234*	D2243	D2251*	D2259*	D2267
D2217*	D2226	D2235	D2244	D2252	D2260	D2268
D2218	D2227	D2236	D2245	D2253	D2261	D2269
D2219	D2228	D2237	D2246	D2254	D2262	D2270
D2220	D2229	D2238	D2247	D2255	D2263	D2271
D2221	D2230	D2239	D2248	D2256*	D2264	D2272
D2222	D2231	D2240	D2249	D2257*	D2265	D2273
D2223	D2232	D2241				

* *These locomotives still carry their original numbers;* D2217 (11123), D2234 (11153), D2251 (11221), D2256 (11226), D2257 (11227), D2258 (11228), D2259 (11229).

Shunter Drewry 0-6-0

Introduced
1959

Engine
Gardner 8L3 of 204 b.h.p. at 1,200 r.p.m.

Weight
29 tons 15 cwt

Maximum tractive effort
16,850 lb

Total b.h.p.
204

Transmission
Mechanical. Vulcan-Sinclair type 23 fluid coupling. Wilson-Drewry C.A.5 type five-speed epicyclic gearbox. Type RF 11 spiral bevel reverse and final drive unit

Driving wheel diameter
3′ 7″

D2274	D2284	D2294	D2304	D2314	D2323	D2332
D2275	D2285	D2295	D2305	D2315	D2324	D2333
D2276	D2286	D2296	D2306	D2316	D2325	D2334
D2277	D2287	D2297	D2307	D2317	D2326	D2335
D2278	D2288	D2298	D2308	D2318	D2327	D2336
D2279	D2289	D2299	D2309	D2319	D2328	D2337
D2280	D2290	D2300	D2310	D2320	D2329	D2338
D2281	D2291	D2301	D2311	D2321	D2330	D2339
D2282	D2292	D2302	D2312	D2322	D2331	D2340
D2283	D2293	D2303	D2313			

Shunter British Railways 0-6-0

Class continued from D2199

D2372	D2376	D2380	D2384	D2388	D2392	D2396
D2373	D2377	D2381	D2385	D2389	D2393	D2397
D2374	D2378	D2382	D2386	D2390	D2394	D2398
D2375	D2379	D2383	D2387	D2391	D2395	D2399

Shunter Barclay 0-6-0

Introduced
1956

Engine
Gardner 8L3 of 204 b.h.p. at 1,200 r.p.m.

Weight
32 tons 0 cwt

Maximum tractive effort
15,340 lb

Total b.h.p.
204

Transmission
Mechanical. Vulcan-Sinclair type 23 fluid coupling. Wilson C.A.4 type four-speed epicyclic gearbox. Wiseman type 15 RLGB reverse and final drive unit

Driving wheel diameter
3′ 6″

Drewry 204 b.h.p. diesel-mechanical 0-6-0 No. D2293 (with 3ft 7in wheels) [*R. K. Evans*

Barclay 204 b.h.p. diesel-mechanical 0-6-0 No. 11177 (since renumbered D2400) [*P. J. Sharpe*

D2400	D2402	D2404	D2406	D2407	D2408	D2409
D2401	D2403	D2405				

Shunter Barclay 0-4-0

Introduced
1958

Engine
Gardner 8L3 of 204 b.h.p. at 1,200 r.p.m.

Weight
35 tons 0 cwt

Maximum tractive effort
20,000 lb

Total b.h.p.
204

Transmission
Mechanical. Vulcan-Sinclair type 23 fluid coupling. Wilson-Drewry C.A.5 type five-speed epicyclic gearbox. Wiseman type 15 R.L.G.B. reverse and final drive unit

Driving wheel diameter
3′ 7″

D2410	D2415	D2420	D2425	D2430	D2435	D2440
D2411	D2416	D2421	D2426	D2431	D2436	D2441
D2412	D2417	D2422	D2427	D2432	D2437	D2442
D2413	D2418	D2423	D2428	D2433	D2438	D2443
D2414	D2419	D2424	D2429	D2434	D2439	D2444

Shunter Hudswell-Clarke 0-6-0

Introduced
1956

Engine
Gardner 8L3 of 204 b.h.p. at 1,200 r.p.m.

Weight
36 tons 7 cwt

Maximum tractive effort
16,100 lb

Total b.h.p.
204

Transmission
Mechanical. S.C.R.5 type, size 23 scoop control fluid coupling. Three-speed "SSS Power-flow" double synchro-type gearbox and final drive

Driving wheel diameter
3′ 6″

D2500	D2503	D2506	D2509	D2512	D2515	D2518
D2501	D2504*	D2507	D2510	D2513	D2516	D2519
D2502	D2505	D2508	D2511	D2514	D2517	

* *D2504 still carries its original number, 11120*

Barclay 204 b.h.p. diesel-mechanical 0-4-0 No. D2418 [*R. J. Buckley*

Hudswell-Clarke 204 b.h.p. diesel-mechanical 0-6-0 No. 11146 (since renumbered D2507) [*B. Stephenson*

Shunter Hunslet 0-6-0

Introduced
1955

Engine
Gardner 8L3 of 204 b.h.p. at 1,200 r.p.m.

Weight
30 tons 0 cwt

Maximum tractive effort
14,500 lb

Total b.h.p.
204

Transmission
Mechanical. Hunslet patent friction clutch. Hunslet four-speed gearbox incorporating reverse and final drive gears

Driving wheel diameter
3′ 4″
3′ 9″*

D2550	D2560†	D2570	D2580*	D2590*	D2600*	D2609*
D2551	D2561	D2571	D2581*	D2591*	D2601*	D2610*
D2552	D2562	D2572	D2582*	D2592*	D2602*	D2611*
D2553	D2563†	D2573	D2583*	D2593*	D2603*	D2613*
D2554	D2564	D2574*	D2584*	D2594*	D2604*	D2614*
D2555	D2565†	D2575*	D2585*	D2595*	D2605*	D2615*
D2556	D2566†	D2576*	D2586*	D2596*	D2606*	D2616*
D2557	D2567	D2577*	D2587*	D2597*	D2607*	D2617*
D2558	D2568	D2578*	D2588*	D2598*	D2608*	D2618*
D2559	D2569†	D2579*	D2589*	D2599*		

† *These locomotives still carry their original numbers;* D2560 (11163), D2563 (11166), D2565 (11168), D2566 (11169), D2569 (11172)

Shunter North British 0-4-0

Introduced
1953

Engine
Paxman 6RPH of 200 b.h.p. at 1,000 r.p.m.

Weight
32 tons 0 cwt

Maximum tractive effort
21,500 lb

Total b.h.p.
200

Transmission
Hydraulic. Voith-North British hydraulic torque converter type L33YU. North British bevel gears and reversing dog clutch coupled through reduction gearing to jackshaft

Driving wheel diameter
3′ 6″

D2700	D2702	D2703	D2704	D2705	D2706	D2707
D2701						

Top: Hunslet 204 b.h.p. diesel-mechanical 0-6-0 No. D2558
[*P. H. Groom*

Centre: Hunslet 204 b.h.p. diesel-mechanical 0-6-0 No. D2594 (with 3ft 9in wheels)
[*N. E. Preedy*

Left: North British 200 b.h.p. diesel-hydraulic 0-4-0 No. D2705

Shunter North British 0-4-0

Introduced
1957

Engine
N.B.L./M.A.N. W6V 17.5/22A of 225 b.h.p. at 1,100 r.p.m. (12 hr rating)

Weight
30 tons 0 cwt

Maximum tractive effort
20,080 lb

Total b.h.p.
225

Transmission
Hydraulic. Voith-North British hydraulic torque converter type LCCYU. North British bevel gears and reversing dog clutch coupled through reduction gearing to jackshaft

Driving wheel diameter
3′ 6″

D2708	D2719	D2730	D2741	D2751	D2761	D2771
D2709	D2720	D2731	D2742	D2752	D2762	D2772
D2710	D2721	D2732	D2743	D2753	D2763	D2773
D2711	D2722	D2733	D2744	D2754	D2764	D2774
D2712	D2723	D2734	D2745	D2755	D2765	D2775
D2713	D2724	D2735	D2746	D2756	D2766	D2776
D2714	D2725	D2736	D2747	D2757	D2767	D2777
D2715	D2726	D2737	D2748	D2758	D2768	D2778
D2716	D2727	D2738	D2749	D2759	D2769	D2779
D2717	D2728	D2739	D2750	D2760	D2770	D2780
D2718*	D2729	D2740				

** D2718 still carries its original number,* 11718

Shunter Yorkshire Engine Co. 0-4-0

Introduced
1960

Engine
Rolls-Royce C6NFL of 179 h.p. at 1,800 r.p.m.

Weight
28 tons 0 cwt

Maximum tractive effort
15,000 lb

Total b.h.p.
170

Transmission
Hydraulic. Rolls-Royce 3-stage torque converter, Series 10,000. Yorkshire Engine Co. axle-hung double-reduction final drive with reversing mechanism

Driving wheel diameter
3′ 6″

D2850	D2853	D2856	D2859	D2862	D2865	D2868
D2851	D2854	D2857	D2860	D2863	D2866	D2869
D2852	D2855	D2858	D2861	D2864	D2867	

North British 225 b.h.p. diesel-hydraulic 0-4-0 No. D2757 [*C. P. Boocock*

Yorkshire Engine Co. 170 b.h.p. diesel-hydraulic 0-4-0 No. D2858 [*R. J. Smith*

Shunter North British 0-4-0

Introduced
1958

Engine
N.B.L./M.A.N. W6V 17.5/22 AS, super-charged

Weight
36 tons 0 cwt

Maximum tractive effort
24,100 lb

Total b.h.p.
330

Transmission
Hydraulic. Voith-North British hydraulic torque converter type L24V. North British spiral bevel gears, reversing and reduction gears to jackshaft

Driving wheel diameter
3′ 9″

D2900 D2902 D2904 D2906 D2908 D2910 D2912
D2901 D2903 D2905 D2907 D2909 D2911 D2913

Shunter Hunslet 0-4-0

Introduced
1955

Engine
Gardner 6L3 of 153 b.h.p. at 1,200 r.p.m.

Weight
22 tons 9 cwt

Maximum tractive effort
10,800 lb

Total b.h.p.
153

Transmission
Mechanical. Hunslet patent friction clutch and four-speed gearbox incorporating reverse and final drive gears

Driving wheel diameter
3′ 4″

D2950 D2951 D2952

Shunter Barclay 0-4-0

Introduced
1956

Engine
Gardner 6L3 of 153 b.h p. at 1,200 r.p.m.

Weight
25 tons 0 cwt

Maximum tractive effort
12,750 lb

Total b.h.p.
153

Transmission
Mechanical. Vulcan-Sinclair rigid type hydraulic coupling. Wilson S.E. 4 type four-speed epicyclic gearbox. Wiseman type 15 RLGB reverse and final drive unit

Driving wheel diameter
3′ 2″

D2953 D2954 D2955 D2956

North British 330 b.h.p. diesel-hydraulic 0-4-0 No. D2904 [*C. P. Boococ*

Hunslet 153 b.h.p. diesel-mechanical 0-4-0 No. D2952

Shunter Ruston & Hornsby 0-4-0

Introduced
1956

Engine
Ruston 6VPHL of 165 b.h.p. at 1,250 r.p.m. (1 hr rating)

Weight
28 tons 0 cwt

Maximum tractive effort
14,350 lb

Total b.h.p.
165

Transmission
Mechanical. Oil pressure-operated S.L.M. type friction clutches incorporated in Ruston constant mesh type gearbox. Reverse gear and final drive unit incorporating bevel gears and dog clutches and reduction gear to final drive

Driving wheel diameter
3′ 4″

D2957 D2958

Shunter Ruston & Hornsby 0-6-0

Introduced
1962

Engine
Paxman 6-cyl RPHL

Weight
42 tons 5 cwt

Maximum tractive effort
28,240 lb

Total b.h.p.
275

Transmission
Electric. A.E.I. type RTA 6652 traction motor, spigot-mounted on a double-reduction axle-hung final drive gearbox

Driving wheel diameter
3′ 6″

D2985	D2987	D2989	D2991	D2993	D2995	D2997
D2986	D2988	D2990	D2992	D2994	D2996	D2998

Shunter Brush 0-4-0

Introduced
1960

Engine
Petter-McLaren 6-cyl LE6 of 180 b.h.p. at 1,800 r.p m.

Weight
30 tons 0 cwt

Maximum tractive effort
19,200 lb

Total b.h.p.
180

Transmission
Electric. One axle-hung nose-suspended traction motor

Driving wheel diameter
3′ 6″

D2999

Left: Barclay 153 b.h.p. diesel-mechanical 0-4-0 No. 11505 (since renumbered D2955)
[*C. P. Boocock*

Centre: Ruston & Hornsby 165 b.h.p. diesel-mechanical 0-4-0 No. 11508 (since renumbered D2958)
[*B. K. B. Green*

Bottom: Ruston & Hornsby 275 b.h.p. diesel-electric 0-6-0 No. D2990
[*G. T. Storer*

Shunter British Railways 0-6-0

Locomotives D3000-D3336 were originally numbered 13000-13336 and are being renumbered as they are overhauled.

Introduced
1953

Engine
English Electric 6-cyl 6KT of 350 b.h.p. at 630 r.p.m.

Weight
49 tons 0 cwt

Maximum tractive effort
35,000 lb

Total b.h.p.
350

Transmission
Electric. Two English Electric nose-suspended traction motors. Double reduction gear drive

Driving wheel diameter
4′ 6″

Note: Nos. D3000-91 and D3102-3116 fitted for vacuum brake operation.

D3000	D3017	D3034	D3051	D3068	D3085	D3101
D3001	D3018	D3035	D3052	D3069	D3086	D3102
D3002	D3019	D3036	D3053	D3070	D3087	D3103
D3003	D3020	D3037	D3054	D3071	D3088	D3104
D3004	D3021	D3038	D3055	D3072	D3089	D3105
D3005	D3022	D3039	D3056	D3073	D3090	D3106
D3006	D3023	D3040	D3057	D3074	D3091	D3107
D3007	D3024	D3041	D3058	D3075	D3092	D3108
D3008	D3025	D3042	D3059	D3076	D3093	D3109
D3009	D3026	D3043	D3060	D3077	D3094	D3110
D3010	D3027	D3044	D3061	D3078	D3095	D3111
D3011	D3028	D3045	D3062	D3079	D3096	D3112
D3012	D3029	D3046	D3063	D3080	D3097	D3113
D3013	D3030	D3047	D3064	D3081	D3098	D3114
D3014	D3031	D3048	D3065	D3082	D3099	D3115
D3015	D3032	D3049	D3066	D3083	D3100	D3116
D3016	D3033	D3050	D3067	D3084		

Shunter British Railways 0-6-0

Introduced
1955

Engine
Crossley 6-cyl ESNT 6 of 350 b.h.p. at 825 r.p.m. (continuous rating)

Weight
47 tons 10 cwt

Maximum tractive effort
35,000 lb

Total b.h.p.
350

Transmission
Electric. Two Crompton Parkinson nose-suspended traction motors. Double reduction gear drive

Driving wheel diameter
4′ 6″

D3117	D3119	D3121	D3123	D3124	D3125	D3126
D3118	D3120	D3122				

Shunter British Railways 0-6-0

Introduced
1953

Engine
English Electric 6-cyl 6KT of 350 b.h.p. at 680 r.p.m.

Weight
48 tons 0 cwt

Maximum tractive effort
35,000 lb

Total b.h.p.
350

Transmission
Electric. Two English Electric nose-suspended traction motors. Double reduction gear drive

Driving wheel diameter
4′ 6″

Fitted for vacuum brake operation

D3127	D3129	D3131	D3133	D3134	D3135	D3136
D3128	D3130	D3132				

Shunter British Railways 0-6-0

Introduced
1955

Engine
Blackstone 6-cyl ER6T of 350 b.h.p. at 750 r.p.m.

Weight
47 tons 10 cwt

Maximum tractive effort
35,000 lb

Total b.h.p.
350

Transmission
Electric. Two G.E.C. nose-suspended traction motors. Double reduction gear drive

Driving wheel diameter
4′ 6″

Fitted for vacuum brake operation

D3137	D3140	D3142	D3144	D3146	D3148	D3150
D3138	D3141	D3143	D3145	D3147	D3149	D3151
D3139						

Shunter British Railways 0-6-0

Introduced
1955

Engine
Blackstone 6-cyl ER6T of 350 b.h.p. at 750 r.p.m.

Weight
47 tons 0 cwt

Maximum tractive effort
35,000 lb

Total b.h.p.
350

Transmission
Electric. Two B.T.H. nose-suspended traction motors. Double reduction gear drive

Driving wheel diameter
4′ 6″

D3152	D3155	D3157	D3159	D3161	D3163	D3165
D3153	D3156	D3158	D3160	D3162	D3164	D3166
D3154						

D3167-D3438: for particulars see D3127-D3136

D3167	D3206	D3245	D3284	D3323	D3362	D3401
D3168	D3207	D3246	D3285	D3324	D3363	D3402
D3169	D3208	D3247	D3286	D3325	D3364	D3403
D3170	D3209	D3248	D3287	D3326	D3365	D3404
D3171	D3210	D3249	D3288	D3327	D3366	D3405
D3172	D3211	D3250	D3289	D3328	D3367	D3406
D3173	D3212	D3251	D3290	D3329	D3368	D3407
D3174	D3213	D3252	D3291	D3330	D3369	D3408
D3175	D3214	D3253	D3292	D3331	D3370	D3409
D3176	D3215	D3254	D3293	D3332	D3371	D3410
D3177	D3216	D3255	D3294	D3333	D3372	D3411
D3178	D3217	D3256	D3295	D3334	D3373	D3412
D3179	D3218	D3257	D3296	D3335	D3374	D3413
D3180	D3219	D3258	D3297	D3336	D3375	D3414
D3181	D3220	D3259	D3298	D3337	D3376	D3415
D3182	D3221	D3260	D3299	D3338	D3377	D3416
D3183	D3222	D3261	D3300	D3339	D3378	D3417
D3184	D3223	D3262	D3301	D3340	D3379	D3418
D3185	D3224	D3263	D3302	D3341	D3380	D3419
D3186	D3225	D3264	D3303	D3342	D3381	D3420
D3187	D3226	D3265	D3304	D3343	D3382	D3421
D3188	D3227	D3266	D3305	D3344	D3383	D3422
D3189	D3228	D3267	D3306	D3345	D3384	D3423
D3190	D3229	D3268	D3307	D3346	D3385	D3424
D3191	D3230	D3269	D3308	D3347	D3386	D3425
D3192	D3231	D3270	D3309	D3348	D3387	D3426
D3193	D3232	D3271	D3310	D3349	D3388	D3427
D3194	D3233	D3272	D3311	D3350	D3389	D3428
D3195	D3234	D3273	D3312	D3351	D3390	D3429
D3196	D3235	D3274	D3313	D3352	D3391	D3430
D3197	D3236	D3275	D3314	D3353	D3392	D3431
D3198	D3237	D3276	D3315	D3354	D3393	D3432
D3199	D3238	D3277	D3316	D3355	D3394	D3433
D3200	D3239	D3278	D3317	D3356	D3395	D3434
D3201	D3240	D3279	D3318	D3357	D3396	D3435
D3202	D3241	D3280	D3319	D3358	D3397	D3436
D3203	D3242	D3281	D3320	D3359	D3398	D3437
D3204	D3243	D3282	D3321	D3360	D3399	D3438
D3205	D3244	D3283	D3322	D3361	D3400	

D3439-D3453: for particulars see D3137-D3151

D3439	D3442	D3444	D3446	D3448	D3450	D3452
D3440	D3443	D3445	D3447	D3449	D3451	D3453
D3441						

D3454-D3472: for particulars see D3127-D3136

D3454	D3457	D3460	D3463	D3466	D3469	D3471
D3455	D3458	D3461	D3464	D3467	D3470	D3472
D3456	D3459	D3462	D3465	D3468		

D3473-D3502: for particulars see D3137-D3151

D3473	D3478	D3483	D3487	D3491	D3495	D3499
D3474	D3479	D3484	D3488	D3492	D3496	D3500
D3475	D3480	D3485	D3489	D3493	D3497	D3501
D3476	D3481	D3486	D3490	D3494	D3498	D3502
D3477	D3482					

D3503-D3611: for particulars see D3127-D3136

D3503	D3519	D3535	D3551	D3567	D3582	D3597
D3504	D3520	D3536	D3552	D3568	D3583	D3598
D3505	D3521	D3537	D3553	D3569	D3584	D3599
D3506	D3522	D3538	D3554	D3570	D3585	D3600
D3507	D3523	D3539	D3555	D3571	D3586	D3601
D3508	D3524	D3540	D3556	D3572	D3587	D3602
D3509	D3525	D3541	D3557	D3573	D3588	D3603
D3510	D3526	D3542	D3558	D3574	D3589	D3604
D3511	D3527	D3543	D3559	D3575	D3590	D3605
D3512	D3528	D3544	D3560	D3576	D3591	D3606
D3513	D3529	D3545	D3561	D3577	D3592	D3607
D3514	D3530	D3546	D3562	D3578	D3593	D3608
D3515	D3531	D3547	D3563	D3579	D3594	D3609
D3516	D3532	D3548	D3564	D3580	D3595	D3610
D3517	D3533	D3549	D3565	D3581	D3596	D3611
D3518	D3534	D3550	D3566			

D3612-D3651: for particulars see D3137-D3151

D3612	D3618	D3624	D3630	D3636	D3642	D3647
D3613	D3619	D3625	D3631	D3637	D3643	D3648
D3614	D3620	D3626	D3632	D3638	D3644	D3649
D3615	D3621	D3627	D3633	D3639	D3645	D3650
D3616	D3622	D3628	D3634	D3640	D3646	D3651
D3617	D3623	D3629	D3635	D3641		

D3652-D4048: for particulars see D3127-D3136

D3652	D3658	D3664	D3670	D3676	D3682	D3688
D3653	D3659	D3665	D3671	D3677	D3683	D3689
D3654	D3660	D3666	D3672	D3678	D3684	D3690
D3655	D3661	D3667	D3673	D3679	D3685	D3691
D3656	D3662	D3668	D3674	D3680	D3686	D3692
D3657	D3663	D3669	D3675	D3681	D3687	D3693

Brush 180 b.h.p. diesel-electric 0-4-0 No. D2999 [*C. P. Boocock*

British Railways 350 b.h.p. diesel-electric 0-6-0 No. D3964 [*J. C. Haydon*

D3694
D3695
D3696
D3697
D3698
D3699
D3700
D3701
D3702
D3703
D3704
D3705
D3706
D3707
D3708
D3709
D3710
D3711
D3712
D3713
D3714
D3715
D3716
D3717
D3718
D3719
D3720
D3721
D3722
D3723
D3724
D3725
D3726
D3727
D3728
D3729
D3730
D3731
D3732
D3733
D3734
D3735
D3736
D3737
D3738
D3739
D3740
D3741
D3742
D3743
D3744
D3745
D3746
D3747
D3748
D3749
D3750
D3751
D3752
D3753
D3754
D3755
D3756
D3757
D3758
D3759
D3760
D3761
D3762
D3763
D3764
D3765
D3766
D3767
D3768
D3769
D3770
D3771
D3772
D3773
D3774
D3775
D3776
D3777
D3778
D3779
D3780
D3781
D3782
D3783
D3784
D3785
D3786
D3787
D3788
D3789
D3790
D3791
D3792
D3793
D3794
D3795
D3796
D3797
D3798
D3799
D3800
D3801
D3802
D3803
D3804
D3805
D3806
D3807
D3808
D3809
D3810
D3811
D3812
D3813
D3814
D3815
D3816
D3817
D3818
D3819
D3820
D3821
D3822
D3823
D3824
D3825
D3826
D3827
D3828
D3829
D3830
D3831
D3832
D3833
D3834
D3835
D3836
D3837
D3838
D3839
D3840
D3841
D3842
D3843
D3844
D3845
D3846
D3847
D3848
D3849
D3850
D3851
D3852
D3853
D3854
D3855
D3856
D3857
D3858
D3859
D3860
D3861
D3862
D3863
D3864
D3865
D3866
D3867
D3868
D3869
D3870
D3871
D3872
D3873
D3874
D3875
D3876
D3877
D3878
D3879
D3880
D3881
D3882
D3883
D3884
D3885
D3886
D3887
D3888
D3889
D3890
D3891
D3892
D3893
D3894
D3895
D3896
D3897
D3898
D3899
D3900
D3901
D3902
D3903
D3904
D3905
D3906
D3907
D3908
D3909
D3910
D3911
D3912
D3913
D3914
D3915
D3916
D3917
D3918
D3919
D3920
D3921
D3922
D3923
D3924
D3925
D3926
D3927
D3928
D3929
D3930
D3931
D3932
D3933
D3934
D3935
D3936
D3937
D3938
D3939
D3940
D3941
D3942
D3943
D3944
D3945
D3946
D3947
D3948
D3949
D3950
D3951
D3952
D3953
D3954
D3955
D3956
D3957
D3958
D3959
D3960
D3961
D3962
D3963
D3964
D3965
D3966
D3967
D3968
D3969
D3970
D3971
D3972
D3973
D3974
D3975
D3976
D3977
D3978
D3979
D3980
D3981
D3982
D3983
D3984
D3985
D3986
D3987
D3988
D3989
D3990
D3991
D3992
D3993
D3994
D3995
D3996
D3997
D3998
D3999
D4000
D4001
D4002
D4003
D4004
D4005
D4006
D4007
D4008
D4009
D4010
D4011
D4012
D4013
D4014
D4015
D4016
D4017
D4018
D4019
D4020
D4021
D4022
D4023
D4024
D4025
D4026
D4027
D4028
D4029

D4030	D4033	D4036	D4039	D4042	D4045	D4047
D4031	D4034	D4037	D4040	D4043	D4046	D4048
D4032	D4035	D4038	D4041	D4044		

D4049-D4094: for particulars see D3137-D3151

D4049	D4056	D4063	D4070	D4077	D4083	D4089
D4050	D4057	D4064	D4071	D4078	D4084	D4090
D4051	D4058	D4065	D4072	D4079	D4085	D4091
D4052	D4059	D4066	D4073	D4080	D4086	D4092
D4053	D4060	D4067	D4074	D4081	D4087	D4093
D4054	D4061	D4068	D4075	D4082	D4088	D4094
D4055	D4062	D4069	D4076			

D4095-D4235

D4095	D4116	D4136	D4156	D4176	D4196	D4216
D4096	D4117	D4137	D4157	D4177	D4197	D4217
D4097	D4118	D4138	D4158	D4178	D4198	D4218
D4098	D4119	D4139	D4159	D4179	D4199	D4219
D4099	D4120	D4140	D4160	D4180	D4200	D4220
D4100	D4121	D4141	D4161	D4181	D4201	D4221
D4101	D4122	D4142	D4162	D4182	D4202	D4222
D4102	D4123	D4143	D4163	D4183	D4203	D4223
D4103	D4124	D4144	D4164	D4184	D4204	D4224
D4104	D4125	D4145	D4165	D4185	D4205	D4225
D4105	D4126	D4146	D4166	D4186	D4206	D4226
D4106	D4127	D4147	D4167	D4187	D4207	D4227
D4107	D4128	D4148	D4168	D4188	D4208	D4228
D4108	D4129	D4149	D4169	D4189	D4209	D4229
D4109	D4130	D4150	D4170	D4190	D4210	D4230
D4110	D4131	D4151	D4171	D4191	D4211	D4231
D4111	D4132	D4152	D4172	D4192	D4212	D4232
D4112	D4133	D4153	D4173	D4193	D4213	D4233
D4113	D4134	D4154	D4174	D4194	D4214	D4234
D4114	D4135	D4155	D4175	D4195	D4215	D4235
D4115						

Type 2 British Railways Bo-Bo

★

Introduced
1958

Engine
Sulzer 6-cyl 6LDA28 of 1,160 b.h.p. at 750 r.p.m.
†‡Sulzer 6-cyl 6LDA28-B of 1,250 b.h.p. at 750 r.p.m.

Weight
75 tons 0 cwt
72 tons 17 cwt*†

Maximum tractive effort
40,000 lb
‡45,000 lb

Total b.h.p.
1,160
1,160*
1,250†‡§

Transmission
Electric. Four B.T.H. axle-hung, nose-suspended traction motors of 213 h.p. (continuous rating)
‡Four A.E.I. 253 AY nose-suspended traction motors

Driving wheel diameter
3′ 9″

D5000	D5034	D5068	D5102*	D5136*	D5170†	D5204‡
D5001	D5035	D5069	D5103*	D5137*	D5171†	D5205‡
D5002	D5036	D5070	D5104*	D5138*	D5172†	D5206‡
D5003	D5037	D5071	D5105*	D5139*	D5173†	D5207‡
D5004	D5038	D5072	D5106*	D5140*	D5174†	D5208‡
D5005	D5039	D5073	D5107*	D5141*	D5175†	D5209‡
D5006	D5040	D5074	D5108*	D5142*	D5176‡	D5210‡
D5007	D5041	D5075	D5109*	D5143*	D5177‡	D5211‡
D5008	D5042	D5076	D5110*	D5144*	D5178‡	D5212‡
D5009	D5043	D5077	D5111*	D5145*	D5179‡	D5213‡
D5010	D5044	D5078	D5112*	D5146*	D5180‡	D5214‡
D5011	D5045	D5079	D5113*	D5147*	D5181‡	D5215‡
D5012	D5046	D5080	D5114*	D5148*	D5182‡	D5216‡
D5013	D5047	D5081	D5115*	D5149*	D5183‡	D5217‡
D5014	D5048	D5082	D5116*	D5150*	D5184‡	D5218‡
D5015	D5049	D5083	D5117*	D5151†	D5185‡	D5219‡
D5016	D5050	D5084	D5118*	D5152†	D5186‡	D5220‡
D5017	D5051	D5085	D5119*	D5153†	D5187‡	D5221‡
D5018	D5052	D5086	D5120*	D5154†	D5188‡	D5222‡
D5019	D5053	D5087	D5121*	D5155†	D5189‡	D5223‡
D5020	D5054	D5088	D5122*	D5156†	D5190‡	D5224‡
D5021	D5055	D5089	D5123*	D5157†	D5191‡	D5225‡
D5022	D5056	D5090	D5124*	D5158†	D5192‡	D5226‡
D5023	D5057	D5091	D5125*	D5159†	D5193‡	D5227‡
D5024	D5058	D5092	D5126*	D5160†	D5194‡	D5228‡
D5025	D5059	D5093	D5127*	D5161†	D5195‡	D5229‡
D5026	D5060	D5094*	D5128*	D5162†	D5196‡	D5230‡
D5027	D5061	D5095*	D5129*	D5163†	D5197‡	D5231‡
D5028	D5062	D5096*	D5130*	D5164†	D5198‡	D5232‡
D5029	D5063	D5097*	D5131*	D5165†	D5199‡	D5233§
D5030	D5064	D5098*	D5132*	D5166†	D5200‡	D5234§
D5031	D5065	D5099*	D5133*	D5167†	D5201‡	D5235§
D5032	D5066	D5100*	D5134*	D5168†	D5202‡	D5236§
D5033	D5067	D5101*	D5135*	D5169†	D5203‡	D5237§

D5238§ D5247§ D5256§ D5265§ D5274§ D5283§ D5292§
D5239§ D5248§ D5257§ D5266§ D5275§ D5284§ D5293§
D5240§ D5249§ D5258§ D5267§ D5276§ D5285§ D5294§
D5241§ D5250§ D5259§ D5268§ D5277§ D5286§ D5295§
D5242§ D5251§ D5260§ D5269§ D5278§ D5287§ D5296§
D5243§ D5252§ D5261§ D5270§ D5279§ D5288§ D5297§
D5244§ D5253§ D5262§ D5271§ D5280§ D5289§ D5298§
D5245§ D5254§ D5263§ D5272§ D5281§ D5290§ D5299§
D5246§ D5255§ D5264§ D5273§ D5282§ D5291§

Class continued with D7500

Type 2 Birmingham R.C. & W. Co. Bo-Bo ★

Introduced
1958

Engine
Sulzer 6-cyl 6LDA28 of 1,160 b.h.p. at 750 r.p.m.
† Sulzer 6-cyl 6LDA28-B of 1,250 b.h.p. at 750 r.p.m.

Weight
74 tons 0 cwt
77 tons 10 cwt*
72 tons 10 cwt†

Maximum tractive effort
42,000 lb

Total b.h.p.
1,160
1,250†

Transmission
Electric. Four Crompton Parkinson axle-hung, nose-suspended traction motors
†Four G.E.C. axle-hung, nose-suspended traction motors

Driving wheel diameter
3′ 7″

D5300* D5317* D5334 D5351† D5368† D5384† D5400†
D5301* D5318* D5335 D5352† D5369† D5385† D5401†
D5302* D5319* D5336 D5353† D5370† D5386† D5402†
D5303* D5320 D5337 D5354† D5371† D5387† D5403†
D5304* D5321 D5338 D5355† D5372† D5388† D5404†
D5305* D5322 D5339 D5356† D5373† D5389† D5405†
D5306* D5323 D5340 D5357† D5374† D5390† D5406†
D5307* D5324 D5341 D5358† D5375† D5391† D5407†
D5308* D5325 D5342 D5359† D5376† D5392† D5408†
D5309* D5326 D5343 D5360† D5377† D5393† D5409†
D5310* D5327 D5344 D5361† D5378† D5394† D5410†
D5311* D5328 D5345 D5362† D5379† D5395† D5411†
D5312* D5329 D5346 D5363† D5380† D5396† D5412†
D5313* D5330 D5347† D5364† D5381† D5397† D5413†
D5314* D5331 D5348† D5365† D5382† D5398† D5414†
D5315* D5332 D5349† D5366† D5383† D5399† D5415†
D5316* D5333 D5350† D5367†

British Railways Type 2 1,160 b.h.p. diesel-electric Bo-Bo No. D5068 [*M. Edwards*

Birmingham R. C. & W. Co. Type 2 1,250 b.h.p. diesel-electric Bo-Bo No. D5384 [*A. Swain*

Brush Type 2 1,365 b.h.p. diesel-electric A1A-A1A No. D5581 [***D. J. Dippie***

Type 2 or 3† Brush A1A-A1A

●*, ★

Introduced
1957

Engine
Mirrlees, Bickerton & Day 12-cyl JVS12T of 1,250*, 1,365 or 1,600† b.h.p. at 850*, 900 or 950† r.p.m. ‡Temporarily uprated to 2,000 b.h.p.

Weight
104 tons 0 cwt

Maximum tractive effort
42,000 lb

Total b.h.p.
1,250*
1,365
1,600†
2,000‡

Transmission
Electric. Four Brush traction motors, single reduction gear drive

Driving wheel diameter
3′ 7″

D5500*	D5529	D5558	D5587	D5616	D5644	D5672
D5501*	D5530	D5559	D5588	D5617	D5645	D5673
D5502*	D5531	D5560	D5589	D5618	D5646	D5674
D5503*	D5532	D5561	D5590	D5619	D5647	D5675
D5504*	D5533	D5562	D5591	D5620	D5648	D5676
D5505*	D5534	D5563	D5592	D5621	D5649	D5677
D5506*	D5535	D5564	D5593	D5622	D5650	D5678
D5507*	D5536	D5565	D5594	D5623	D5651	D5679
D5508*	D5537	D5566	D5595	D5624	D5652	D5680
D5509*	D5538	D5567	D5596	D5625	D5653	D5681
D5510*	D5539	D5568	D5597	D5626	D5654	D5682
D5511*	D5540	D5569	D5598	D5627	D5655†	D5683
D5512*	D5541	D5570	D5599	D5628	D5656†	D5684
D5513*	D5542	D5571	D5600	D5629	D5657†	D5685
D5514*	D5543	D5572	D5601	D5630	D5658†	D5686
D5515*	D5544	D5573	D5602	D5631	D5659†	D5687
D5516*	D5545†	D5574	D5603	D5632	D5660†	D5688
D5517*	D5546	D5575	D5604	D5633	D5661†	D5689
D5518*	D5547	D5576	D5605	D5634	D5662†	D5690
D5519*	D5548	D5577	D5606	D5635	D5663†	D5691
D5520	D5549	D5578	D5607	D5636	D5664†	D5692
D5521	D5550	D5579	D5608	D5637	D5665†	D5693
D5522	D5551	D5580	D5609	D5638	D5666†	D5694
D5523	D5552	D5581	D5610	D5639	D5667†	D5695
D5524	D5553	D5582	D5611	D5640	D5668†	D5696
D5525	D5554	D5583	D5612	D5641	D5669†	D5697
D5526	D5555	D5584	D5613	D5642	D5670†	D5698
D5527	D5556	D5585	D5614	D5643	D5671	D5699
D5528	D5557	D5586	D5615			

Class continued with D5800

Type 2 Metropolitan Vickers Co-Bo

●

Introduced
1958

Engine
Crossley 8-cyl HST V8 of 1,200 b.h.p. at 625 r.p.m. (continuous)

Weight
97 tons 0 cwt

Maximum tractive effort
50,000 lb

Total b.h.p.
1,200

Transmission
Electric. Five Metropolitan-Vickers axle-hung nose-suspended traction motors

Driving wheel diameter
3′ 3½″

D5700	D5703	D5706	D5709	D5712	D5715	D5718
D5701	D5704	D5707	D5710	D5713	D5716	D5719
D5702	D5705	D5708	D5711	D5714	D5717	

Type 2 Brush A1A-A1A

Class continued from D5699

★

D5800	D5809	D5818	D5827	D5836	D5845	D5854
D5801	D5810	D5819	D5828	D5837	D5846	D5855
D5802	D5811	D5820	D5829	D5838	D5847	D5856
D5803	D5812	D5821	D5830	D5839	D5848	D5857
D5804	D5813	D5822	D5831	D5840	D5849	D5858
D5805	D5814	D5823	D5832	D5841	D5850	D5859
D5806	D5815	D5824	D5833	D5842	D5851	D5860
D5807	D5816	D5825	D5834	D5843	D5852	D5861
D5808	D5817	D5826	D5835 ‡	D5844	D5853	D5862

Type 2 English Electric Bo-Bo

★

Introduced
1959

Engine
Napier 9-cyl "Deltic" T9-29 two-stroke, pressure-charged, of 1,100 b.h.p. at 1,600 r.p.m.

Weight
73 tons 17 cwt

Maximum tractive effort
47,000 lb

Total b.h.p.
1,100

Transmission
Electric. Four English Electric axle-hung nose-suspended traction motors

Driving wheel diameter
3′ 7″

D5900	D5902	D5904	D5906	D5907	D5908	D5909
D5901	D5903	D5905				

Metropolitan Vickers Type 2 1,200 b.h.p. diesel-electric Co-Bo No. D5700 [*C. P. Boocock*

English Electric Type 2 1,100 b.h.p. diesel-electric Bo-Bo No. D5907 [*P. J. Sharpe*

North British Type 2 1,000 b.h.p. diesel-electric Bo-Bo No. D6116 [*R. K. Evans*

Type 2 North British Bo-Bo

●, ★*

Introduced
1959

Engine
N.B.L./M.A.N. 12-cyl L12V18/21S, pressure-charged, of 1,000 or 1,100* b.h.p.

Weight
72 tons 10 cwt

Maximum tractive effort
45,000 lb

Total b.h.p.
1,000
1,100*

Transmission
Electric. Four G.E.C. nose-suspended traction motors

Driving wheel diameter
3′ 7″

D6100	D6109	D6118	D6126	D6134	D6142*	D6150*
D6101	D6110	D6119	D6127	D6135	D6143*	D6151*
D6102	D6111	D6120	D6128	D6136	D6144*	D6152*
D6103	D6112	D6121	D6129	D6137	D6145*	D6153*
D6104*	D6113	D6122	D6130	D6138*	D6146*	D6154*
D6105	D6114	D6123	D6131	D6139*	D6147*	D6155*
D6106	D6115	D6124	D6132	D6140*	D6148*	D6156*
D6107	D6116	D6125	D6133*	D6141*	D6149*	D6157*
D6108	D6117					

Type 2 North British B-B

□*, ◇

Introduced
1959

Engine
N.B.L./M.A.N. 12-cyl L12V18/21M of 1,000* or 1,100 b.h.p.

Weight
68 tons 0 cwt*
65 tons 0 cwt

Maximum tractive effort
40,000 lb

Total b.h.p.
1,000*
1,100

Transmission
Hydraulic. Voith-N.B.L. L.T.306r hydraulic transmission and cardan shafts to primary gear-boxes on the inner axles and secondary gear-boxes on the outer axles

Driving wheel diameter
3′ 7″

D6300*	D6309	D6318	D6326	D6334	D6342	D6350
D6301*	D6310	D6319	D6327	D6335	D6343	D6351
D6302*	D6311	D6320	D6328	D6336	D6344	D6352
D6303*	D6312	D6321	D6329	D6337	D6345	D6353
D6304*	D6313	D6322	D6330	D6338	D6346	D6354
D6305*	D6314	D6323	D6331	D6339	D6347	D6355
D6306	D6315	D6324	D6332	D6340	D6348	D6356
D6307	D6316	D6325	D6333	D6341	D6349	D6357
D6308	D6317					

North British Type 2 1,100 b.h.p. diesel-hydraulic B-B No. D6330 [*J. B. Bucknall*

Birmingham R. C. & W. Co. Type 3 1,550 b.h.p. diesel-electric Bo-Bo No. D6549 [*G. T. Storer*

Birmingham R. C. & W. Co. Type 3 1,550 b.h.p. diesel-electric Bo-Bo No. D6591 (built to Hastings line gauge) [*D. L. Percival*

Type 3 Birmingham R.C. & W. Co. Bo-Bo ★

Introduced
1960

Engine
Sulzer 8-cyl 8LDA28 pressure-charged of 1,550 b.h.p. at 750 r.p.m. (continuous)

Weight
73 tons 8 cwt

Maximum tractive effort
45,000 lb

Total b.h.p.
1,550

Transmission
Electric. Four Crompton Parkinson 305 h.p. axle-hung nose-suspended traction motors

Driving wheel diameter
3′ 7″

*Built to Hastings line gauge

D6500	D6514	D6528	D6542	D6556	D6570	D6584
D6501	D6515	D6529	D6543	D6557	D6571	D6585
D6502	D6516	D6530	D6544	D6558	D6572	D6586*
D6503	D6517	D6531	D6545	D6559	D6573	D6587*
D6504	D6518	D6532	D6546	D6560	D6574	D6588*
D6505	D6519	D6533	D6547	D6561	D6575	D6589*
D6506	D6520	D6534	D6548	D6562	D6576	D6590*
D6507	D6521	D6535	D6549	D6563	D6577	D6591*
D6508	D6522	D6536	D6550	D6564	D6578	D6592*
D6509	D6523	D6537	D6551	D6565	D6579	D6593*
D6510	D6524	D6538	D6552	D6566	D6580	D6594*
D6511	D6525	D6539	D6553	D6567	D6581	D6595*
D6512	D6526	D6540	D6554	D6568	D6582	D6596*
D6513	D6527	D6541	D6555	D6569	D6583	D6597*

Type 3 English Electric Co-Co ★

Introduced
1961

Engine
English Electric 12-cyl 12CSVT of 1,750 b.h.p. at 850 r.p.m.

Weight
108 tons 0 cwt

Maximum tractive effort
55,500 lb

Total b.h.p.
1,750

Transmission
Electric. Six English Electric axle-hung nose-suspended traction motors

Driving wheel diameter
3′ 7″

D6700	D6707	D6714	D6721	D6728	D6735	D6742
D6701	D6708	D6715	D6722	D6729	D6736	D6743
D6702	D6709	D6716	D6723	D6730	D6737	D6744
D6703	D6710	D6717	D6724	D6731	D6738	D6745
D6704	D6711	D6718	D6725	D6732	D6739	D6746
D6705	D6712	D6719	D6726	D6733	D6740	D6747
D6706	D6713	D6720	D6727	D6734	D6741	D6748

D6749	D6774	D6799	D6823	D6847	D6871	D6895
D6750	D6775	D6800	D6824	D6848	D6872	D6896
D6751	D6776	D6801	D6825	D6849	D6873	D6897
D6752	D6777	D6802	D6826	D6850	D6874	D6898
D6753	D6778	D6803	D6827	D6851	D6875	D6899
D6754	D6779	D6804	D6828	D6852	D6876	D6900
D6755	D6780	D6805	D6829	D6853	D6877	D6901
D6756	D6781	D6806	D6830	D6854	D6878	D6902
D6757	D6782	D6807	D6831	D6855	D6879	D6903
D6758	D6783	D6808	D6832	D6856	D6880	D6904
D6759	D6784	D6809	D6833	D6857	D6881	D6905
D6760	D6785	D6810	D6834	D6858	D6882	D6906
D6761	D6786	D6811	D6835	D6859	D6883	D6907
D6762	D6787	D6812	D6836	D6860	D6884	D6908
D6763	D6788	D6813	D6837	D6861	D6885	D6909
D6764	D6789	D6814	D6838	D6862	D6886	D6910
D6765	D6790	D6815	D6839	D6863	D6887	D6911
D6766	D6791	D6816	D6840	D6864	D6888	D6912
D6767	D6792	D6817	D6841	D6865	D6889	D6913
D6768	D6793	D6818	D6842	D6866	D6890	D6914
D6769	D6794	D6819	D6843	D6867	D6891	D6915
D6770	D6795	D6820	D6844	D6868	D6892	D6916
D6771	D6796	D6821	D6845	D6869	D6893	D6917
D6772	D6797	D6822	D6846	D6870	D6894	D6918
D6773	D6798					

Type 3 Beyer Peacock (Hymek) B-B

Introduced
1961

Engine
Bristol-Siddeley/Maybach MD870 of 1,700 b.h.p.

Weight
74 tons 0 cwt

Maximum tractive effort
49,700 lb

Total b.h.p. △
1,700

Transmission
Hydraulic. Stone-Maybach Mekydro type 6184U

Driving wheel diameter
3′ 9″

D7000	D7009	D7018	D7027	D7036	D7045	D7054
D7001	D7010	D7019	D7028	D7037	D7046	D7055
D7002	D7011	D7020	D7029	D7038	D7047	D7056
D7003	D7012	D7021	D7030	D7039	D7048	D7057
D7004	D7013	D7022	D7031	D7040	D7049	D7058
D7005	D7014	D7023	D7032	D7041	D7050	D7059
D7006	D7015	D7024	D7033	D7042	D7051	D7060
D7007	D7016	D7025	D7034	D7043	D7052	D7061
D7008	D7017	D7026	D7035	D7044	D7053	D7062

D7063	D7069	D7075	D7081	D7086	D7091	D7096
D7064	D7070	D7076	D7082	D7087	D7092	D7097
D7065	D7071	D7077	D7083	D7088	D7093	D7098
D7066	D7072	D7078	D7084	D7089	D7094	D7099
D7067	D7073	D7079	D7085	D7090	D7095	D7100
D7068	D7074	D7080				

Type 2 British Railways Bo-Bo

Class continued from D5299 ★

D7500§	D7514§	D7528§	D7542§	D7556§	D7570§	D7584§
D7501§	D7515§	D7529§	D7543§	D7557§	D7571§	D7585§
D7502§	D7516§	D7530§	D7544§	D7558§	D7572§	D7586§
D7503§	D7517§	D7531§	D7545§	D7559§	D7573§	D7587§
D7504§	D7518§	D7532§	D7546§	D7560§	D7574§	D7588§
D7505§	D7519§	D7533§	D7547§	D7561§	D7575§	D7589§
D7506§	D7520§	D7534§	D7548§	D7562§	D7576§	D7590§
D7507§	D7521§	D7535§	D7549§	D7563§	D7577§	D7591§
D7508§	D7522§	D7536§	D7550§	D7564§	D7578§	D7592§
D7509§	D7523§	D7537§	D7551§	D7565§	D7579§	D7593§
D7510§	D7524§	D7538§	D7552§	D7566§	D7580§	D7594§
D7511§	D7525§	D7539§	D7553§	D7567§	D7581§	D7595§
D7512§	D7526§	D7540§	D7554§	D7568§	D7582§	D7596§
D7513§	D7527§	D7541§	D7555§	D7569§	D7583§	D7597§

Type 1 English Electric Bo-Bo

★

Introduced
1957

Total b.h.p.
1,000

Engine
English Electric 8 SVT Mk. II of 1,000 b.h.p. at 850 r.p.m. (continuous)

Transmission
Electric. Four axle-hung, nose-suspended d.c. traction motors

Weight
72 tons 0 cwt

Driving wheel diameter
3′ 7″

Maximum tractive effort
42,000 lb

English Electric Type 3 1,750 b.h.p. diesel-electric Co-Co No. D6735 [*D. J. Dippie*

Beyer Peacock (Hymek) Type 3 1,700 b.h.p. diesel-hydraulic B-B No. D7006 [*C. F. Verrall*

English Electric Type 1 1,000 b.h.p. diesel-electric Bo-Bo No. D8040 [*R. K. Evans*

D8000	D8019	D8038	D8056	D8074	D8092	D8110
D8001	D8020	D8039	D8057	D8075	D8093	D8111
D8002	D8021	D8040	D8058	D8076	D8094	D8112
D8003	D8022	D8041	D8059	D8077	D8095	D8113
D8004	D8023	D8042	D8060	D8078	D8096	D8114
D8005	D8024	D8043	D8061	D8079	D8097	D8115
D8006	D8025	D8044	D8062	D8080	D8098	D8116
D8007	D8026	D8045	D8063	D8081	D8099	D8117
D8008	D8027	D8046	D8064	D8082	D8100	D8118
D8009	D8028	D8047	D8065	D8083	D8101	D8119
D8010	D8029	D8048	D8066	D8084	D8102	D8120
D8011	D8030	D8049	D8067	D8085	D8103	D8121
D8012	D8031	D8050	D8068	D8086	D8104	D8122
D8013	D8032	D8051	D8069	D8087	D8105	D8123
D8014	D8033	D8052	D8070	D8088	D8106	D8124
D8015	D8034	D8053	D8071	D8089	D8107	D8125
D8016	D8035	D8054	D8072	D8090	D8108	D8126
D8017	D8036	D8055	D8073	D8091	D8109	D8127
D8018	D8037					

Type 1 — British Thomson-Houston — Bo-Bo

Introduced
1957

Engine
Paxman 16-cyl YHXL V-type, pressure charged, of 800 b.h.p. at 1,250 r.p.m.

Weight
68 tons 0 cwt

Maximum tractive effort
37,500 lb

Total b.h.p.
800

★

Transmission
Electric. Four B.T.H. nose-suspended traction motors with single reduction gear drive

Driving wheel diameter
3′ 3½″

D8200	D8207	D8214	D8220	D8226	D8232	D8238
D8201	D8208	D8215	D8221	D8227	D8233	D8239
D8202	D8209	D8216	D8222	D8228	D8234	D8240
D8203	D8210	D8217	D8223	D8229	D8235	D8241
D8204	D8211	D8218	D8224	D8230	D8236	D8242
D8205	D8212	D8219	D8225	D8231	D8237	D8243
D8206	D8213					

British Thomson-Houston Type I 800 b.h.p. diesel-electric Bo-Bo No. D8201 [*J. C. Haydon*

North British Type I 800 b.h.p. diesel-electric Bo-Bo No. D8401 [*R. J. Buckley*

Clayton Type I 900 b.h.p. diesel-electric Bo-Bo No. D8500 [*D. L. Percival*

Type 1 North British Bo-Bo

●

Introduced
1958

Total b.h.p.
800

Engine
Paxman 16-cyl 16YHXL of 800 b.h.p. at 1,250 r.p.m.

Transmission
Electric. Four G.E.C. axle-hung nose-suspended traction motors

Weight
68 tons 0 cwt

Driving wheel diameter
3′ 7″

Maximum tractive effort
42,000 lb

D8400	D8402	D8404	D8406	D8407	D8408	D8409
D8401	D8403	D8405				

Type 1 Clayton Bo-Bo

★

Introduced
1962

Total b.h.p.
900

Engines
Two Paxman 6-cyl 6ZHXL of 450 b.h.p. at 1,500 r.p.m.

Transmission
Electric. 4 G.E.C. axle-hung, nose-suspended traction motors

Weight
68 tons 0 cwt

Driving wheel diameter
3′ 3½″

Maximum tractive effort
40,000 lb

D8500	D8513	D8526	D8539	D8552	D8564	D8576
D8501	D8514	D8527	D8540	D8553	D8565	D8577
D8502	D8515	D8528	D8541	D8554	D8566	D8578
D8503	D8516	D8529	D8542	D8555	D8567	D8579
D8504	D8517	D8530	D8543	D8556	D8568	D8580
D8505	D8518	D8531	D8544	D8557	D8569	D8581
D8506	D8519	D8532	D8545	D8558	D8570	D8582
D8507	D8520	D8533	D8546	D8559	D8571	D8583
D8508	D8521	D8534	D8547	D8560	D8572	D8584
D8509	D8522	D8535	D8548	D8561	D8573	D8585
D8510	D8523	D8536	D8549	D8562	D8574	D8586
D8511	D8524	D8537	D8550	D8563	D8575	D8587
D8512	D8525	D8538	D8551			

Type 5 English Electric Co-Co

"Deltic"

Introduced
1961

Engines
Two 18-cyl Napier "Deltic" 18-25 of 1,650 b.h.p. at 1,500 r.p.m.

Weight
99 tons 0 cwt

Maximum tractive effort
50,000 lb

Total b.h.p.
3,300

Transmission
Electric. Six English Electric EE750/25G axle-hung nose-suspended traction motors

Driving wheel diameter
3′ 7″

D9000 *Royal Scots Grey*
D9001 *St. Paddy*
D9002
D9003 *Meld*
D9004
D9005
D9006
D9007 *Pinza*
D9008
D9009 *Alycidon*
D9010
D9011
D9012 *Crepello*
D9013 *The Black Watch*
D9014
D9015 *Tulyar*
D9016
D9017
D9018 *Ballymoss*
D9019
D9020 *Nimbus*
D9021

Type 3 L.M.S. Co-Co

Introduced
1947

Engine
English Electric 16-cyl of 1,600 b.h.p. at 750 r.p.m. (continuous rating)

Weight
127 tons 13 cwt

Maximum tractive effort
41,400 lb

Total b.h.p. ◆
1,600

Transmission
Electric. Six nose-suspended motors single reduction gear drive

Driving wheel diameter
3′ 6″

10000 10001

English Electric Type 5 3,300 b.h.p. diesel-electric Co-Co No. D9000 *Royal Scots Grey*
[*D. L. Percival*

L.M.S. Type 3 1,600 b.h.p. diesel-electric Co-Co No. 10001 [*R. Puntis*

British Railways Type 3 1,600 b.h.p. diesel-electric 1Co-Co1 No. 10202 [*J. B. Bucknall*

Type 3 or 4* 1Co-Co1
British Railways

Introduced
1951
1954*

Engine
English Electric 16-cyl of 1,600 or 2,000* b.h.p.

Weight
135 tons 0 cwt
132 tons 0 cwt*

Maximum tractive effort
48,000 lb
50,000 lb*

Total b.h.p. ■, ★*
1,600
2,000*

Transmission
Electric. Six axle-hung, nose-suspended motors

Driving wheel diameter
3′ 7″

10201 10202 10203*

Shunter L.M.S. 0-6-0

Introduced
1939

Engine
English Electric 6-cyl of 350 b.h.p.

Weight
54 tons 16 cwt

Maximum tractive effort
33,000 lb

Total b.h.p.
350

Transmission
Electric. Single motor, jackshaft drive

Driving wheel diameter
4′ 3″

12003	12008	12013	12017	12021	12025	12029
12004	12009	12014	12018	12022	12026	12030
12005	12010	12015	12019	12023	12027	12031
12006	12011	12016	12020	12024	12028	12032
12007	12012					

Shunter L.M.S. and 0-6-0
British Railways

Introduced
1945

Engine
English Electric 6-cyl of 350 b.h.p.

Weight
47 tons 5 cwt

Maximum tractive effort
35,000 lb

Total b.h.p.
350

Transmission
Electric. Two nose-suspended motors, double reduction gear drive

Driving wheel diameter
4′ 0½″

L.M.S. 350 b.h.p. diesel-electric 0-6-0 No. 12013 [A. Swain

L.M.S./British Railways 350 b.h.p. diesel-electric 0-6-0 No. 12070 [C. P. Boocock

12033	12049	12064	12079	12094	12109	12124
12034	12050	12065	12080	12095	12110	12125
12035	12051	12066	12081	12096	12111	12126
12036	12052	12067	12082	12097	12112	12127
12037	12053	12068	12083	12098	12113	12128
12038	12054	12069	12084	12099	12114	12129
12039	12055	12070	12085	12100	12115	12130
12040	12056	12071	12086	12101	12116	12131
12041	12057	12072	12087	12102	12117	12132
12042	12058	12073	12088	12103	12118	12133
12043	12059	12074	12089	12104	12119	12134
12044	12060	12075	12090	12105	12120	12135
12045	12061	12076	12091	12106	12121	12136
12046	12062	12077	12092	12107	12122	12137
12047	12063	12078	12093	12108	12123	12138
12048						

Shunter L.N.E.R. 0-6-0

Introduced
1944

Engine
English Electric 6-cyl of 350 b.h.p.

Weight
50 tons 0 cwt

Maximum tractive effort
32,000 lb

Total b.h.p.
350

Transmission
Electric. Two nose-suspended motors, double reduction gear drive

Driving wheel diameter
4′ 0″

15000 15001 15002 15003

Shunter English Electric 0-6-0

Introduced
1936

Engine
English Electric 6-cyl of 350 b.h.p.

Weight
51 tons 10 cwt

Maximum tractive effort
30,000 lb

Total b.h.p.
350

Transmission
Electric. Two nose-suspended motors, single reduction gear drive

Driving wheel diameter
4′ 1″

15100

Shunter British Railways 0-6-0

Introduced
1948

Engine
English Electric 6-cyl of 350 b.h.p.

Weight
50 tons 0 cwt

Maximum tractive effort
33,500 lb

Total b.h.p.
350

Transmission
Electric. Two nose-suspended motors, double reduction gear drive

Driving wheel diameter
4′ 0½″

15101 15102 15103 15104 15105 15106

Shunter S.R. 0-6-0

Introduced
1937

Engine
English Electric 6-cyl of 350 b.h.p.

Weight
55 tons 5 cwt

Maximum tractive effort
30,000 lb

Total b.h.p.
350

Transmission
Electric. Two nose-suspended motors, single reduction gear drive

Driving wheel diameter
4′ 6″

15201 15202 15203

Shunter British Railways 0-6-0

Introduced
1949

Engine
English Electric 6-cyl of 350 b.h.p.

Weight
45 tons 0 cwt

Maximum tractive effort
24,000 lb

Total b.h.p.
350

Transmission
Electric. Two nose-suspended motors, double reduction gear drive

Driving wheel diameter
4′ 6″

15211	15215	15219	15223	15227	15231	15234
15212	15216	15220	15224	15228	15232	15235
15213	15217	15221	15225	15229	15233	15236
15214	15218	15222	15226	15230		

British Railways 350 b.h.p. diesel-electric 0-6-0 No. 15106 [*R. J. Henly*

Birmingham R. C. & W. Co. Type 4 2,750 b.h.p. diesel-electric Co-Co No. D0260 *Lion* [*N. R. Burton*

Brush Type 4 2,700 b.h.p. diesel-electric Co-Co No. D0280 *Falcon* [*D. J. Dippie*

LOCOMOTIVES ON TRIAL

British Railways are providing facilities for road tests of the following seven locomotives, which remain the property of the manufacturers and are not included in B.R. stock.

Shunter English Electric 0-6-0

Introduced
1957

Engine
English Electric 6RKT of 500 b.h.p. at 750 r.p.m.

Weight
48 tons 0 cwt

Maximum tractive effort
33,000 lb

Total b.h.p.
500

Transmission
Electric. One English Electric traction motor coupled to double-reduction gear box final drive

Driving wheel diameter
4′ 0″

D0226

Shunter English Electric 0-6-0

Introduced
1957

Engine
English Electric 6RKT of 500 b.h.p. at 750 r.p.m.

Weight
48 tons 0 cwt

Maximum tractive effort
33,000 lb

Total b.h.p.
500

Transmission
Hydraulic. Lysholm-Smith torque-converter and three-speed reduction gear to final drive

Driving wheel diameter
4′ 0″

D0227

Type 4 Birmingham R.C. & W. Co. Co-Co

Introduced
1962

Engine
Sulzer 12-cyl 12LDA28-C, inter-cooled, of 2,750 b.h.p. at 800 r.p.m.

Weight
114 tons 0 cwt

Maximum tractive effort
55,000 lb

Total b.h.p.
2,750

Transmission
Electric. Six A.E.I. axle-hung, nose-suspended traction motors

Driving wheel diameter
3′ 9″

D0260 *Lion*

Type 4 Brush Co-Co

Introduced
1961

Engines
Two Maybach MD655 V-type of 1,440 b.h.p. at 1,500 r.p.m.

Weight
115 tons 0 cwt

Maximum tractive effort
60,000 lb

Total b.h.p.
2,700

Transmission
Electric. Six Brush traction motors

Driving wheel diameter
3′ 7″

D0280 *Falcon*

Type 4 English Electric Co-Co

Introduced
1962

Engine
English Electric 16-cyl 16CSVT, after-cooled, of 2,700 b.h.p.

Weight
105 tons 0 cwt

Maximum tractive effort
50,000 lb

Total b.h.p.
2,700

Transmission
Electric

Driving wheel diameter
3′ 6″

DP2

Gas Turbine English Electric 4-6-0

Introduced
1961

Engine
English Electric gas turbine of 2,750 b.h.p. at 9,000 r.p.m.

Weight
Locomotive: 79 tons 16 cwt
Tender: 44 tons 0 cwt

Maximum tractive effort
38,000 lb

Total b.h.p.
2,750

Transmission
Mechanical. Gearbox and flexible drive to coupled axles

Driving wheel diameter
5′ 9″

GT3

Shunter — Yorkshire Engine Co. — 0-8-0

Introduced
1961

Engines
2 Rolls-Royce C8SFL of 311 b.h.p. at 1,800 r.p.m.

Weight
58 tons 0 cwt

Maximum tractive effort
45,000 lb

Total b.h.p.
600

Transmission
Hydraulic

Driving wheel diameter
3′ 9″

Taurus

DEPARTMENTAL LOCOMOTIVES

EASTERN & NORTH EASTERN REGIONS

Shunter — Hibberd & Co. — 0-4-0

Introduced
1950

Engine
English National 4-cyl Gas type DA4 of 52 b.h.p. at 1,250 r.p.m.

Weight
11 tons 0 cwt

Maximum tractive effort

Total b.h.p.
52

Transmission
Mechanical. Spur-type three-speed gearbox with roller chains

Driving wheel diameter

(Original number in brackets)

52 (11104)

Shunter — Ruston & Hornsby — 0-4-0

Introduced
1955

Engine
Ruston & Hornsby Mark 4V vertical 4-cyl of 88 b.h.p.

Weight
17 tons 0 cwt

Maximum tractive effort
9,500 lb

Total b.h.p.
88

Transmission
Mechanical

Driving wheel diameter
3′ 0″

56

Shunter Barclay 0-4-0

Introduced
1958

Engine

Weight

Maximum tractive effort

Total b.h.p.
150

Transmission
Mechanical

Driving wheel diameter

81 82 83 84 87

Shunter Ruston & Hornsby 0-4-0

Introduced
1959

Engine

Weight

Maximum tractive effort

Total b.h.p.

Transmission

Driving wheel diameter

85

Shunter Hunslet 0-6-0

Introduced
1955

Engine
Gardner 8L3 of 204 b.h.p. at 1,200 r.p.m.

Weight
30 tons 0 cwt

Maximum tractive effort
14,500 lb

Total b.h.p.
204

Transmission
Mechanical. Hunslet patent friction clutch. Hunslet four-speed gearbox incorporating reverse and final drive gears

Driving wheel diameter
3′ 4″

(Original number in brackets)

88 (D2612)

Shunter British Railways 0-6-0

Introduced
1958

Engine
Gardner 8L3 of 204 b.h.p. at 1,200 r.p.m.

Weight
30 tons 4 cwt

Maximum tractive effort
15,000 lb

Total b.h.p.
200

Transmission
Mechanical. Wilson-Drewry Director air-operated epicyclic gearbox. R.F.11 spiral bevel reverse/final drive unit

Driving wheel diameter
3′ 7″

91 92

LONDON MIDLAND REGION

Shunter John Fowler & Co. 0-4-0

Introduced
1936

Engine
Fowler 4C vertical of 150 b.h.p. at 1,000 r.p.m. (1 hr rating)

Weight
29 tons 0 cwt

Maximum tractive effort
15,000 lb

Total b.h.p.
150

Transmission
Mechanical. Four-speed gearbox

Driving wheel diameter
3′ 3″

ED2 ED3 ED4 ED5 ED6

Shunter John Fowler & Co. 0-4-0

Introduced
1955

Engine
Fowler 4C of 150 b.h.p.

Weight
29 tons 0 cwt

Maximum tractive effort
15,000 lb

Total b.h.p.
150

Transmission
Mechanical. Three-lobe synchromesh gearbox with multiple disc dry clutch manually operated

Driving wheel diameter
3′ 3″

ED7

Shunter Ruston & Hornsby 0-4-0

Introduced
1958

Engine
Ruston 4YCL

Weight
8 tons 4 cwt

Maximum tractive effort
4,200 lb

Total b.h.p.

Transmission
Mechanical. Chain drive

Driving wheel diameter
2′ 6″

Gauge
3′ 0″

ED10

Shunter Ruston & Hornsby 0-4-0

Introduced
1958

Engine

Weight
3 tons 10 cwt

Maximum tractive effort
1,890 lb

Total b.h.p.
20

Transmission

Driving wheel diameter

Gauge
1′ 6″

ZM32

SOUTHERN REGION

Shunter Ruston & Hornsby 0-4-0

Introduced
1946

Engine
Ruston 4VRH

Weight
7 tons 10 cwt

Maximum tractive effort
3,480 lb

Total b.h.p.
48

Transmission
Mechanical. Chain

Driving wheel diameter
2′ 6″

This locomotive was supplied to the Bristol Aviation Co. in 1946 and was later purchased by British Railways.

DS1169

Ruston & Hornsby 48 b.h.p. diesel-mechanical 0-4-0 No. DS1169 [*W. M. J. Jackson*

Ruston & Hornsby 165 b.h.p. diesel-electric 0-6-0 No. PWM653 [*A. Swain*

Shunter Drewry 0-6-0

Introduced
1947

Engine
Gardner 8L3 of 204 b.h.p.

Weight
24 tons 15 cwt

Maximum tractive effort
16,850 lb

Total b.h.p.
204

Transmission
Mechanical. Five-speed gearbox

Driving wheel diameter
3′ 3″

DS1173

WESTERN REGION

Shunter Ruston & Hornsby 0-4-0

Introduced
1957

Engine
Ruston & Hornsby 4-cyl of 88 b.h.p.

Weight
17 tons 0 cwt

Maximum tractive effort
9,500 lb

Total b.h.p.
88

Transmission
Mechanical. Chain driven from gearbox

Driving wheel diameter
3′ 0″

20

Shunter Ruston & Hornsby 0-6-0

Introduced
1953

Engine
Ruston & Hornsby 6-cyl of 165 b.h.p.

Weight
30 tons 0 cwt

Maximum tractive effort
17,000 lb

Total b.h.p.
165

Transmission
Electric. One B.T.H. nose-suspended traction motor

Driving wheel diameter
3′ 2½″

PWM650 PWM651 PWM652 PWM653 PWM654

EASTERN REGION DIESEL
LOCOMOTIVE CLASSIFICATION

Horse-power	Description	Loco. Nos.	Code
153	Hunslet/Gardner	D2950–2	1/15
153	Barclay/Gardner	D2953–6	1/12
165	Ruston & Hornsby	D2957–8	1/16
170	Yorkshire Engine Co.	D2850–69	1/17
200	N.B. Loco. Co./Paxman	D2700–7	2/4A
200	Brush/Petter	D2999	2/2
204	B.R./Gardner	D2000–2199, 2372–99	2/1
204	Drewry/Gardner (3′ 3″ wheel) ...	D2200–14	2/13A
204	Drewry/Gardner (3′ 6″ wheel) ...	D2215–73	2/13
204	Drewry/Gardner (3′ 7″ wheel) ...	D2274–2340 ...	2/13
204	Barclay/Gardner (4-speed) ...	D2400–9	2/12A
204	Barclay/Gardner (5-speed) ...	D2410–44	2/12
204	Hudswell-Clarke/Gardner ...	D2500–19	2/14
204	Hunslet/Gardner (3′ 4″ wheel) ...	D2550–73	2/15A
204	Hunslet/Gardner (3′ 9″ wheel) ...	D2574–D2618 ...	2/15
225	N.B. Loco. Co./M.A.N.	D2708–80	2/4
330	N.B. Loco. Co./M.A.N.	D2900–13	3/4
350	B.R./English Electric	D3000–3116/27-36/67 –3438/54–72, 3503–3611/52-64/72–3718/22–4048	3/1
350	B.R./Crossley	D3117–26	3/1B
350	B.R./Blackstone/G.E.C.	D3137–51, 3439–53/73–3502, 3612–51 4049–94	3/1C
350	B.R./Blackstone/B.T.H.	D3152–66	3/1D
350	B.R./E.E. (max. speed 27 m.p.h.)	D3665–71, 3719–21	3/1A
350	L.M.S./English Electric (4′ 3″ wheel)	12003–32	3/8
350	L.M.S./English Electric (4′ 0½″ wheel)	12033–12138 ...	3/8A
350	L.N.E./English Electric	15000–3	3/10
350	G.W./English Electric (4′ 1″ wheel)	15100	3/11A
350	G.W./English Electric (4′0½″wheel)	15101–6	3/11
350	S.R./English Electric	15201–3	3/9A
350	S.R./English Electric	15211-36	3/9
800	B.T.H./Paxman	D8200–43	8/5
800	N.B. Loco. Co./Paxman	D8400–9	8/4
900	Clayton/Paxman	D8500–87	9/18
1,000	N.B. Loco. Co./M.A.N./G.E.C. ...	D6100–37	10/4
1,000	N.B. Loco. Co./M.A.N./Voith ...	D6300–5	10/4A
1,000	English Electric	D8000–8127 ...	10/3
1,100	English Electric/Napier	D5900–9	11/3
1,100	N.B. Loco. Co./M.A.N./G.E.C. ...	D6138–57	11/4
1,160	B.R./Sulzer...	D5000–48	11/1
1,160	B.R./Sulzer...	D5049–5150 ...	11/1A
1,160	Birmingham/Sulzer	D5300–46	11/6
1,100	N.B. Loco. Co./M.A.N./Voith ...	D6306–57	11/4A
1,200	Metro. Vickers/Crossley	D5700–19	12/5
1,250	Brush/Mirrlees	D5500–19	12/2
1,250	Birmingham/Sulzer	D5347–5415 ...	12/6
1,250	B.R./Sulzer...	D5151–5232 ...	12/1

EASTERN REGION DIESEL

LOCOMOTIVE CLASSIFICATION—*continued*

Horse-power	Description	Loco. Nos.	Code
1,365	Brush/Mirrlees	D5520–44/6–5654/ 71–99, 5800–62 ...	13/2
1,550	Birmingham/Sulzer	D6500–85	15/6
1,550	Birmingham/Sulzer	D6586–97	15/6A
1,600	L.M.S./English Electric	10000–1	16/8
1,600	S.R./English Electric	10201–2	16/9
1,600	Brush/Mirrlees	D5545, 5655–70 ...	16/2
1,750	English Electric	D6700–6818 ...	17/3
1,700	Beyer Peacock/Maybach	D7000–7100 ...	17/7
2,000	B.R./Maybach/Mekydro	D800–2	20/1
2,000	English Electric	D200–399	20/3
2,000	N.B. Loco. Co./M.A.N./Voith ...	D600–4	20/4
2,000	S.R./English Electric	10203	20/9
2,200	B.R./Maybach/Mekydro	D803–29/31/2/66–70	22/1
2,200	N.B. Loco. Co.	D833–65	22/4
2,300	B.R./Sulzer...	D1, 3–10	23/1
2,500	B.R./Sulzer...	D2, 11–137... ...	25/1
2,500	B.R./Sulzer/Brush	D138–93	25/1A
2,700	B.R./Maybach/Voith	D1000–73	27/1
2,750	Brush/Sulzer	D1500–49	27/2
3,300	English Electric/Napier Deltic ...	D9000–21	33/3

B.R. DIESEL MULTIPLE-UNITS

UNLESS otherwise stated, all multiple-unit trains are gangwayed within each set, with guard's and luggage compartment at the inner end of motor brake coaches, and seating is in open saloons with centre and/or end doors. The letter L in the headings indicates an open vehicle fitted with toilet facilities: K indicates a side corridor vehicle with toilet. Two standard lengths of underframe are in use, namely 56 ft. 11 in. and 63 ft. 5 in. but the actual body lengths vary by a few inches for the same type of underframe. The dimensions shown are the length over body and the overall width.

Several of the types listed are sub-divided by reason of detail or mechanical differences. For example, a certain number of cars in a class may have a different seating arrangement or a different make of engine but are otherwise similar to the main batch. Such differences are noted in the heading to the class and given a reference mark by which the relevant dimensions or details and the cars concerned can be identified. The type of set in which each class is formed on delivery, together with the principal manufacturer, is shown at the head of the details for that class, although it should be noted that changes may occur owing to varying operating conditions, even to the extent of coupling different makes of car in the same set or running power cars without intermediate trailers. Most railcars are fitted with a standard Mechanical transmission of a cardan shaft and freewheel to a four-speed epicyclic gearbox, and a further cardan shaft to the final drive. Where a non-standard transmission is employed, full details are shown under the relevant heading. Cars are listed in numerical order by type and not by set formation.

COUPLING CODES

Although several multiple-unit diesel sets can be coupled together and driven by one man in the leading cab, for various reasons it is not possible for all types of diesel unit to work together. In order to distinguish cars that can run together, all have painted at each end above the buffers a colour code symbol. A miniature symbol also appears on the plug socket covers. Only units bearing the same symbol may be coupled together.

▲ **RED TRIANGLE** ● **WHITE CIRCLE**

◆ **YELLOW DIAMOND** ■ **BLUE SQUARE**

★ **ORANGE STAR**

NUMERICAL LIST OF
DIESEL MULTIPLE-UNITS

Derby Works, B.R. (2)

MOTOR BRAKE SECOND ■

Engines
Two B.U.T. (Leyland) 6-cyl. horizontal type of 230 b.h.p.
*Two Rolls-Royce 8-cyl. horizontal type of 238 b.h.p.
†Two B.U.T. (Leyland) 6-cyl. horizontal type of 230 b.h.p.

Transmission
Mechanical. Standard
*Hydraulic. Twin-disc Torque converter
†Mechanical. Standard. Fitted with Self Changing Gears Ltd. automatic four-speed gearbox.

Body: 64′ 6″ × 9′ 3″ **Weight:** 35 tons 10 cwt, 37 tons 10 cwt†

Seats: 2nd, 62

E50000*	E50009	E50018	E50026	E50035	E50043
E50001	E50010	E50019	E50027	E50036	E50044
E50002	E50011	E50020	E50029	E50037	E50045
E50003	E50012	E50021	E50030	E50038	E50046
E50004	E50013	E50022	E50031	E50039	E50047
E50005	E50014	E50023	E50032	E50040	E50048
E50006	E50015	E50024	E50033	E50041	E50049†
E50007	E50016	E50025	E50034	E50042	
E50008	E50017				

Derby Works, B.R. (3 Suburban)

MOTOR BRAKE SECOND ■

Engines
Two B.U.T. (Leyland) 6-cyl. horizontal type of 150 b.h.p.

Transmission
Mechanical. Standard

Body: 64′ 0″ × 9′ 3″. Non-gangwayed, side doors to each seating bay

Weight: 35 tons 10 cwt **Seats: 2nd,** 65

W50050	W50057	W50064	W50071	W50078	W50085
W50051	W50058	W50065	W50072	W50079	W50086
W50052	W50059	W50066	W50073	W50080	W50087
W50053	W50060	W50067	W50074	W50081	W50088
W50054	W50061	W50068	W50075	W50082	W50089
W50055	W50062	W50069	W50076	W50083	W50090
W50056	W50063	W50070	W50077	W50084	W50091

Derby Works, B.R. (3 Suburban)

MOTOR SECOND ■

Engines
Two B.U.T. (Leyland) 6-cyl. horizontal type of 150 b.h.p.

Transmission
Mechanical. Standard

Body: 64′ 0″ × 9′ 3″. Non-gangwayed, side doors to each seating bay

Weight: 35 tons 10 cwt **Seats: 2nd,** 95

W50092	W50099	W50106	W50113	W50120	W50128
W50093	W50100	W50107	W50114	W50121	W50129
W50094	W50101	W50108	W50115	W50122	W50130
W50095	W50102	W50109	W50116	W50123	W50131
W50096	W50103	W50110	W50117	W50124	W50132
W50097	W50104	W50111	W50118	W50126	W50133
W50098	W50105	W50112	W50119	W50127	

Metropolitan-Cammell (2)

MOTOR BRAKE SECOND ■

Engines
Two Rolls-Royce 6-cyl. horizontal type of 180 b.h.p.
*Two Rolls-Royce 6-cyl. type super-charged to 230 b.h.p.

Transmission
Mechanical. Standard

Body: 57′ 0″ × 9′ 3″ **Weight:** 33 tons **Seats: 2nd,** 52

M50134 M50135 M50136* M50137

Metropolitan-Cammell (4)

MOTOR COMPOSITE (L) ■

Engines
Two B.U.T. (A.E.C.) 6-cyl. horizontal type of 150 b.h.p.

Transmission
Mechanical. Standard

Body: 57′ 0″ × 9′ 3″ **Weight:** 32 tons **Seats: 1st,** 12; **2nd,** 45

E50138	E50141	E50144	E50146	E50148	E50150
E50139	E50142	E50145	E50147	E50149	E50151
E50140	E50143				

Metropolitan-Cammell (2)

MOTOR BRAKE SECOND ■

Engines
Two B.U.T. (A.E.C.) 6-cyl. horizontal type of 150 b.h.p.

Transmission
Mechanical. Standard

Body: 57′ 0″ × 9′ 3″ **Weight:** 32 tons **Seats: 2nd,** 52

E50152 E50153 E50154 E50155 E50156 E50157

Metropolitan-Cammell (2)

MOTOR COMPOSITE (L) ■

Engines
Two B.U.T. (A.E.C.) 6-cyl. horizontal type of 150 b.h.p.

Transmission
Mechanical. Standard

Body: 57′ 0″ × 9′ 3″ **Weight:** 32 tons **Seats: 1st,** 12; **2nd,** 53

E50158 E50159 E50160 E50161 E50162 E50163

Western Region Derby three-car suburban unit with Motor Second No. W50121 leading [M. Mensing

Metropolitan-Cammell Motor Composite No. E50179 [P. J. Sharpe

Gloucester R. C. & W. Co. Motor Brake Second No. M50352 at Birmingham (New Street) [M. Mensing

Metropolitan-Cammell (2)

MOTOR BRAKE SECOND ■

For details see E50152-7

E50164 E50165 E50166 E50167

Metropolitan-Cammell (2)

MOTOR COMPOSITE (L) ■

For details see E50158-63

E50168 E50169 E50170 E50171

Metropolitan-Cammell (4)

MOTOR COMPOSITE (L) ■

For details see E50158-63

E50172	E50178	E50182	E50186	E50190	E50194
E50174	E50179	E50183	E50187	E50191	E50195
E50175	E50180	E50184	E50188	E50192	E50196
E50176	E50181	E50185	E50189	E50193	E50197
E50177					

Metropolitan-Cammell (2)

MOTOR BRAKE SECOND ■

For details see E50152-7

E50198	E50204	E50210	E50216	E50222	E50228
E50199	E50205	E50211	E50217	E50223	E50229
E50200	E50206	E50212	E50218	E50224	E50230
E50201	E50207	E50213	E50219	E50225	E50231
E50202	E50208	E50214	E50220	E50226	E50232
E50203	E50209	E50215	E50221	E50227	E50233

Metropolitan-Cammell (4)

MOTOR COMPOSITE (L) ■

For details see E50138-51

E50234	E50236	E50238	E50240	E50242	E50244
E50235	E50237	E50239	E50241	E50243	E50245

Metropolitan-Cammell (2)

MOTOR BRAKE SECOND ■

Engines
Two B.U.T. (A.E.C.) 6-cyl. horizontal type of 150 b.h.p.

Transmission
Mechanical. Standard

Body: 57′ 0″ × 9′ 3″ **Weight:** 32 tons **Seats:** 2nd, 44

E50246 E50247 E50248

Cravens (4)

MOTOR BRAKE SECOND ■

Engines
Two B.U.T. (A.E.C.) 6-cyl. horizontal type of 150 b.h.p.

Transmission
Mechanical. Standard

Body: 57′ 6″ × 9′ 2″ **Weight:** 30 tons 10 cwt **Seats:** 2nd, 52

E50249

Metropolitan-Cammell (2)

MOTOR BRAKE SECOND ■

Engines
Two B.U.T. (A.E.C.) 6-cyl. horizontal type of 150 b.h.p.

Transmission
Mechanical. Standard

Body: 57′ 0″ × 9′ 3″ **Weight:** 32 tons **Seats:** 2nd, 52

E50250 E50252 E50254 E50256 E50258 E50259
E50251 E50253 E50255 E50257

Metropolitan-Cammell (2)

MOTOR COMPOSITE (L) ■

Engines
Two B.U.T. (A.E.C.) 6-cyl. horizontal type of 150 b.h.p.

Transmission
Mechanical. Standard

Body: 57′ 0″ × 9′ 3″ **Weight:** 32 tons **Seats:** 1st, 12; 2nd, 53

E50260 E50262 E50264 E50266 E50268 E50269
E50261 E50263 E50265 E50267

Metropolitan-Cammell (3)

MOTOR COMPOSITE (L) ■

Engines
Two Rolls-Royce 6-cyl. horizontal type of 180 b.h.p.

Transmission
Mechanical. Standard

Body: 57′ 0″ × 9′ 3″ **Weight:** 33 tons **Seats:** 1st, 12; 2nd, 53

E50270 E50272 E50274 E50276 E50278 E50279
E50271 E50273 E50275 E50277

Metropolitan-Cammell (3)

MOTOR BRAKE SECOND ■

Engines
Two Rolls-Royce 6-cyl. horizontal type of 180 b.h.p.

Transmission
Mechanical Standard

Body: 57′ 0″ × 9′ 3″ **Weight:** 33 tons **Seats: 2nd,** 52

E50280	E50283	E50285	E50287	E50289	E50291
E50281	E50284	E50286	E50288	E50290	E50292
E50282					

Metropolitan-Cammell (2)

MOTOR BRAKE SECOND ■

Engines
Two B.U.T. (A.E.C.) 6-cyl. horizontal type of 150 b.h.p.

Transmission
Mechanical. Standard

Body: 57′ 0″ × 9′ 3″ **Weight:** 32 tons **Seats: 2nd,** 52

E50293 E50294 E50295 E50296

Metropolitan-Cammell (3)

MOTOR BRAKE SECOND ■

Engines
Two B.U.T. 6-cyl. horizontal type of 150 b.h.p.

Transmission
Mechanical. Standard

Body: 57′ 0″ × 9′ 3″ **Weight:** 31 tons 10 cwt **Seats: 2nd,** 52

M50303	M50306	M50309	M50312	M50315	M50318
M50304	M50307	M50310	M50313	M50316	M50319
M50305	M50308	M50311	M50314	M50317	M50320

Metropolitan-Cammell (3)

MOTOR COMPOSITE (L) ■

Engines
Two B.U.T. 6-cyl. horizontal type of 150 b.h.p.

Transmission
Mechanical. Standard

Body: 57′ 0″ × 9′ 3″ **Weight:** 32 tons **Seats: 1st,** 12; **2nd,** 53

M50321	M50324	M50327	M50330	M50333	M50336
M50322	M50325	M50328	M50331	M50334	M50337
M50323	M50326	M50329	M50332	M50335	M50338

Gloucester R. C. & W. Co. (2)

MOTOR BRAKE SECOND ■

Engines
Two B.U.T. (A.E.C.) 6-cyl. horizontal type of 150 b.h.p.

Transmission
Mechanical. Standard
* Fitted with C.A.V. Ltd. automatic gear change equipment

Body: 57′ 6″ × 9′ 3″ **Weight:** 30 tons 5 cwt **Seats: 2nd,** 52

SC50339	SC50343	SC50347	M50350	M50353	M50356
SC50340	SC50344	M50348	M50351	M50354	M50357
SC50341	SC50345	M50349	M50352	M50355	M50358 *
SC50342	SC50346				

Cravens (2)

MOTOR BRAKE SECOND ■

Engines
Two B.U.T. (Leyland) (A.E.C.*) 6-cyl. horizontal type of 150 b.h.p.

Transmission
Mechanical. Standard

Body: 57′ 6″ × 9′ 2″ **Weight:** 29 tons **Seats:** 2nd, 52

E50359	E50365	E50371*	E50377*	E50383*	E50389*
E50360	E50366	E50372*	E50378*	E50384*	M50390*
E50361	E50367	E50373*	E50379*	E50385*	M50391*
E50362	E50368	E50374*	E50380*	E50386*	M50392*
E50363	E50369	E50375*	E50381*	E50387*	M50393*
E50364	E50370	E50376*	E50382*	E50388*	M50394*

Park Royal Vehicles (2)

MOTOR BRAKE SECOND ■

Engines
Two B.U.T. (A.E.C.) 6-cyl. horizontal type of 150 b.h.p.

Transmission
Mechanical. Standard

Body: 57′ 6″ × 9′ 3″ **Weight:** 33 tons 8 cwt **Seats:** 2nd, 52

M50395	M50399	M50403	M50406	M50409	M50412
M50396	M50400	M50404	M50407	M50410	M50413
M50397	M50401	M50405	M50408	M50411	M50414
M50398	M50402				

D. Wickham & Co. (2)

MOTOR BRAKE SECOND ■

Engines
Two B.U.T. (Leyland) 6-cyl. horizontal type of 150 b.h.p.

Transmission
Mechanical. Standard

Body: 57′ 0″ × 9′ 3″ **Weight:** 27 tons 10 cwt **Seats:** 2nd, 59

E50416 E50417 E50418

Birmingham R. C. & W. Co. (3)

MOTOR BRAKE SECOND ■

Engines
Two B.U.T. (Leyland) 6-cyl. horizontal type of 150 b.h.p.

Transmission
Mechanical. Standard

Body: 57′ 6″ × 9′ 3″ **Weight:** 31 tons **Seats:** 2nd, 52

M50420 M50421 M50422 M50423

D. Wickham & Co. twin unit at Histon [*N. Barratt*

Birmingham R. C. & W. Co. three-car unit with Motor Composite No. M50523 leading [*P. J. Lynch*

Derby Motor Composite No. E50630 [*P. J. Sharpe*

Birmingham R. C. & W. Co. (3)

MOTOR COMPOSITE (L) ■

Engines
Two B.U.T. (Leyland) 6-cyl. horizontal type of 150 b.h.p.

Transmission
Mechanical. Standard

Body: 57′ 6″ × 9′ 3″ **Weight:** 31 tons **Seats: 1st,** 12; **2nd,** 54

M50424 M50425 M50426 M50427

Birmingham R. C. & W. Co. (3)

MOTOR BRAKE SECOND ■

For details see M50420-3

M50428	M50437	M50446	M50455	M50464	M50472
M50429	M50438	M50447	M50456	M50465	M50473
M50430	M50439	M50448	M50457	M50466	M50474
M50431	M50440	M50449	M50458	M50467	M50475
M50432	M50441	M50450	M50459	M50468	M50476
M50433	M50442	M50451	M50460	M50469	M50477
M50434	M50443	M50452	M50461	M50470	M50478
M50435	M50444	M50453	M50462	M50471	M50479
M50436	M50445	M50454	M50463		

Birmingham R. C. & W. Co. (3)

MOTOR COMPOSITE (L) ■

For details see M50424-7

M50480	M50489	M50498	M50507	M50516	M50524
M50481	M50490	M50499	M50508	M50517	M50525
M50482	M50491	M50500	M50509	M50518	M50526
M50483	M50492	M50501	M50510	M50519	M50527
M50484	M50493	M50502	M50511	M50520	M50528
M50485	M50494	M50503	M50512	M50521	M50529
M50486	M50495	M50504	M50513	M50522	M50530
M50487	M50496	M50505	M50514	M50523	M50531
M50488	M50497	M50506	M50515		

Birmingham R. C. & W. Co. (2)

MOTOR BRAKE SECOND ■

Engines
Two B.U.T. (Leyland) 6-cyl. horizontal type of 150 b.h.p.

Transmission
Mechanical. Standard

Body: 57′ 6″ × 9′ 3″ **Weight:** 31 tons **Seats: 2nd,** 52

M50532	M50534	M50536	M50538	M50540	M50541
M50533	M50535	M50537	M50539		

Birmingham R. C. & W. Co. (4)

MOTOR COMPOSITE (L) ■

Engines
Two B.U.T. (Leyland) 6-cyl. horizontal type of 150 b h.p.

Transmission
Mechanical. Standard

Body: 57′ 6″ × 9′ 3″ **Weight**: 31 tons **Seats: 1st**, 12; **2nd**, 5

E50542	E50551	E50560	E50569	E50578	E50586
E50543	E50552	E50561	E50570	E50579	E50587
E50544	E50553	E50562	E50571	E50580	E50588
E50545	E50554	E50563	E50572	E50581	E50589
E50546	E50555	E50564	E50573	E50582	E50590
E50547	E50556	E50565	E50574	E50583	E50591
E50548	E50557	E50566	E50575	E50584	E50592
E50549	E50558	E50567	E50576	E50585	E50593
E50550	E50559	E50568	E50577		

Birmingham R. C. & W. Co. (2)

MOTOR BRAKE SECOND ■

Engines
Two B.U.T. (Leyland) 6-cyl. horizontal type of 160 b.h.p.

Transmission
Mechanical. Standard

Body: 57′ 6″ × 9′ 3″ **Weight**: 31 tons **Seats: 2nd**, 52

E50594	E50595	E50596	E50597	E50598

Derby Works, B.R. (2 or 3*)

MOTOR BRAKE SECOND ■

Engines
Two B.U.T. (Leyland) 6-cyl. horizontal type of 150 b.h.p.

Transmission
Mechanical. Standard

Body: 57′ 6″ × 9′ 2″ **Weight**: 28 tons 10 cwt **Seats: 2nd**, 52

E50599	E50605	E50610	E50615	E50620*	M50625
E50600	E50606	E50611	E50616	E50621*	M50626
E50601	E50607	E50612	E50617	E50622*	M50627
E50602	E50608	E50613	E50618	E50623*	M50628
E50603	E50609	E50614	E50619	E50624*	M50629
E50604					

Derby Works, B.R. (3* or 4)

MOTOR COMPOSITE (L) ■

Engines
Two B.U.T. (Leyland) 6-cyl. horizontal type of 150 b.h.p.

Transmission
Mechanical. Standard

Body: 57′ 6″ × 9′ 2″ **Weight:** 28 tons **Seats:** 1st, 12; 2nd, 50

E50630	E50633	E50636	E50639	E50642*	E50645*
E50631	E50634	E50637	E50640	E50643*	E50646*
E50632	E50635	E50638	E50641	E50644*	

Swindon Works, B.R. (3 Cross Country)

MOTOR SECOND (L) ■

Engines
Two B.U.T. (A.E.C.) 6-cyl. horizontal type of 150 b.h.p.

Transmission
Mechanical. Standard

Body: 64′ 6″ × 9′ 3″ **Weight:** 36 tons 10 cwt **Seats:** 2nd, 68

W50647	W50656	W50664	W50672	W50680	W50688
W50648	W50657	W50665	W50673	W50681	W50689
W50649	W50658	W50666	W50674	W50682	W50690
W50650	W50659	W50667	W50675	W50683	W50691
W50651	W50660	W50668	W50676	W50684	W50692
W50652	W50661	W50669	W50677	W50685	W50693
W50653	W50662	W50670	W50678	W50686	W50694
W50654	W50663	W50671	W50679	W50687	W50695
W50655					

Swindon Works, B.R. (3 Cross Country)

MOTOR BRAKE COMPOSITE ■

Engines
Two B.U.T. (A.E.C.) 6-cyl. horizontal type of 150 b.h.p.

Transmission
Mechanical. Standard

Body: 64′ 6″ × 9′ 3″ **Weight:** 36 tons **Seats:** 1st, 18; 2nd, 16

W50696	W50705	W50713	W50721	W50729	W50737
W50697	W50706	W50714	W50722	W50730	W50738
W50698	W50707	W50715	W50723	W50731	W50739
W50699	W50708	W50716	W50724	W50732	W50740
W50700	W50709	W50717	W50725	W50733	W50741
W50701	W50710	W50718	W50726	W50734	W50742
W50702	W50711	W50719	W50727	W50735	W50743
W50703	W50712	W50720	W50728	W50736	W50744
W50704					

Metropolitan-Cammell (3)

MOTOR COMPOSITE (L) ■

Engines
Two Rolls-Royce 6-cyl. horizontal type of 180 b.h.p.

Transmission
Mechanical. Standard

Body: 57′ 0″ × 9′ 3″ **Weight:** 32 tons **Seats: 1st,** 12; **2nd,** 53

E50745 E50746 E50747

Metropolitan-Cammell (4)

MOTOR COMPOSITE (L) ■

Engines
Two B.U.T. (A.E.C.) 6-cyl. horizonta type of 150 b.h.p.

Transmission
Mechanical. Standard

Body: 57′ 0″ × 9′ 3″ **Weight:** 32 tons **Seats: 1st,** 12; **2nd,** 53

E50748 E50749 E50750 E50751

Cravens (3)

MOTOR BRAKE SECOND ■

Engines
Two B.U.T. (Leyland) 6-cyl. horizontal type of 150 b.h.p.

Transmission
Mechanical. Standard

Body: 57′ 6″ × 9′ 2″ **Weight:** 30 tons **Seats: 2nd,** 52

M50752	M50756	M50759	M50762	M50765	M50768
M50753	M50757	M50760	M50763	M50766	M50769
M50754	M50758	M50761	M50764	M50767	M50770
M50755					

Cravens (2)

MOTOR BRAKE SECOND ■

Engines
Two B.U.T. (A.E.C.) 6-cyl. horizontal type of 150 b.h.p.

Transmission
Mechanical. Standard

Body: 57′ 6″ × 9′ 2″ **Weight:** 30 tons **Seats: 2nd,** 52

M50771	M50774	M50776	M50778	M50780	M50782
M50772	M50775	M50777	M50779	M50781	M50784
M50773					

Cravens (3)

MOTOR COMPOSITE (L) ■

Engines
Two B.U.T. (Leyland) 6-cyl. horizontal type of 150 b.h.p.

Transmission
Mechanical. Standard

Body: 57′ 6″ × 9′ 2″ **Weight:** 30 tons **Seats: 1st,** 12; **2nd,** 51

Original Swindon three-car Cross Country unit. The leading vehicle is Motor Brake Second No. W50710 [*M. Mensing*

Cravens Motor Brake Second No. M50778 [*A. Swain*

Swindon Inter-City Intermediate Motor Second No. SC50936 [*P. J. Sharpe*

M50785	M50789	M50792	M50795	M50798	M50801
M50786	M50790	M50793	M50796	M50799	M50802
M50787	M50791	M50794	M50797	M50800	M50803
M50788					

Cravens (2)

MOTOR COMPOSITE (L) ■

Engines
Two B.U.T. (A.E.C.) 6-cyl. horizontal type of 150 b.h.p.

Transmission
Mechanical. Standard

Body: 57′ 6″ × 9′ 2″ **Weight:** 30 tons **Seats:** 1st, 12; 2nd, 51

M50804	M50807	M50810	M50812	M50814	M50816
M50805	M50809	M50811	M50813	M50815	M50817
M50806					

Derby Works, B.R. (3 Suburban)

MOTOR BRAKE SECOND ■

For details see W50050-91

W50818	W50827	W50836	W50845	W50854	W50863
W50819	W50828	W50837	W50846	W50855	W50864
W50820	W50829	W50838	W50847	W50856	W50865
W50821	W50830	W50839	W50848	W50857	W50866
W50822	W50831	W50840	W50849	W50858	W50867
W50823	W50832	W50841	W50850	W50859	W50868
W50824	W50833	W50842	W50851	W50860	W50869
W50825	W50834	W50843	W50852	W50861	W50870
W50826	W50835	W50844	W50853	W50862	

Derby Works, B.R. (3 Suburban)

MOTOR SECOND ■

For details see W50092-50133

W50871	W50880	W50889	W50898	W50907	W50916
W50872	W50881	W50890	W50899	W50908	W50917
W50873	W50882	W50891	W50900	W50909	W50918
W50874	W50883	W50892	W50901	W50910	W50919
W50875	W50884	W50893	W50902	W50911	W50920
W50876	W50885	W50894	W50903	W50912	W50921
W50877	W50886	W50895	W50904	W50913	W50922
W50878	W50887	W50896	W50905	W50914	W50923
W50879	W50888	W50897	W50906	W50915	

Derby Works, B.R. (2)

MOTOR BRAKE SECOND ■

Engines
Two B.U.T. (A.E.C.) 6-cyl. horizontal type of 150 b.h.p.

Transmission
Mechanical. Standard

Body: 57′ 6″ × 9′ 2″ **Weight:** 28 tons 10 cwt **Seats: 2nd,** 52

M50924	M50926	M50928	M50930	M50932	M50934
M50925	M50927	M50929	M50931	M50933	M50935

Swindon Works, B.R. (6 Inter-City)

MOTOR SECOND (L) ●

Engines
Two B.U.T. 6-cyl. horizontal type of 150 b.h.p.

Transmission
Mechanical. Standard

Body: 64′ 6″ × 9′ 3″. Gangwayed both ends, side driving compartment at one end

Weight: 38 tons **Seats: 2nd,** 64

SC50936

Derby Works, B.R. (2)

MOTOR BRAKE SECOND ■

Engines
Two B.U.T. (Leyland) 6-cyl. horizontal type of 150 b.h.p.

Transmission
Mechanical. Standard

Body: 57′ 6″ × 9′ 2″ **Weight:** 28 tons 10 cwt **Seats: 2nd,** 52

M50938	M50947	M50956	M50964	M50972	M50980
M50939	M50948	M50957	M50965	M50973	M50981
M50940	M50949	M50958	M50966	M50974	M50982
M50941	M50950	M50959	M50967	M50975	M50983
M50942	M50951	M50960	M50968	M50976	M50984
M50943	M50952	M50961	M50969	M50977	M50985
M50944	M50953	M50962	M50970	M50978	M50986
M50945	M50954	M50963	M50971	M50979	M50987
M50946	M50955				

Derby Works, B.R. (3 Suburban)

MOTOR SECOND ★

Engines
Two Rolls-Royce horizontal type of 238 b.h.p.

Transmission
Hydraulic. Twin-disc torque converter

Body: 64′ 0″ × 9′ 3″. Non-gangwayed, side doors to each seating bay

Weight: 39 tons 10 cwt **Seats: 2nd,** 95

E50988	E50992	E50996	E50999	E51002	E51005
E50989	E50993	E50997	E51000	E51003	E51006
E50990	E50994	E50998	E51001	E51004	E51007
E50991	E50995				

Swindon Works, B.R. (6 Inter-City)

MOTOR SECOND (L) ●

Engines
Two B.U.T. 6-cyl. horizontal type of 150 b.h.p.

Transmission
Mechanical. Standard

Body: 64′ 6″ × 9′ 3″. Gangwayed both ends, side driving compartment at one end

Weight: 38 tons **Seats: 2nd,** 64

SC51008	SC51012	SC51016	SC51020	SC51024	SC51027
SC51009	SC51013	SC51017	SC51021	SC51025	SC51028
SC51010	SC51014	SC51018	SC51022	SC51026	SC51029
SC51011	SC51015	SC51019	SC51023		

Swindon Works, B.R. (3 or 6 Inter-City)

MOTOR BRAKE SECOND (L) ●

Engines
Two B.U.T. (A.E.C.) 6-cyl. horizontal type of 150 b.h.p.

Transmission
Mechanical. Standard

Body: 64′ 6″ × 9′ 3″ **Weight:** 38 tons **Seats: 2nd,** 52

SC51030	SC51034	SC51038	SC51042	SC51046	SC51049
SC51031	SC51035	SC51039	SC51043	SC51047	SC51050
SC51032	SC51036	SC51040	SC51044	SC51048	SC51051
SC51033	SC51037	SC51041	SC51045		

Gloucester R. C. & W. Co. (3 Cross Country)

MOTOR BRAKE COMPOSITE ■

Engines
Two B.U.T. 6-cyl. horizontal type of 150 b.h.p.

Transmission
Mechanical. Standard

Body: 64′ 6″ × 9′ 3″ **Weight:** 36 tons 19 cwt **Seats: 1st,** 18; **2nd,** 16

W51052	W51057	W51062	W51067	W51072	W51076
W51053	W51058	W51063	W51068	W51073	W51077
W51054	W51059	W51064	W51069	W51074	W51078
W51055	W51060	W51065	W51070	W51075	W51079
W51056	W51061	W51066	W51071		

Swindon Inter-City Motor Brake Second No. SC51045 [*D. L. Percival*

Gloucester R. C. & W. Co. Motor Brake Composite No. W51070 [*P. J. Sharpe*

Liverpool Street–Hertford East train formed of two Derby three-car suburban units [*K. L. Cook*

Gloucester R. C. & W. Co. (3 Cross Country)

MOTOR SECOND (L) ■

Engines
Two B.U.T. 6-cyl. horizontal type of 150 b.h.p.

Transmission
Mechanical. Standard

Body: 64′ 6″ × 9′ 3″ **Weight:** 37 tons 10 cwt **Seats:** 2nd, 68

W51080	W51085	W51090	W51095	W51100	W51104
W51081	W51086	W51091	W51096	W51101	W51105
W51082	W51087	W51092	W51097	W51102	W51106
W51083	W51088	W51093	W51098	W51103	W51107
W51084	W51089	W51094	W51099		

Gloucester R. C. & W. Co. (2)

MOTOR BRAKE SECOND ■

For details see SC50339-M50357

SC51108	SC51112	SC51116	SC51119	SC51122	SC51125
SC51109	SC51113	SC51117	SC51120	SC51123	SC51126
SC51110	SC51114	SC51118	SC51121	SC51124	SC51127
SC51111	SC51115				

Derby Works, B.R. (3 Suburban)

MOTOR BRAKE SECOND ■

For details see W50050-91

W51128	W51131	W51133	W51135	W51137	W51139
W51129	W51132	W51134	W51136	W51138	W51140
W51130					

Derby Works, B.R. (3 Suburban)

MOTOR SECOND ■

For details see W50092-50133

W51141	W51144	W51146	W51148	W51150	W51152
W51142	W51145	W51147	W51149	W51151	W51153
W51143					

Derby Works, B.R. (3 Suburban)

MOTOR BRAKE SECOND ★

Engines
Two Rolls-Royce horizontal type of 238 b.h.p.

Transmission
Hydraulic. Twin-disc torque converter

Body: 64′ 0″ × 9′ 3″. Non-gangwayed, side doors to each seating bay

Weight: 39 tons 10 cwt **Seats:** 2nd, 65

E51154	E51158	E51162	E51165	E51168	E51171
E51155	E51159	E51163	E51166	E51169	E51172
E51156	E51160	E51164	E51167	E51170	E51173
E51157	E51161				

Metropolitan-Cammell (2)

MOTOR BRAKE SECOND ■

Engines
Two B.U T. (A.E.C.) 6-cyl. horizontal type of 150 b.h.p.

Transmission
Mechanical. Standard

Body: 57′ 0″ × 9′ 3″ **Weight:** 32 tons **Seats:** 2nd, 52

M51174	M51188	M51202	E51215	SC51228	SC51241
M51175	M51189	M51203	E51216	SC51229	SC51242
M51176	M51190	E51204	E51217	SC51230	SC51243
M51177	M51191	E51205	E51218	SC51231	SC51244
M51178	M51192	E51206	E51219	SC51232	SC51245
M51179	M51193	E51207	E51220	SC51233	SC51246
M51180	M51194	E51208	E51221	SC51234	SC51247
M51181	M51195	E51209	E51222	SC51235	SC51248
M51182	M51196	E51210	E51223	SC51236	SC51249
M51183	M51197	E51211	SC51224	SC51237	SC51250
M51184	M51198	E51212	SC51225	SC51238	SC51251
M51185	M51199	E51213	SC51226	SC51239	SC51252
M51186	M51200	E51214	SC51227	SC51240	SC51253
M51187	M51201				

Cravens (2)

MOTOR BRAKE SECOND ■

Engines
Two B.U.T. (A.E.C.) 6-cyl. horizontal type of 150 b.h.p.

Transmission
Mechanical. Standard

Body: 57′ 6″ × 9′ 2″ **Weight:** 30 tons **Seats:** 2nd, 52

E51254	E51262	E51270	E51278	E51286	E51294
E51255	E51263	E51271	E51279	E51287	E51295
E51256	E51264	E51272	E51280	E51288	E51296
E51257	E51265	E51273	E51281	E51289	E51297
E51258	E51266	E51274	E51282	E51290	E51298
E51259	E51267	E51275	E51283	E51291	E51299
E51260	E51268	E51276	E51284	E51292	E51300
E51261	E51269	E51277	E51285	E51293	E51301

Birmingham R. C. & W. Co. (3 Suburban)

MOTOR BRAKE SECOND ■

Engines

Transmission
Mechanical. Standard

Body: 64′ 0″ × 9′ 3″. Non-gangwayed, side doors to each seating bay

Weight: 36 tons **Seats:** 2nd, 65

Birmingham R. C. & W. Co. Western Region three-car suburban unit on a Reading–Kingham service [*M. Mensing*

Pressed Steel three-car suburban unit at West Ealing [*Alan Williams*

W51302 W51305 W51308 W51311 W51313 W51315
W51303 W51306 W51309 W51312 W51314 W51316
W51304 W51307 W51310

Birmingham R. C. & W. Co. (3 Suburban)

MOTOR SECOND ■

Engines

Transmission
Mechanical. Standard

Body: 64′ 0″ × 9 3″. Non-gangwayed, side doors to each seating bay

Weight: 36 tons **Seats:** 2nd, 91

W51317 W51320 W51323 W51326 W51328 W51330
W51318 W51321 W51324 W51327 W51329 W51331
W51319 W51322 W51325

Pressed Steel Co. (3 Suburban)

MOTOR BRAKE SECOND ■

Engines
Two B.U.T. (Leyland) 6-cyl. horizontal type of 150 b.h.p.

Transmission
Mechanical. Standard

Body: 64′ 0″ × 9′ 3″. Non-gangwayed, side doors to each seating bay

Weight: 36 tons **Seats:** 2nd, 65

W51332 W51339 W51346 W51353 W51360 W51367
W51333 W51340 W51347 W51354 W51361 W51368
W51334 W51341 W51348 W51355 W51362 W51369
W51335 W51342 W51349 W51356 W51363 W51370
W51336 W51343 W51350 W51357 W51364 W51371
W51337 W51344 W51351 W51358 W51365 W51372
W51338 W51345 W51352 W51359 W51366 W51373

Pressed Steel Co. (3 Suburban)

MOTOR SECOND ■

Engines
Two B.U.T. (Leyland) 6-cyl. horizontal type of 150 b.h.p.

Transmission
Mechanical. Standard

Body: 64′ 0″ × 9′ 3″. Non-gangwayed, side doors to each seating bay

Weight: 36 tons **Seats:** 2nd, 91

W51374 W51381 W51388 W51395 W51402 W51409
W51375 W51382 W51389 W51396 W51403 W51410
W51376 W51383 W51390 W51397 W51404 W51411
W51377 W51384 W51391 W51398 W51405 W51412
W51378 W51385 W51392 W51399 W51406 W51413
W51379 W51386 W51393 W51400 W51407 W51414
W51380 W51387 W51394 W51401 W51408 W51415

Derby Works, B.R. (2)

MOTOR BRAKE SECOND ■

Engines
Two B.U.T (A.E.C.) 6-cyl. horizontal type of 150 b.h.p.

Transmission
Mechanical. Standard

Body: 57′ 6″ × 9′ 2″ **Weight:** 29 tons **Seats:** 2nd, 52

M51416	M51418	M51420	M51422	M51423	M51424
M51417	M51419	M51421			

Metropolitan-Cammell (2)

MOTOR BRAKE SECOND ■

Engines
Two B.U.T. (Leyland) 6-cyl. horizontal type of 150 b.h.p.

Transmission
Mechanical. Standard

Body: 57′ 0″ × 9′ 3″ **Weight:** 32 tons **Seats:** 2nd, 52

E51425	E51427	E51429	E51431	E51433	E51434
E51426	E51428	E51430	E51432		

Metropolitan-Cammell (3 or 4*)

MOTOR BRAKE SECOND ■

Engines
Two B.U.T. (Leyland) 6-cyl. horizontal type of 150 b.h.p.

Transmission
Mechanical. Standard

Body: 57′ 0″ × 9′ 3″ **Weight:** 32 tons **Seats:** 2nd, 52

E51435*	E51441*	SC51447	SC51453	SC51459	SC51465
E51436*	E51442*	SC51448	SC51454	SC51460	SC51466
E51437*	E51443*	SC51449	SC51455	SC51461	SC51467
E51438*	E51444*	SC51450	SC51456	SC51462	SC51468
E51439*	SC51445	SC51451	SC51457	SC51463	SC51469
E51440*	SC51446	SC51452	SC51458	SC51464	SC51470

Cravens (2)

MOTOR BRAKE SECOND ■

Engines
Two B.U.T. (A.E.C.) 6-cyl. horizontal type of 150 b.h.p.

Transmission
Mechanical. Standard

Body: 57′ 6″ × 9′ 2″ **Weight:** 30 tons 10 cwt **Seats:** 2nd, 52

E51471	SC51475	SC51479	SC51483	SC51487	SC51491
E51472	SC51476	SC51480	SC51484	SC51488	SC51492
SC51473	SC51477	SC51481	SC51485	SC51489	SC51493
SC51474	SC51478	SC51482	SC51486	SC51490	SC51494

Cravens Motor Brake Second No. SC51490 [*P. J. Sharpe*

Later Swindon three-car Cross Country unit, with four-character headcode panel, on a Stratford-upon-Avon–Leamington service. The leading vehicle is Motor Brake Composite No. W51581 [*M. Mensing*

Metropolitan-Cammell (2)

MOTOR COMPOSITE (L) ■

Engines
Two B.U.T. (Leyland) 6-cyl. horizontal type of 150 b.h.p.

Transmission
Mechanical. Standard

Body: 57′ 0″ × 9′ 3″ **Weight:** 32 tons **Seats: 1st,** 12; **2nd,** 53

E51495 E51497 E51499 E51501 E51503 E51504
E51496 E51498 E51500 E51502

Metropolitan-Cammell (3 or 4*)

MOTOR COMPOSITE (L) ■

Engines
Two B.U.T. (Leyland) 6-cyl. horizontal type of 150 b.h.p.

Transmission
Mechanical. Standard

Body: 57′ 0″ × 9′ 3″ **Weight:** 32 tons **Seats: 1st,** 12; **2nd,** 53

E51505* E51511* SC51517 SC51523 SC51529 SC51535
E51506* E51512* SC51518 SC51524 SC51530 SC51536
E51507* E51513* SC51519 SC51525 SC51531 SC51537
E51508* E51514* SC51520 SC51526 SC51532 SC51538
E51509* SC51515 SC51521 SC51527 SC51533 SC51539
E51510* SC51516 SC51522 SC51528 SC51534 SC51540

Metropolitan-Cammell (3)

MOTOR BRAKE SECOND ■

For details see E51435-SC51470

E51541 E51543 E51544 E51545 E51546 E51547
E51542

Metropolitan-Cammell (2)

MOTOR BRAKE SECOND ■

Engines
Two B.U.T. (A.E.C.) 6-cyl. horizontal type of 150 b.h.p.

Transmission
Mechanical. Standard

Body: 57′ 0″ × 9′ 3″ **Weight:** 31 tons 10 cwt **Seats: 2nd,** 52

E51548 E51549 E51550

Metropolitan-Cammell (3)

MOTOR COMPOSITE (L) ■

For details see E51505-SC515 40

E51551 E51553 E51554 E51555 E51556 E51557
E51552

Metropolitan-Cammell (2)

MOTOR COMPOSITE (L) ■

Engines
Two B.U.T. (A.E.C.) 6-cyl. horizontal type of 150 b.h.p.

Transmission
Mechanical. Standard

Body: 57′ 0″ × 9′ 3″ **Weight:** 31 tons 10 cwt **Seats: 1st,** 12; **2nd,** 53

E51558 E51559 E51560

Derby Works, B.R. (2)

MOTOR COMPOSITE (L) ■

Engines
Two B.U.T. (A.E.C.) 6-cyl. horizontal type of 150 b.h.p.

Transmission
Mechanical. Standard

Body: 57′ 6″ × 9′ 2″ **Weight:** 27 tons **Seats: 1st,** 12; **2nd,** 53

M51561 M51563 M51565 M51567 M51569 M51571
M51562 M51564 M51566 M51568 M51570 M51572

Swindon Works, B.R. (3 Cross Country)

MOTOR BRAKE COMPOSITE (L) ■

Engines
Two B.U.T. 6-cyl. horizontal type of 150 b.h.p.

Transmission
Mechanical. Standard

Body: 64′ 6″ × 9′ 3″ **Weight:** 36 tons 7 cwt **Seats: 1st,** 18; **2nd,** 16

W51573 W51575 W51577 W51579 W51580 W51581
W51574 W51576 W51578

Swindon Works, B.R. (3 Cross Country)

MOTOR SECOND (L) ■

Engines
Two B.U.T. 6-cyl. horizontal type of 150 b.h.p.

Transmission
Mechanical. Standard

Body: 64′ 6″ × 9′ 3″ **Weight:** 36 tons 10 cwt **Seats: 2nd,** 68

W51582 W51584 W51586 W51588 W51589 W51590
W51583 W51585 W51587

Derby Works, B.R. (4 Suburban)

MOTOR BRAKE SECOND ■

Engines
Two Rolls-Royce 8-cyl. horizontal type of 238 b.h.p.

Transmission
Hydraulic. Torque converter

Body: 64′ 0″ × 9′ 3″. Non-gangwayed, side doors to each seating bay

Weight: 40 tons **Seats: 2nd,** 76

M51591	M51601	M51611	M51621	M51631	M51641
M51592	M51602	M51612	M51622	M51632	M51642
M51593	M51603	M51613	M51623	M51633	M51643
M51594	M51604	M51614	M51624	M51634	M51644
M51595	M51605	M51615	M51625	M51635	M51645
M51596	M51606	M51616	M51626	M51636	M51646
M51597	M51607	M51617	M51627	M51637	M51647
M51598	M51608	M51618	M51628	M51638	M51648
M51599	M51609	M51619	M51629	M51639	M51649
M51600	M51610	M51620	M51630	M51640	M51650

Derby Works, B.R. (4 Suburban)

MOTOR BRAKE SECOND ■

Engines
Two B.U.T. (Leyland) 6-cyl. horizontal type of 230 b.h.p.

Transmission
Mechanical. Standard

Body: 64′ 0″ × 9′ 3″. Non-gangwayed, side doors to each seating bay

Weight: 38 tons **Seats:** 2nd, 78

M51651	M51656	M51661	M51666	M51671	M51676
M51652	M51657	M51662	M51667	M51672	M51677
M51653	M51658	M51663	M51668	M51673	M51678
M51654	M51659	M51664	M51669	M51674	M51679
M51655	M51660	M51665	M51670	M51675	M51680

Cravens (2)

MOTOR BRAKE SECOND ■

Engine
One Rolls-Royce 8-cyl. horizontal type of 238 b.h.p.

Transmission
Mechanical. Standard

Body: 57′ 6″ × 9′ 2″ **Weight:** 29 tons 10 cwt **Seats:** 2nd, 52

M51681	M51686	M51690	M51694	M51698	M51702
M51682	M51687	M51691	M51695	M51699	M51703
M51683	M51688	M51692	M51696	M51700	M51704
M51684	M51689	M51693	M51697	M51701	M51705
M51685					

Cravens (2)

MOTOR COMPOSITE (L) ■

Engine
One Rolls-Royce 8-cyl. horizontal type of 238 b.h.p.

Transmission
Mechanical. Standard

Body: 57′ 6″ × 9′ 2″ **Weight:** 29 tons **Seats:** 1st, 12; 2nd, 51

M51706 M51711 M51715 M51719 M51723 M51727
M51707 M51712 M51716 M51720 M51724 M51728
M51708 M51713 M51717 M51721 M51725 M51729
M51709 M51714 M51718 M51722 M51726 M51730
M51710

Cravens (2)

MOTOR BRAKE SECOND ■

Engine
One Rolls-Royce 8-cyl. horizontal type of 238 b.h.p.

Transmission
Hydraulic. Torque converter

Body: 57′ 6″ × 9′ 2″ **Weight:** 29 tons 10 cwt **Seats:** 2nd, 52

M51731 M51736 M51740 M51744 M51748 M51752
M51732 M51737 M51741 M51745 M51749 M51753
M51733 M51738 M51742 M51746 M51750 M51754
M51734 M51739 M51743 M51747 M51751 M51755
M51735

Cravens (2)

MOTOR COMPOSITE (L) ■

Engine
One Rolls-Royce 8-cyl. horizontal type of 238 b.h.p.

Transmission
Hydraulic. Torque converter

Body: 57′ 6″ × 9′ 2″ **Weight:** 29 tons **Seats:** 1st, 12; 2nd, 51

M51756 M51760 M51764 M51768 M51772 M51776
M51757 M51761 M51765 M51769 M51773 M51777
M51758 M51762 M51766 M51770 M51774 M51778
M51759 M51763 M51767 M51771 M51775 M51779

Swindon Works, B.R. (3 Cross Country)

MOTOR BRAKE COMPOSITE ■

Engines
Two B.U.T. 6-cyl. horizontal type of 150 b.h.p.

Transmission
Mechanical. Standard

Body: 64′ 6″ × 9′ 3″ **Weight:** 36 tons 7 cwt **Seats:** 1st, 18; 2nd, 16

SC51781 SC51783 SC51784 SC51785 SC51786 SC51787
SC51782

Swindon Works, B.R. (3 Cross Country)

MOTOR SECOND (L) ■

Engines
Two B.U.T. 6-cyl. horizontal type of 150 b.h.p.

Transmission
Mechanical. Standard

Body: 64′ 6″ × 9′ 3″ **Weight:** 36 tons 10 cwt **Seats:** 2nd, 68

SC51788 SC51790 SC51791 SC51792 SC51793 SC51794
SC51789

Metropolitan-Cammell (3)

MOTOR BRAKE SECOND ■

Engines
Two B.U.T. (A.E.C.) 6-cyl. horizontal type of 150 b.h.p.

Transmission
Mechanical. Standard

Body: 57′ 0″ × 9′ 3″ **Weight:** 32 tons **Seats: 2nd,** 52

SC51795 SC51797 SC51798 SC51799 SC51800 SC51801
SC51796

Metropolitan-Cammell (3)

MOTOR COMPOSITE (L) ■

Engines
Two B.U.T. (A.E.C.) 6-cyl. horizontal type of 150 b.h.p.

Transmission
Mechanical. Standard

Body: 57′ 0″ × 9′ 3″ **Weight:** 32 tons **Seats: 1st,** 12; **2nd,** 53

SC51802 SC51804 SC51805 SC51806 SC51807 SC51808
SC51803

Birmingham R. C. & W. Co. (3)

MOTOR BRAKE COMPOSITE ■

Engines
Two Rolls-Royce Series 130D of 180 b.h.p.

Transmission
Mechanical. Standard

Body: 57′ 6″ × 9′ 3″ **Weight:** 32 tons **Seats: 1st,** 12; **2nd,** 33

E51809 E51813 E51817 E51820 E51823 E51826
E51810 E51814 E51818 E51821 E51824 E51827
E51811 E51815 E51819 E51822 E51825 E51828
E51812 E51816

Birmingham R. C. & W. Co. (3)

MOTOR COMPOSITE (L) ■

Engines
Two Rolls-Royce Series 130D of 180 b.h.p.

Transmission
Mechanical. Standard

Body: 57′ 6″ × 9′ 3″ **Weight:** 31 tons 10 cwt **Seats: 1st,** 12; **2nd,** 54

E51829	E51833	E51837	E51840	E51843	E51846
E51830	E51834	E51838	E51841	E51844	E51847
E51831	E51835	E51839	E51842	E51845	E51848
E51832	E51836				

Derby Works, B.R. (4 Suburban)

MOTOR BRAKE SECOND ■

Engines
Two B.U.T. 6-cyl. horizontal type of 230 b.h.p.

Transmission
Mechanical. Standard

Body: 64′ 0″ × 9′ 3″. Non-gangwayed, side doors to each seating bay

Weight: 38 tons **Seats: 2nd,** 78

M51849	M51858	M51867	M51876	M51885	M51893
M51850	M51859	M51868	M51877	M51886	M51894
M51851	M51860	M51869	M51878	M51887	M51895
M51852	M51861	M51870	M51879	M51888	M51896
M51853	M51862	M51871	M51880	M51889	M51897
M51854	M51863	M51872	M51881	M51890	M51898
M51855	M51864	M51873	M51882	M51891	M51899
M51856	M51865	M51874	M51883	M51892	M51900
M51857	M51866	M51875	M51884		

Derby Works, B.R. (2)

MOTOR BRAKE SECOND ■

Engines
Two B.U.T. (A.E.C.) 6-cyl. horizontal type of 150 b.h.p.

Transmission
Mechanical. Standard

Body: 57′ 6″ × 9′ 2″ **Weight:** 28 tons 10 cwt **Seats: 2nd,** 52

M51901	M51910	M51919	M51927	M51935	M51943
M51902	M51911	M51920	M51928	M51936	M51944
M51903	M51912	M51921	M51929	M51937	M51945
M51904	M51913	M51922	M51930	M51938	M51946
M51905	M51914	M51923	M51931	M51939	M51947
M51906	M51915	M51924	M51932	M51940	M51948
M51907	M51916	M51925	M51933	M51941	M51949
M51908	M51917	M51926	M51934	M51942	M51950
M51909	M51918				

Swindon Works, B.R. (6 Trans-Pennine)

MOTOR COMPOSITE ■

Engines
Two B.U.T. (Leyland) 6-cyl. horizontal type of 230 b.h.p.

Transmission
Mechanical. Standard

Body: 64′ 6″ × 9′ 3″ **Weight:** **Seats: 1st,** 21; **2nd,** 36

Derby four-car suburban unit for the St. Pancras area, with Motor Brake Second No. M51649 leading, on a Bedford-Henlow Camp special working [*P. Thatcher*

Swindon six-car Trans-Pennine unit leaving Huddersfield, with Motor Composite No. E51952 leading [*P. J. Sharpe*

Non-driving Motor Brake Second No. E51974 of a six-car Trans-Pennine unit [*P. J. Sharpe*

E51951	E51954	E51957	E51960	E51963	E51966
E51952	E51955	E51958	E51961	E51964	E51967
E51953	E51956	E51959	E51962	E51965	

Swindon Works, B.R. (6 Trans-Pennine)

MOTOR BRAKE SECOND (K) ■

(non-driving)

Engines
Two B.U.T. (Leyland) 6-cyl. horizontal type of 230 b.h.p.

Transmission
Mechanical. Standard

Body: 64′ 6″ × 9′ 3″ **Weight:** **Seats: 2nd, 48**

E51968	E51971	E51974	E51977	E51980	E51983
E51969	E51972	E51975	E51978	E51981	E51984
E51970	E51973	E51976	E51979	E51982	

Derby Works, B.R. (3)

MOTOR BRAKE SECOND ■

Engines
Two B.U.T. 6-cyl. horizontal type of 150 b.h.p.

Transmission
Mechanical. Standard

Body: 58′ 1″ × 9′ 3″ **Weight:** 34 tons 10 cwt **Seats: 2nd, 52**

SC51985	SC51990	SC51995	SC51999	SC52003	SC52007
SC51986	SC51991	SC51996	SC52000	SC52004	SC52008
SC51987	SC51992	SC51997	SC52001	SC52005	SC52009
SC51988	SC51993	SC51998	SC52002	SC52006	SC52010
SC51989	SC51994				

Derby Works, B.R. (3)

MOTOR COMPOSITE (L) ■

Engines
Two B.U.T. 6-cyl. horizontal type of 150 b.h.p.

Transmission
Mechanical. Standard

Body: 58′ 1″ × 9′ 3″ **Weight:** 35 tons **Seats: 1st,** 12; **2nd,** 53

SC52011	SC52016	SC52021	SC52025	SC52029	SC52033
SC52012	SC52017	SC52022	SC52026	SC52030	SC52034
SC52013	SC52018	SC52023	SC52027	SC52031	SC52035
SC52014	SC52019	SC52024	SC52028	SC52032	SC52036
SC52015	SC52020				

Derby Works, B.R. (2)

MOTOR COMPOSITE (L) ■

Engines
Two B.U.T. 6-cyl. horizontal type of 150 b.h.p.

Transmission
Mechanical. Standard

Body: 57′ 6″ × 9′ 2″ **Weight:** 28 tons **Seats: 1st,** 12; **2nd,** 53

M52037	M52042	M52047	M52052	M52057	M52062
M52038	M52043	M52048	M52053	M52058	M52063
M52039	M52044	M52049	M52054	M52059	M52064
M52040	M52045	M52050	M52055	M52060	M52065
M52041	M52046	M52051	M52056	M52061	

Birmingham R. C. & W. Co. (3)

MOTOR BRAKE COMPOSITE ■

Engines: Two Rolls-Royce Series 130D of 180 b.h.p.

Transmission Mechanical. Standard

Body: 57′ 6″ × 9′ 3″ **Weight:** 32 tons **Seats: 1st,** 12; **2nd,** 33

M52066	M52068	M52070	M52072	M52074	M52075
M52067	M52069	M52071	M52073		

Birmingham R. C. & W. Co. (3)

MOTOR COMPOSITE (L) ■

Engines: Two Rolls-Royce Series 130D of 180 b.h.p.

Transmission Mechanical. Standard

Body: 57′ 6″ × 9′ 3″ **Weight:** 31 tons 10 cwt **Seats: 1st,** 12; **2nd,** 54

M52076	M52078	M52080	M52082	M52084	M52085
M52077	M52079	M52081	M52083		

Gloucester R. C. & W. Co. (1)

MOTOR BRAKE SECOND ■

Engines Two B.U.T. (A.E.C.) 6-cyl. horizontal type of 150 b.h.p.

Transmission Mechanical. Standard

Body: 64′ 6″ × 9′ 3″. Non-gangwayed, side doors to each seating bay

Weight: 35 tons **Seats: 2nd,** 65

W55000	W55004	W55008	W55011	W55014	W55017
W55001	W55005	W55009	W55012	W55015	W55018
W55002	W55006	W55010	W55013	W55016	W55019
W55003	W55007				

Pressed Steel Co. (1)

MOTOR BRAKE SECOND ■

Engines Two B.U.T. 6-cyl. horizontal type of 150 b.h.p.

Transmission Mechanical. Standard

Body: 64′ 6″ × 9′ 3″. Non-gangwayed, side doors to each seating bay

Weight: 37 tons **Seats: 2nd,** 65

Later Birmingham R. C. & W. Co. Motor Composite No. M52082 [*D. L. Percival*

Gloucester R. C. & W. Co. single-unit Motor Brake Second No. W55004 [*M. Mensing*

W55020	W55023	W55026	W55029	W55032	W55034
W55021	W55024	W55027	W55030	W55033	W55035
W55022	W55025	W55028	W55031		

Gloucester R. C. & W. Co. (1)

MOTOR PARCELS VAN ■

Engines
Two B.U.T. (A.E.C.) 6-cyl. horizontal type of 230 b.h.p.

Transmission
Mechanical. Standard

Body: 64′ 6″ × 9′ 3″. Non-gangwayed* **Weight:** 40 tons*, 41 tons

M55987*	M55989*	W55991	W55993	W55995	W55996
M55988*	M55990*	W55992	W55994		

Cravens (1)

MOTOR PARCELS VAN ♦

Engines
Two B.U.T. (A.E.C.) 6-cyl. horizontal type of 150 b.h.p.

Transmission
Mechanical. Standard

Body: 57′ 6″ × 9′ 3″. Non-gangwayed **Weight:** 30 tons

M55997 M55998 M55999

Derby Works, B.R. (2)

DRIVING TRAILER COMPOSITE (L) ■

Body: 64′ 6″ × 9′ 3″ **Weight:** 29 tons, 31 tons* **Seats: 1st,** 12; **2nd,** 62

E56000	E56009*	E56018	E56026	E56034	E56042
E56001*	E56010	E56019	E56027*	E56035	E56043
E56002	E56011	E56020	E56028	E56036	E56044
E56003	E56012	E56021	E56029	E56037	E56045
E56004*	E56013	E56022	E56030	E56038	E56046
E56005*	E56014	E56023*	E56031	E56039	E56047
E56006	E56015	E56024	E56032	E56040	E56048
E56007*	E56016	E56025	E56033	E56041	E56049
E56008*	E56017				

Metropolitan-Cammell (2)

DRIVING TRAILER COMPOSITE (L) ■

Body: 57′ 0″ × 9′ 3″ **Weight:** 25 tons **Seats: 1st,** 12; **2nd,** 53

E56050 E56058 E56066 E56073 E56080 E56087
E56051 E56059 E56067 E56074 E56081 E56088
E56052 E56060 E56068 E56075 E56082 E56089
E56053 E56061 E56069 E56076 E56083 M56090
E56054 E56062 E56070 E56077 E56084 M56091
E56055 E56063 E56071 E56078 E56085 M56092
E56056 E56064 E56072 E56079 E56086 M56093
E56057 E56065

Gloucester R. C. & W. Co. (2)

DRIVING TRAILER COMPOSITE (L) ■

Body: 57′ 6″ × 9′ 3″ **Weight:** 25 tons **Seats:** **1st,** 12; **2nd,** 54

SC56094 SC56098 SC56102 M56105 M56108 M56111
SC56095 SC56099 M56103 M56106 M56109 M56112
SC56096 SC56100 M56104 M56107 M56110 M56113
SC56097 SC56101

Cravens (2)

DRIVING TRAILER COMPOSITE (L) ■

Body: 57′ 6″ × 9′ 2″ **Weight:** 23 tons **Seats:** **1st,** 12; **2nd,** 51, 54*

E56114 E56120 E56126 E56132 E56138 E56144
E56115 E56121 E56127 E56133 E56139 M56145*
E56116 E56122 E56128 E56134 E56140 M56146*
E56117 E56123 E56129 E56135 E56141 M56147*
E56118 E56124 E56130 E56136 E56142 M56148*
E56119 E56125 E56131 E56137 E56143 M56149*

Park Royal Vehicles (2)

DRIVING TRAILER COMPOSITE (L) ■

Body: 57′ 6″ × 9′ 3″ **Weight:** 26 tons 7 cwt **Seats:** **1st,** 16; **2nd,** 48

M56150 M56154 M56158 M56161 M56164 M56167
M56151 M56155 M56159 M56162 M56165 M56168
M56152 M56156 M56160 M56163 M56166 M56169
M56153 M56157

D. Wickham & Co. (2)

DRIVING TRAILER COMPOSITE (L) ■

Body: 57′ 0″ × 9′ 3″ **Weight:** 20 tons 10 cwt **Seats:** **1st,** 16; **2nd,** 50

E56171 E56172 E56173

Gloucester R. C. & W. Co. Motor Parcels Van No. W55993 [M. Mensing

Cravens Motor Parcels Van No. M55999 [J. B. Bucknall

Birmingham R. C. & W. Co. (2)

DRIVING TRAILER COMPOSITE (L) ■

Body: 57′ 6″ × 9′ 3″ **Weight:** **Seats:** 1st, 12; 2nd, 54

M56175	M56177	M56179	M56181	M56183	M56184
M56176	M56178	M56180	M56182		

Birmingham R. C. & W. Co. (2)

DRIVING TRAILER COMPOSITE (L) ■

Body: 57′ 6″ × 9′ 3″ **Weight:** 24 tons **Seats:** 1st, 12; 2nd, 54

E56185 E56186 E56187 E56188 E56189

Derby Works, B.R. (2)

DRIVING TRAILER COMPOSITE (L) ■

Body: 57′ 6″ × 9′ 2″ **Weight:** 22 tons **Seats:** 1st, 12; 2nd, 53

E56190	E56195	E56200	E56204	E56208	M56212
E56191	E56196	E56201	E56205	E56209	M56213
E56192	E56197	E56202	E56206	E56210	M56214
E56193	E56198	E56203	E56207	M56211	M56215
E56194	E56199				

Metropolitan-Cammell (2)

DRIVING TRAILER COMPOSITE (L) ■

Body: 57′ 0″ × 9′ 3″ **Weight:** 25 tons **Seats:** 1st, 12; 2nd, 45

E56218 E56219 E56220

Derby Works, B.R. (2)

DRIVING TRAILER COMPOSITE (L) ■

Body: 57′ 6″ × 9′ 2″ **Weight:** 22 tons **Seats:** 1st, 12; 2nd, 53

M56221	M56231	M56241	M56251	M56261	M56271
M56222	M56232	M56242	M56252	M56262	M56272
M56223	M56233	M56243	M56253	M56263	M56273
M56224	M56234	M56244	M56254	M56264	M56274
M56225	M56235	M56245	M56255	M56265	M56275
M56226	M56236	M56246	M56256	M56266	M56276
M56227	M56237	M56247	M56257	M56267	M56277
M56228	M56238	M56248	M56258	M56268	M56278
M56229	M56239	M56249	M56259	M56269	M56279
M56230	M56240	M56250	M56260	M56270	

Derby "heavyweight" twin unit at Worksop on a Lincoln–Sheffield working
[*P. Ransome-Wallis*

Gloucester R. C. & W. Co. twin unit at Birmingham (New Street) with Driving Trailer Composite No. M56110 leading
[*M. Mensing*

Park Royal twin unit on a Northampton–Birmingham service
[*M. Mensing*

Pressed Steel Co. (2)

DRIVING TRAILER SECOND ■

(For use with Single Unit cars Nos. W55000-35)

Body: 64′ 0″ × 9′ 3″. Non-gangwayed, side doors to each seating bay
Weight: **Seats:** **2nd,** 95

W56280 W56282 W56284 W56286 W56288 W56289
W56281 W56283 W56285 W56287

Gloucester R. C. & W. Co. (2)

DRIVING TRAILER SECOND ■

(For use with Single Unit cars Nos. W55000-35)

Body: 64′ 0″ × 9′ 3″. Non-gangwayed, side doors to each seating bay
Weight: 29 tons **Seats:** **2nd,** 95

W56291 W56293 W56295 W56297 W56298 W56299
W56292 W56294 W56296

Gloucester R. C. & W. Co. (2)

DRIVING TRAILER COMPOSITE (L) ■

For Details see SC56094-M56113

SC56300 SC56304 SC56308 SC56311 SC56314 SC56317
SC56301 SC56305 SC56309 SC56312 SC56315 SC56318
SC56302 SC56306 SC56310 SC56313 SC56316 SC56319
SC56303 SC56307

Metropolitan-Cammell (2)

DRIVING TRAILER COMPOSITE (L) ■

Body: 57′ 0″ × 9′ 3″ **Weight:** 25 tons **Seats:** **1st,** 12; **2nd,** 53

M56332 M56346 M56360 E56373 SC56386 SC56399
M56333 M56347 M56361 E56374 SC56387 SC56400
M56334 M56348 E56362 E56375 SC56388 SC56401
M56335 M56349 E56363 E56376 SC56389 SC56402
M56336 M56350 E56364 E56377 SC56390 SC56403
M56337 M56351 E56365 E56378 SC56391 SC56404
M56338 M56352 E56366 E56379 SC56392 SC56405
M56339 M56353 E56367 E56380 SC56393 SC56406
M56340 M56354 E56368 E56381 SC56394 SC56407
M56341 M56355 E56369 SC56382 SC56395 SC56408
M56342 M56356 E56370 SC56383 SC56396 SC56409
M56343 M56357 E56371 SC56384 SC56397 SC56410
M56344 M56358 E56372 SC56385 SC56398 SC56411
M56345 M56359

Derby twin unit at Sandy on a Cambridge–Bletchley service with Driving Trailer Composite No. M56225 leading [*M. Mensing*

Later Derby twin unit on a Chester–Liverpool service. The leading vehicle is Driving Trailer Composite No. M56275 [*M. Mensing*

Cravens (2)

DRIVING TRAILER COMPOSITE (L) ■

Body: 57′ 6″ × 9′ 2″ **Weight:** 24 tons **Seats:** **1st,** 12; **2nd,** 51

E56412	E56424	E56436	E56448	E56460	SC56472
E56413	E56425	E56437	E56449	E56461	SC56473
E56414	E56426	E56438	E56450	SC56462	SC56474
E56415	E56427	E56439	E56451	SC56463	SC56475
E56416	E56428	E56440	E56452	SC56464	SC56476
E56417	E56429	E56441	E56453	SC56465	SC56477
E56418	E56430	E56442	E56454	SC56466	SC56478
E56419	E56431	E56443	E56455	SC56467	SC56479
E56420	E56432	E56444	E56456	SC56468	SC56480
E56421	E56433	E56445	E56457	SC56469	SC56481
E56422	E56434	E56446	E56458	SC56470	SC56482
E56423	E56435	E56447	E56459	SC56471	SC56483

Derby Works, B.R. (2)

DRIVING TRAILER COMPOSITE (L) ■

Body: 57′ 6″ × 9′ 2″ **Weight:** 22 tons **Seats:** **1st,** 12; **2nd,** 53

M56484	M56488	M56492	M56496	M56499	M56502
M56485	M56489	M56493	M56497	M56500	M56503
M56486	M56490	M56494	M56498	M56501	M56504
M56487	M56491	M56495			

Derby Works, B.R. (3 Suburban)

TRAILER COMPOSITE ■

Body: 63′ 8¾″ × 9′ 3″. Non-gangwayed, side doors to each seating bay

Weight: 28 tons 10 cwt **Seats:** **1st,** 28; **2nd,** 74

W59000	W59006	W59012	W59017	W59022	W59027
W59001	W59007	W59013	W59018	W59023	W59028
W59002	W59008	W59014	W59019	W59024	W59029
W59003	W59009	W59015	W59020	W59025	W59030
W59004	W59010	W59016	W59021	W59026	W59031
W59005	W59011				

Derby Works, B.R. (3 Suburban)

TRAILER SECOND ■

Body: 63′ 8¾″ × 9′ 3″. Non-gangwayed, side doors to each seating bay

Weight: 28 tons 10 cwt **Seats:** **2nd,** 106

Gloucester R. C. & W. Co. Driving Trailer Second No. W56295 leading a single-unit Motor Brake Second and three-car Cross Country unit [*M. Mensing*

Metropolitan-Cammell twin unit on a Birmingham–Rugby service, with Driving Trailer Composite No. M56342 leading [*M. Mensing*

Cravens twin unit formed of Driving Trailer Composite No. E56460 and Motor Brake Second No. E51471 [*A. H. Bryant*

W59032 W59034 W59036 W59038 W59040 W59041
W59033 W59035 W59037 W59039

Metropolitan-Cammell (4)

TRAILER SECOND (L) ■

Body: 57′ 0″ × 9′ 3″ **Weight:** 25 tons **Seats:** 2nd, 61

E59042 E59044 E59045 E59046 E59047 E59048
E59043

Metropolitan-Cammell (4)

TRAILER BRAKE SECOND (L) ■

Body: 57′ 0″ × 9′ 3″ **Weight:** 25 tons **Seats:** 2nd, 45

E59049 E59051 E59052 E59053 E59054 E59055
E59050

Metropolitan-Cammell (4)

TRAILER SECOND (L) ■

Body: 57′ 0″ × 9′ 3″ **Weight:** 25 tons **Seats:** 2nd, 71

E59060 E59063 E59065 E59067 E59069 E59071
E59061 E59064 E59066 E59068 E59070 E59072
E59062

Metropolitan-Cammell (4)

TRAILER BRAKE SECOND (L) ■

Body: 57′ 0″ × 9′ 3″ **Weight:** 25 tons **Seats:** 2nd, 53

E59073 E59076 E59078 E59080 E59082 E59084
E59074 E59077 E59079 E59081 E59083 E59085
E59075

Metropolitan-Cammell (4)

TRAILER SECOND (L) ■

For details see E59042-8

E59086 E59087 E59088 E59089 E59090 E59091

Metropolitan-Cammell (4)

TRAILER BRAKE SECOND (L) ■

For details see E59049-55

E59092 E59093 E59094 E59095 E59096 E59097

Swindon Works, B.R. (3 or 6 Inter-City)

TRAILER BUFFET FIRST (L) ●

Body: **Weight:** **Seats:** **1st,; Buffet,**

SC59098 SC59099

Metropolitan-Cammell (3)

TRAILER SECOND (L) ■

Body: 57′ 0″ × 9′ 3″ **Weight:** 24 tons 10 cwt **Seats: 2nd,** 71

E59100 E59102 E59104 E59106 E59108 E59109
E59101 E59103 E59105 E59107

Metropolitan-Cammell (4)

TRAILER BRAKE SECOND (L) ■

Body: 57′ 0″ × 9′ 3″ **Weight:** 25 tons **Seats: 2nd,** 53

E59112 E59113

Metropolitan-Cammell (3)

TRAILER COMPOSITE (L) ■

Body: 57′ 0″ × 9′ 3″ **Weight:** 25 tons **Seats: 1st,** 12; **2nd,** 53

M59114 M59117 M59120 M59123 M59126 M59129
M59115 M59118 M59121 M59124 M59127 M59130
M59116 M59119 M59122 M59125 M59128 M59131

Birmingham R. C. & W. Co. (3)

TRAILER COMPOSITE (L) ■

Body: 57′ 0″ × 9′ 3″ **Weight:** 24 tons **Seats: 1st,** 12; **2nd,** 54

M59132 M59142 M59152 M59161 M59170 M59179
M59133 M59143 M59153 M59162 M59171 M59180
M59134 M59144 M59154 M59163 M59172 M59181
M59135 M59145 M59155 M59164 M59173 M59182
M59136 M59146 M59156 M59165 M59174 M59183
M59137 M59147 M59157 M59166 M59175 M59184
M59138 M59148 M59158 M59167 M59176 M59185
M59139 M59149 M59159 M59168 M59177 M59186
M59140 M59150 M59160 M59169 M59178 M59187
M59141 M59151

Birmingham R. C. & W. Co. (4)

TRAILER SECOND (L) ■

Body: 57′ 0″ × 9′ 3″ **Weight:** 24 tons **Seats:** 2nd, 69

E59188	E59192	E59196	E59200	E59203	E59206
E59189	E59193	E59197	E59201	E59204	E59207
E59190	E59194	E59198	E59202	E59205	E59208
E59191	E59195	E59199			

Birmingham R. C. & W. Co. (4)

TRAILER BRAKE SECOND (L) ■

Body: 57′ 0″ × 9′ 3″ **Weight:** 25 tons **Seats:** 2nd, 51

E59209	E59213	E59217	E59221	E59224	E59227
E59210	E59214	E59218	E59222	E59225	E59228
E59211	E59215	E59219	E59223	E59226	E59229
E59212	E59216	E59220			

Birmingham R. C. & W. Co. (4)

TRAILER SECOND (L) ■

For details see E59188-E59208

E59230 E59231 E59232 E59233 E59234

Birmingham R. C. & W. Co. (4)

TRAILER BRAKE SECOND (L) ■

For details see E59209-29

E59240 E59241 E59242 E59243 E59244

Derby Works, B.R. (4)

TRAILER BRAKE SECOND (L) ■

Body: 57′ 6″ × 9′ 2″ **Weight:** 22 tons 10 cwt **Seats:** 2nd, 50

E59245 E59246 E59247 E59248 E59249 E59250

Swindon Works, B.R. (3 Cross Country)

TRAILER BUFFET SECOND (L) ■

Body: 64′ 6″ × 9′ 3″ Open second with miniature buffet at one end

Weight: 31 tons **Seats:** 2nd, 60; **Buffet**, 4

W59255 W59263 W59271 W59279 W59287 W59295
W59256 W59264 W59272 W59280 W59288 W59296
W59257 W59265 W59273 W59281 W59289 W59297
W59258 W59266 W59274 W59282 W59290 W59298
W59259 W59267 W59275 W59283 W59291 W59299
W59260 W59268 W59276 W59284 W59292 W59300
W59261 W59269 W59277 W59285 W59293 W59301
W59262 W59270 W59278 W59286 W59294

Metropolitan-Cammell (3)

TRAILER SECOND (L) ■

Body: 57′ 0″ × 9′ 3″ **Weight:** 25 tons **Seats:** 2nd, 71

E59302 E59303 E59304

Metropolitan-Cammell (4)

TRAILER SECOND (L) ■

Body: 57′ 0″ × 9′ 3″ **Weight:** 25 tons **Seats:** 2nd, 71

E59305 E59306

Cravens (3)

TRAILER SECOND (L) ■
OR TRAILER COMPOSITE (L)*

Body: 57′ 6″ × 9′ 2″ **Weight:** 23 tons **Seats:** 2nd, 69; 1st, 12*; 2nd, 54*

M59307* M59311 M59314 M59317* M59320* M59323
M59308 M59312 M59315 M59318* M59321* M59324
M59309 M59313 M59316* M59319 M59322* M59325
M59310*

Derby Works, B.R. (3 Suburban)

TRAILER COMPOSITE ■

For details see W59000-31

W59326 W59335 W59344 W59353 W59361 W59369
W59327 W59336 W59345 W59354 W59362 W59370
W59328 W59337 W59346 W59355 W59363 W59371
W59329 W59338 W59347 W59356 W59364 W59372
W59330 W59339 W59348 W59357 W59365 W59373
W59331 W59340 W59349 W59358 W59366 W59374
W59332 W59341 W59350 W59359 W59367 W59375
W59333 W59342 W59351 W59360 W59368 W59376
W59334 W59343 W59352

Derby Works, B.R. (3* or 4)

TRAILER SECOND (L) ■

Body: 57′ 6″ × 9′ 2″ **Weight:** 22 tons, 22 tons 10 cwt* **Seat:** 2nd, 68

E59380 E59382 E59384 E59386* E59388* E59390*
E59381 E59383 E59385 E59387* E59389*

Swindon Works, B.R. (3 or 6 Inter-City)

TRAILER FIRST (K) ●

Body: 64′ 6″ × 9′ 3″ **Weight:** **Seats:** 1st, 42

SC59391 SC59393 SC59395 SC59397 SC59399 SC59400
SC59392 SC59394 SC59396 SC59398

Swindon Works B.R. (3 or 6 Inter-City)

TRAILER COMPOSITE (L) ●

Body: 64′ 6″ × 9′ 3″ **Weight:** **Seats:** 1st, 18; 2nd, 32

SC59402 SC59404 SC59406 SC59408 SC59410 SC59412
SC59403 SC59405 SC59407 SC59409 SC59411

Gloucester R. C. & W. Co. (3 Cross Country)

TRAILER BUFFET SECOND (L) ■

Body: 64′ 6″ × 9′ 3″. Open second with miniature buffet at one end

Weight: 31 tons 8 cwt **Seats:** 2nd, 60; **Buffet**, 4

W59413 W59418 W59422 W59426 W59430 W59434
W59414 W59419 W59423 W59427 W59431 W59435
W59415 W59420 W59424 W59428 W59432 W59436
W59416 W59421 W59425 W59429 W59433 W59437
W59417

Derby Works, B.R. (3 Suburban)

TRAILER COMPOSITE ■

For details see W59000-31

W59438 W59440 W59442 W59444 W59446 W59448
W59439 W59441 W59443 W59445 W59447

Derby Works, B.R. (3 Suburban)

TRAILER SECOND ★

Body: 63′ 8¾″ × 9′ 3″. Non-gangwayed, side doors to each seating bay

Weight: 28 tons 10 cwt **Seats:** 2nd, 110

E59449	E59453	E59457	E59460	E59463	E59466
E59450	E59454	E59458	E59461	E59464	E59467
E59451	E59455	E59459	E59462	E59465	E59468
E59452	E59456				

Birmingham R. C. & W. Co. (3 Suburban)

TRAILER COMPOSITE (L) ■

Body: 63′ 10″ × 9′ 3″. Non-gangwayed, side doors to each seating bay

Weight: **Seats: 1st,** 24; **2nd,** 50

W59469	W59472	W59475	W59478	W59480	W59482
W59470	W59473	W59476	W59479	W59481	W59483
W59471	W59474	W59477			

Pressed Steel Co. (3 Suburban)

TRAILER COMPOSITE (L) ■

Body: 63′ 10″ × 9′ 3″. Non gangwayed, side doors to each seating bay.

Weight: 30 tons **Seats: 1st,** 24; **2nd,** 50

W59484	W59491	W59498	W59505	W59511	W59517
W59485	W59492	W59499	W59506	W59512	W59518
W59486	W59493	W59500	W59507	W59513	W59519
W59487	W59494	W59501	W59508	W59514	W59520
W59488	W59495	W59502	W59509	W59515	W59521
W59489	W59496	W59503	W59510	W59516	W59522
W59490	W59497	W59504			

Metropolitan-Cammell (3 or 4*)

TRAILER COMPOSITE (L) ■

Body: 57′ 0″ × 9′ 3″ **Weight:** 25 tons **Seats: 1st,** 12; **2nd,** 53

E59523*	E59531*	E59539*	SC59547	SC59555	SC59563
E59524*	E59532*	E59540*	SC59548	SC59556	SC59564
E59525*	E59533*	E59541*	SC59549	SC59557	SC59565
E59526*	E59534*	E59542*	SC59550	SC59558	SC59566
E59527*	E59535*	SC59543	SC59551	SC59559	SC59567
E59528*	E59536*	SC59544	SC59552	SC59560	SC59568
E59529*	E59537*	SC59545	SC59553	SC59561	
E59530*	E59538*	SC59546	SC59554	SC59562	

Metropolitan-Cammell (3)

TRAILER SECOND (L) ■

Body: 57′ 0″ × 9′ 3″ **Weight:** 24 tons 10 cwt **Seats: 2nd,** 71

Swindon Trailer Buffet First No. SC59099, formed in a Scottish Region Inter-City unit [*P. J. Sharpe*

Trailer Second No. E59766 of a Swindon six-car Trans-Pennine unit [*P. J. Sharpe*

Metropolitan-Cammell six-car Midland Pullman unit passing Elstree [*Hunnard Morris*

E59569 E59570 E59571 E59572

Metropolitan-Cammell (4)

TRAILER BUFFET SECOND (L) ■

Body: 57′ 0″ × 9′ 3″ Open second with miniature buffet at one end
Weight: 26 tons 10 cwt **Seats:** 2nd, 53; **Buffet,**

E59573 E59574 E59575 E59576 E59577 E59578

Swindon Works, B.R. (3 Cross Country)

TRAILER BUFFET SECOND (L) ■

Body: 64′ 6″ × 9′ 3″. Open second with miniature buffet at one end
Weight: 30 tons 12 cwt **Seats:** 2nd, 60; **Buffet,** 4

W59579	W59581	W59583	W59585	W59587	W59588
W59580	W59582	W59584	W59586		

Derby Works, B.R. (4 Suburban)

TRAILER SECOND (L) ■

Body: 63′ 10″ × 9′ 3″. Non-gangwayed, side doors to each seating bay. Intermediate lavatories on each side of central passageway
Weight: 30 tons **Seats:** 2nd, 90

M59589	M59594	M59599	M59604	M59609	M59614
M59590	M59595	M59600	M59605	M59610	M59615
M59591	M59596	M59601	M59606	M59611	M59616
M59592	M59597	M59602	M59607	M59612	M59617
M59593	M59598	M59603	M59608	M59613	M59618

Derby Works, B.R. (4 Suburban)

TRAILER SECOND ■

Body: 63′ 8¾″ × 9′ 3″. Non-gangwayed, side doors to each seating bay
Weight: 29 tons **Seats:** 2nd, 106

M59619	M59627	M59635	M59643	M59650	M59657
M59620	M59628	M59636	M59644	M59651	M59658
M59621	M59629	M59637	M59645	M59652	M59659
M59622	M59630	M59638	M59646	M59653	M59660
M59623	M59631	M59639	M59647	M59654	M59661
M59624	M59632	M59640	M59648	M59655	M59662
M59625	M59633	M59641	M59649	M59656	M59663
M59626	M59634	M59642			

Derby Works, B.R. (4 Suburban)

TRAILER COMPOSITE (L) ■

Body: 63′ 6″ × 9′ 3″. Non-gangwayed, side doors to each seating bay
Weight: 30 tons **Seats:** **1st**, 30; **2nd**, 40

M59664 M59667 M59670 M59673 M59675 M59677
M59665 M59668 M59671 M59674 M59676 M59678
M59666 M59669 M59672

Swindon Works, B.R. (3 Cross Country)

TRAILER BUFFET SECOND (L) ■

Body: 64′ 6″ × 9′ 3″. Open second with miniature buffet at one end
Weight: 30 tons 12 cwt **Seats:** **2nd**, 60; **Buffet**, 4

SC59679 SC59681 SC59682 SC59683 SC59684 SC59685
SC59680

Metropolitan-Cammell (3)

TRAILER COMPOSITE (L) ■

Body: 57′ 0″ × 9′ 3″ **Weight:** 25 tons **Seats:** **1st**, 12; **2nd**, 53

SC59686 SC59688 SC59689 SC59690 SC59691 SC59692
SC59687

Birmingham R. C. & W. Co. (3)

TRAILER SECOND (L) ■

Body: 57′ 6″ × 9′ 3″ **Weight:** 24 tons **Seats:** **2nd**, 72

E59693 E59697 E59701 E59704 E59707 E59710
E59694 E59698 E59702 E59705 E59708 E59711
E59695 E59699 E59703 E59706 E59709 E59712
E59696 E59700

Derby Works, B.R. (4 Suburban)

TRAILER SECOND ■

Body: 63′ 6″ × 9′ 3″. Non-gangwayed, side doors to each seating bay
Weight: 28 tons **Seats:** **2nd**, 106

M59713 M59714 M59715 M59716 M59717 M59718

Derby Works, B.R. (4 Suburban)

TRAILER COMPOSITE (L) ■

Body: 63′ 6″ × 9′ 3″. Non-gangwayed, side doors to each seating bay
Weight: 30 tons **Seats:** **1st,** 30; **2nd,** 40

M59719 M59720 M59721 M59722 M59723 M59724

Derby Works, B.R. (4 Suburban)

TRAILER SECOND ■

For details see M59713-8

M59725	M59729	M59733	M59736	M59739	M59742
M59726	M59730	M59734	M59737	M59740	M59743
M59727	M59731	M59735	M59738	M59741	M59744
M59728	M59732				

Derby Works, B.R. (4 Suburban)

TRAILER COMPOSITE (L) ■

For details see M59719-24

M59745	M59749	M59753	M59756	M59759	M59762
M59746	M59750	M59754	M59757	M59760	M59763
M59747	M59751	M59755	M59758	M59761	M59764
M59748	M59752				

Swindon Works, B.R. (6 Trans-Pennine)

TRAILER SECOND (L) ■

Body: 64′ 6″ × 9′ 3″ **Weight:** **Seats:** 2nd, 64

E59765	E59767	E59769	E59771	E59772	E59773
E59766	E59768	E59770			

Swindon Works, B.R. (6 Trans-Pennine)

TRAILER BUFFET FIRST (L) ■

Body: 64′ 6″ × 9′ 3″ **Weight:** **Seats:** 1st, 18; **Buffet,** 8

E59774	E59776	E59778	E59779	E59780	E59781
E59775	E59777				

Derby Works, B.R. (3)

TRAILER SECOND (L) ■

Body: 58′ 1″ × 9′ 3″ **Weight:** 28 tons **Seats:** 2nd, 71

SC59782 SC59787 SC59792 SC59796 SC59800 SC59804
SC59783 SC59788 SC59793 SC59797 SC59801 SC59805
SC59784 SC59789 SC59794 SC59798 SC59802 SC59806
SC59785 SC59790 SC59795 SC59799 SC59803 SC59807
SC59786 SC59791

Birmingham R. C. & W. Co. (3)

TRAILER SECOND (L) ■

Body: 57′ 6″ × 9′ 3″ **Weight:** **Seats:** 2nd,

M59808 M59810 M59812 M59814 M59816 M59817
M59809 M59811 M59813 M59815

Metropolitan-Cammell (6 Pullman Units)

MOTOR BRAKE FIRST (L)

Engine
One North British/M.A.N. 12-cyl. pressure-charged V-type L12V18/21BS of 1,000 b.h.p.

Transmission
Electric. Two 425 h.p. G.E.C. traction motors driving through Brown-Boveri spring drive

Body: 66′ 5½″ × 9′ 3″. Guard's, luggage compartment, engine room and full width driving cab at outer end of car

Weight: 67 tons 10 cwt **Seats:** 1st, 12

M60090 M60091 M60092 M60093

Metropolitan-Cammell (8 Pullman Units)

MOTOR BRAKE SECOND (L)

Engine
One North British/M.A.N. 12-cyl. pressure-charged V-type L12V18/21BS of 1,000 b.h.p.

Transmission
Electric. Two 425 h.p. G.E.C. traction motors driving through Brown-Boveri spring drive

Body: 66′ 5½″ × 9′ 3″. Guard's, luggage compartment, engine room and full width driving cab at outer end of car

Weight: 67 tons 10 cwt **Seats:** 2nd, 18

W60094 W60095 W60096 W60097 W60098 W60099

Metropolitan-Cammell (8 Pullman Units)

MOTOR PARLOUR SECOND (L)

(non-driving)

Transmission: Electric. Two 425 h.p. G.E.C. traction motors driving through Brown-Boveri spring drive

Body: 65′ 6″ × 9′ 3″ **Weight:** 45 tons 10 cwt **Seats:** 2nd, 42

W60644 W60645 W60646 W60647 W60648 W60649

Metropolitan-Cammell Motor Brake Second for use in the Western Region diesel-electric Pullman trains [C. P. Boocock

Metropolitan-Cammell Motor Parlour Second No. W60644 [P. J. Sharpe

Original Derby Motor Brake Second No. E79032 [P. Ransome-Wallis

Metropolitan-Cammell (6 Pullman Units)

MOTOR KITCHEN FIRST (L)

(non-driving)

Transmission: Electric. Two 425 h.p. G.E.C. traction motors driving through Brown-Boveri spring drive

Body: 65′ 6″ × 9′ 3″ **Weight:** 49 tons **Seats:** 1st, 18

M60730 M60731 M60732 M60733

Metropolitan-Cammell (8 Pullman Units)

TRAILER KITCHEN FIRST (L)

Body: 65′ 6″ × 9′ 3″ **Weight:** 36 tons **Seats:** 1st, 18

W60734 W60735 W60736 W60737 W60738 W60739

Metropolitan-Cammell (6 or 8* Pullman Units)

TRAILER PARLOUR FIRST (L)

Body: 65′ 6″ × 9′ 3″ **Weight:** 33 tons **Seats:** 1st, 36

M60740 M60742 W60744* W60746* W60748* W60749*
M60741 M60743 W60745* W60747*

Derby Works, B.R. (2)

MOTOR BRAKE SECOND ▲

Engines
Two B.U.T. (Leyland) 6-cyl horizontal type of 125 b.h.p.

Transmission
Hydro-Mechanical. Lysholm Smith (Leyland) torque converter to final drive

Body: 57′ 6″ × 9′ 2″ **Weight:** 26 tons **Seats:** 2nd, 61

E79000 E79002 E79004 E79005 E79006 E79007
E79001 E79003

Derby Works, B.R. (2)

MOTOR BRAKE SECOND ♦

Engines
Two B.U.T. (A.E.C.) 6-cyl. horizontal type of 150 b.h.p.

Transmission
Mechanical. Standard

Body: 57′ 6″ × 9′ 2″ **Weight:** 27 tons **Seats:** 2nd, 61, 56*

M79008 M79015 E79022* E79028* E79034* E79040*
M79009 M79016 E79023* E79029* E79035* E79041*
M79010 M79017 E79024* E79030* E79036* E79043*
M79011 M79018 E79025* E79031* E79037* E79044*
M79012 M79019 E79026* E79032* E79038* E79045*
M79013 M79020 E79027* E79033* E79039* E79046*
M79014 E79021*

Metropolitan-Cammell (2)

MOTOR BRAKE SECOND ♦

Engines
Two B.U.T. (A.E.C.) 6-cyl. horizontal type of 150 b.h.p.

Transmission
Mechanical. Standard

Body: 57′ 0″ × 9′ 3″ **Weight:** 26 tons 10 cwt **Seats:** 2nd, 57, 53*

E79047	E79053	E79059	E79065	E79071	M79077*
E79048	E79054	E79060	E79066	E79072	M79078*
E79049	E79055	E79061	E79067	E79073	M79079*
E79050	E79056	E79062	E79068	E79074	M79080*
E79051	E79057	E79063	E79069	E79075	M79081*
E79052	E79058	E79064	E79070	M79076*	M79082*

Swindon Works, B.R. (3 or 6 Inter-City)

MOTOR BRAKE SECOND (L) ●

Engines
Two B.U.T. (A.E.C.) 6-cyl. horizontal type of 150 b.h.p.

Transmission
Mechanical. Standard

Body: 64′ 6″ × 9′ 3″. Guard's and luggage compartment at outer end. Two types of car; "leading"* with full width driving compartment, gangwayed at inner end only; "intermediate"† with side driving compartment gangwayed at both ends

Weight: 38 tons **Seats:** 2nd, 52

SC79083†	SC79088†	SC79093*	SC79098*	SC79103*	SC79108*
SC79084†	SC79089†	SC79094*	SC79099*	SC79104*	SC79109*
SC79085†	SC79090†	SC79095†	SC79100*	SC79105*	SC79110*
SC79086†	SC79091*	SC79096*	SC79101*	SC79106*	SC79111*
SC79087†	SC79092*	SC79097*	SC79102*	SC79107*	

Derby Works, B.R. (2)

MOTOR BRAKE SECOND (L) ♦

Engines
Two B.U.T. 6-cyl. horizontal type of 150 b.h.p.

Transmission
Mechanical. Standard
*Fitted with Self-Changing Gears Ltd. automatic four-speed gearbox

Body: 57′ 6″ × 9′ 2″ **Weight:** 27 tons **Seats:** 2nd, 52

M79118	M79124	M79130	M79135*	E79140	M79145
M79119	M79125	M79131	M79136	M79141	M79146
M79120	M79126	M79132	E79137	M79142	M79147
M79121	M79127	M79133	E79138	M79143	M79148
M79122	M79128	M79134	E79139	M79144	M79149
M79123	M79129				

Metropolitan-Cammell Motor Brake Second No. E79070 at Wickford [*P. J. Sharpe*

Bristol/Eastern Coach Works Four-Wheel Railbus No. SC79959 [*D. J. Dippie*

Derby Works, B.R. (4)

MOTOR SECOND ♦

Engines
Two B.U.T. (A.E.C.) 6-cyl. horizontal type of 150 b h.p.

Transmission
Mechanical. Standard

Body: 57′ 6″ × 9′ 2″ **Weight:** 26 tons **Seats:** **2nd, 64**

E79150 E79151 E79152 E79153 E79154

Swindon Works, B.R. (6 Inter-City)

MOTOR SECOND (L) ●

Engines
Two B.U.T. (A.E.C.) 6-cyl. horizontal type of 150 b.h.p.

Transmission
Mechanical. Standard

Body: 64′ 6″ × 9′ 3″. Gangwayed both ends. Side driving compartment at one end

Weight: 39 tons 3 cwt **Seats:** **2nd, 64**

SC79155 SC79158 SC79161 SC79163 SC79165 SC79167
SC79156 SC79159 SC79162 SC79164 SC79166 SC79168
SC79157 SC79160

Derby Works, B.R. (2)

MOTOR BRAKE SECOND ♦

For details see M79118-49

M79169 M79172 M79174 M79176 M79178 M79180
M79171 M79173 M79175 M79177 M79179 M79181

Derby Works, B.R. (2)

MOTOR BRAKE SECOND ♦

For details see M79008-20

M79184 M79185 M79186 M79187 M79188

Derby Works, B.R. (2)

MOTOR COMPOSITE (L) ♦

Engines
Two B.U.T. (A.E.C.) 6-cyl. horizontal type of 150 b.h.p.

Transmission
Mechanical. Standard

Body: 57′ 6″ × 9′ 2″ **Weight:** 27 tons **Seats:** **1st, 12; 2nd, 53**

M79189 M79190 M79192

Derby Works, B.R. (2)

DRIVING TRAILER COMPOSITE (L) ♦

Body: 57′ 6″ × 9′ 2″ **Weight:** 20 tons **Seats:** **1st,** 16; **2nd,** 53

E79250 E79253 E79255 E79257 E79259 E79261
E79251 E79254 E79256 E79258 E79260 E79262
E79252

Metropolitan-Cammell (2)

DRIVING TRAILER SECOND (L) ♦

Body: 57′ 0″ × 9′ 3″ **Weight:** 25 tons **Seats:** **2nd,** 71

E79263 E79268 E79273 E79278 E79283 E79288
E79264 E79269 E79274 E79279 E79284 E79289
E79265 E79270 E79275 E79280 E79285 E79290
E79266 E79271 E79276 E79281 E79286 E79291
E79267 E79272 E79277 E79282 E79287

Derby Works, B.R. (4)

TRAILER BRAKE SECOND (L) ♦

Body: 57′ 6″ × 9′ 2″ **Weight:** 20 tons 10 cwt **Seats:** **2nd,** 45

E79325 E79326 E79327 E79328 E79329

Derby Works, B.R. (4)

TRAILER SECOND (L) ♦

Body: 57′ 6″ × 9′ 2″ **Weight:** 20 tons 10 cwt **Seats:** **2nd,** 61

E79400 E79401 E79402 E79403 E79404

Swindon Works, B.R. (3 or 6 Inter-City)

TRAILER BUFFET FIRST (K) ●

Body: 64′ 6″ × 9′ 3″. Side corridor with three first class compartments. Buffet with kitchen, bar and saloon

Weight: 34 tons **Seats:** **1st,** 18; **Buffet,** 12

SC79440 SC79442 SC79444 SC79445 SC79446 SC79447
SC79441 SC79443

Swindon Works, B.R. (3 or 6 Inter-City)

TRAILER FIRST (K) ●

Body: 64′ 6″ × 9′ 3″. Side corridor with seven first class compartments and end doors

Weight: 33 tons 9 cwt **Seats:** **1st,** 42

SC79470 SC79473 SC79475 SC79477 SC79479 SC79481
SC79471 SC79474 SC79476 SC79478 SC79480 SC79482
SC79472

Derby Works, B.R. (2)

MOTOR COMPOSITE (L) ▲

Engines
Two B.U.T. (Leyland) 6-cyl. horizontal type of 125 b.h.p.

Transmission
Hydro-Mechanical. Lysholm Smith (Leyland) torque converter to final drive

Body: 57′ 6″ × 9′ 2″ **Weight:** 27 tons **Seats: 1st,** 16; **2nd,** 53

E79500 E79502 E79504 E79505 E79506 E79507
E79501 E79503

Derby Works, B.R. (4)

MOTOR COMPOSITE ♦

Engines
Two B.U.T. (A.E.C.) 6-cyl. horizontal type of 150 b.h.p.

Transmission
Mechanical. Standard

Body: 57′ 6 × 9′ 2″ **Weight:** 26 tons 10 cwt **Seats: 1st,** 20; **2nd,** 36

E79508 E79509 E79510 E79511 E79512

Derby Works, B.R. (2)

DRIVING TRAILER COMPOSITE (L) ♦

Body: 57′ 6″ × 9′ 2″ **Weight:** 21 tons **Seats: 1st,** 9, 16*; **2nd,** 53

M79600 M79605 M79609 E79613* E79618* E79622*
M79601 M79606 M79610 E79614* E79619* E79623*
M79602 M79607 M79611 E79615* E79620* E79624*
M79603 M79608 M79612 E79617* E79621* E79625*
M79604

Metropolitan-Cammell (2)

DRIVING TRAILER COMPOSITE (L) ♦

Body: 57′ 0″ × 9′ 3″ **Weight:** 25 tons **Seats: 1st,** 12; **2nd,** 53

M79626 M79628 M79629 M79630 M79631 M79632
M79627

Derby Works, B.R. (2)

DRIVING TRAILER COMPOSITE (L) ♦

Body: 57′ 6″ × 9′ 2″ **Weight:** 20 tons **Seats: 1st,** 12; **2nd,** 53

M79633 M79635

Waggon und Maschinenbau Four-Wheel Railbus at White Notley [*P. J. Sharpe*

D. Wickham & Co. Four-Wheel Railbus No. SC79965 [*P. J. Sharpe*

Derby Works, B.R. (2)

DRIVING TRAILER COMPOSITE (L) ♦

For details see M79600-E79625

M79639	M79647	M79655	M79663	M79671	M79678
M79640	M79648	M79656	M79664	M79672	M79679
M79641	M79649†	M79657	M79665	M79673	M79680
M79642	M79650	E79658*	M79666	M79674	M79681
M79643	M79651	E79659*	M79667	M79675	M79682
M79644	M79652	E79660*	M79668	M79676	M79683
M79645	M79653	E79661*	M79669	M79677	M79684
M79646	M79654	M79662	M79670		

† This vehicle has been fitted internally for use as an inspection saloon including a pantry, and is not in public service. It has been rewired to work with "Blue Square" type motor-coaches

> **NOTE** For reasons of clarity the B.U.T. 4-wheel units below are not in strict numerical order. Some of these vehicles are now used by the L.M. Engineer's Dept. and are not in public service.

British United Traction Co.

MOTOR SECOND (Four-wheel units)

Engine
B.U.T. (A.E.C.) 6-cyl. horizontal type of 125 b.h.p.

Transmission
Mechanical. Standard

Body: 37′ 6″ × 9′ 0″. Non-gangwayed. Driving compartment at each end

Weight: 15 tons **Seats:** 2nd, 34

M79740 M79745 M79748

British United Traction Co.

MOTOR BRAKE SECOND (Four-wheel units)

Engine
B.U.T. (A.E.C.) 6-cyl. horizontal type of 125 b.h.p.

Transmission
Mechanical. Standard

Body: 37′ 6″ × 9′ 0″. Non-gangwayed. Driving compartment at each end

Weight: 15 tons **Seats:** 2nd, 28

M79742 M79743 M79744 M79750

British United Traction Co.

TRAILER SECOND (Four-wheel units)

Body: 37′ 6″ × 9′ 0″. Non-gangwayed

Weight: 10 tons 10 cwt **Seats:** 2nd, 48

M79741 M79746 M79747 M79749

Derby Works, B.R. (1)

MOTOR BRAKE SECOND ♦

Engines
Two B.U.T. (A.E.C.) 6-cyl. horizontal type of 150 b.h.p.

Transmission
Mechanical. Standard

Body: 57′ 6″ × 9′ 2″. Non-gangwayed. Driving compartment at each end

Weight: 27 tons **Seats:** 2nd, 52

M79900 M79901

Bristol/E.C.W.

FOUR-WHEEL RAILBUS

Engine
Gardner 6.H.L.W. 6-cyl. type of 112 b.h.p. at 1,700 r.p.m.

Transmission
Mechanical. Standard. Fitted with Self-Changing Gears Ltd. five-speed epicyclic gearbox

Body: 42′ 4″ × 9′ 3″. Non-gangwayed

Weight: 13 tons 10 cwt **Seats:** 2nd, 56

SC79958 SC79959

Waggon und Maschinenbau

FOUR-WHEEL RAILBUS

Engine
Buessing 150 b.h.p. at 1,900 r.p.m.
*A.E.C. A220X type

Transmission
Mechanical. Cardan shaft to ZF electro-magnetic six-speed gearbox

Body: 41′10″ × 8′ $8\frac{5}{16}$″. Non-gangwayed

Weight: 15 tons **Seats:** 2nd, 56

E79960 E79661 E79962 E79963* E79964

D. Wickham & Co.

FOUR-WHEEL RAILBUS

Engine
Meadows 6-cyl. type 6HDT500 of 105 b.h.p. at 1,800 r.p.m.

Transmission
Mechanical. Freeborn-Wickham disc-and-ring coupling driving Self-Changing Gears Ltd. four-speed epicyclic gearbox and cardan shaft to final drive

Body: 38′ 0″ × 9′ 0″. Non-gangwayed

Weight: 11 tons 5 cwt **Seats:** 2nd, 44

SC79965 SC79966 SC79967 SC79968 SC79969

Park Royal Four-Wheel Railbus No. SC79974 [*R. A. Panting*

A. C. Cars Four-Wheel Railbus No. SC79979 [*P. J. Sharpe*

Ex-G.W.R. Railcar No. W20W at Oxford on a Birmingham–Swindon special working [*M. Pope*

Park Royal Vehicles

FOUR-WHEEL RAILBUS

Engine
B.U.T. (A.E.C.) 6-cyl. horizontal type of 150 b.h.p.

Transmission
Mechanical. Standard. Fitted with Self-Changing Gears Ltd. four-speed epicyclic gearbox

Body: 42′ 0″ × 9′ 3″. Non-gangwayed

Weight: 15 tons **Seats:** 2nd, 50

SC79970 SC79971 SC79972 SC79973 SC79974

A.C. Cars

FOUR-WHEEL RAILBUS

Engine
B.U.T. (A.E.C.) 6-cyl. horizontal type of 150 b.h.p.

Transmission
Mechanical. Standard

Body: 36′ 0″ × 8′ 11″. Non-gangwayed

Weight: 11 tons **Seats:** 2nd, 46

W79975 W79976 W79977 W79978 SC79979

G.W.R. Railcars

Car No.	*Date*	*Engines*	*Total b.h.p.*	*Seats 2nd*
20-26/9-32†	1940	2	210	48
33, 38‡	1942	4	420	92
‖1096	—	-	—	64

‡ Twin-coach unit with buffet facilities. Adjoining statistics apply per 2-car unit. These cars work as a three-car set with corridor second W1096W

† These cars may work in pairs with an additional ordinary coach between

‖ This is an ordinary 60ft ex-G.W. corridor second adapted for use between two diesel railcars, and is painted green

W20W W22W W24W W26W W30W W32W W38W
W21W W23W W25W W29W W31W W33W W1096W

TRAILER COMPOSITE (K) ■

(Ex-G.W. vehicles converted for use with diesel units)

W7254W W7804W W7813W

Derby/Cowlairs Works, B.R. (2)

BATTERY ELECTRIC RAILCAR

MOTOR BRAKE SECOND

Electrical Equipment: Two 100 kW Siemens-Schuckert nose-suspended traction motors powered by 216 lead-acid cell batteries of 1070 amp/hour capacity

Body: 57′ 6″ × 9′ 2″ **Weight:** 37 tons 10 cwt **Seats:** 2nd, 52

SC79998

Derby/Cowlairs Works, B.R. (2)

BATTERY ELECTRIC RAILCAR DRIVING TRAILER COMPOSITE

Body: 57′ 6″ × 9′ 2″ **Weight:** 32 tons 10 cwt **Seats:** 1st, 12; 2nd, 53

SC79999

SOUTHERN REGION DIESEL-ELECTRIC MULTIPLE-UNITS

Eastleigh Works, B.R. (6)

HASTINGS

(Gangwayed within set)

MOTOR BRAKE SECOND

Engine
English Electric 4-cyl. type 4SRKT Mark II of 500 b.h.p. at 850 r.p.m.

Transmission
Electric. Two nose-suspended axle-hung traction motors

Body: 58′ 0″ (64′ 6″*) × 8′ $2\frac{1}{2}$″ & 9′ 0″. Guard's, luggage compartment, engine room and full width driving compartment at outer end of car

Weight: 54 tons 2 cwt, 55 tons* **Seats:** 2nd, 22, 30*

TRAILER FIRST (K)

Body: 58′ 0″ (64′ 6″*) × 8′ $2\frac{1}{2}$″ & 9′ 0″. Side corridor with seven (eight*) first class compartments with side door to each compartment

Weight: 30 tons, 31 tons* **Seats:** 1st, 42, 48*

TRAILER SECOND (L)

Body: 58′ 0″ (64′ 6″*) × 8′ $2\frac{1}{2}$″ & 9′ 0″

Weight: 29 tons, 30 tons* **Seats:** 2nd, 52, 60*

TRAILER SECOND (L)

(as above)

TRAILER SECOND (L)

(as above)

MOTOR BRAKE SECOND

(as above)

1001	1004	1007	1013*	1016*	1018*
1002	1005	1011*	1014*	1017*	1019*
1003	1006	1012*	1015*		

Eastleigh six-car Hastings line long underframe unit No. 1011 at Ashford
[*P. Ransome-Wallis*

Eastleigh three-car Hampshire unit No. 1113 at Fratton [*P. H. Wells*

Eastleigh three-car Berkshire unit No. 1129 [*A. J. Wheeler*

Eastleigh Works, B.R. (6)

HASTINGS

(Gangwayed within set)

MOTOR BRAKE SECOND

Engine
English Electric 4-cyl. type 4SRKT Mark II of 500 b.h.p. at 850 r.p.m.

Transmission
Electric. Two nose-suspended axle-hung traction motors

Body: 64′ 6″ × 8′ 2½″ & 9′ 0″. Guard's, luggage compartment, engine room and full-width driving compartment at outer end of car

Weight: 55 tons **Seats:** 2nd, 30

TRAILER SECOND (L)

Body: 64′ 6″ × 8′ 2½″ & 9′ 0″ **Weight:** 30 tons **Seats:** 2nd, 60

TRAILER BUFFET

Body: 64′ 6″ × 8′ 2½″ & 9′ 0″. Buffet with kitchen and bar; self-contained seating saloon

Weight: 35 tons **Seats:** Buffet, 21

TRAILER FIRST (K)

Body: 64′ 6″ × 8′ 2½″ & 9′ 0″. Side corridor with eight first class compartments with side door to each compartment

Weight: 31 tons **Seats:** 1st, 48

TRAILER SECOND (L)

(as above)

MOTOR BRAKE SECOND

(as above)

1031 1033 1034 1035 1036 1037
1032

Eastleigh Works, B.R. (3 or 2*)

HAMPSHIRE
HASTINGS*
BERKSHIRE†

MOTOR BRAKE SECOND

Engine
English Electric 4-cyl. type 4SRKT Mark II of 600 b.h.p. at 850 r.p.m.

Transmission
Electric. Two nose-suspended axle-hung traction motors

Body: 64′ 0″ × 9′ 3″. Guard's, luggage compartment, engine room and full-width driving compartment at outer end of car. Non-gangwayed, side doors to each seating bay

Weight: 56 tons **Seats:** 2nd, 52, 42†

Driving Trailer Composite of Eastleigh three-car Hampshire unit No. 1126 [*P. J. Sharpe*

Eastleigh three-car East Sussex unit No. 1307 leaving Hurst Green on a Victoria–Tunbridge Wells (West) working [*B. Stephenson*

TRAILER SEMI-SALOON SECOND

(three-car units only)

Body: 63′ 6″ × 9′ 3″. Non-gangwayed, side doors to each seating bay

Weight: **Seats: 2nd,** 104

DRIVING TRAILER COMPOSITE (L)

Body: 64′ 0″ × 9′ 3″. Non-gangwayed, side doors to each seating bay or compartment. 5-bay 2nd class saloon and 2 1st class compartments with intermediate lavatories, also a 2nd class compartment next to driving compartment

Weight: 32 tons **Seats: 1st,** 13; **2nd,** 62

1101	1107	1113	1119*	1124	1129†
1102	1108	1114	1120*	1125	1130†
1103	1109	1115	1121*	1126	1131†
1104	1110	1116	1122*	1127†	1132†
1105	1111	1117	1123	1128†	1133†
1106	1112	1118			

Eastleigh Works, B.R. (3)

EAST SUSSEX

MOTOR BRAKE SECOND

Engine	**Transmission**
English Electric 4-cyl. type 4SRKT Mark II of 600 b.h.p. at 850 r.p.m.	Electric. Two nose-suspended axle-hung traction motors

Body: 64′ 0″ × 8′ 6″ & 9′ 0″. Guard's, luggage compartment, engine room and full-width driving compartment at outer end of car. Non-gangwayed, side doors to each seating bay

Weight: 56 tons **Seats: 2nd,** 42

TRAILER COMPOSITE

Body: 63′ 6″ × 8′ 6″ & 9′ 0″. Non-gangwayed, side doors to each seating bay or compartment. 3-bay 2nd class saloon, 4 1st class compartments, side lavatory and further 2-bay 2nd class saloon connected by side corridor.

Weight: 31 tons **Seats: 1st,** 24; **2nd,** 42

DRIVING TRAILER SEMI-SALOON SECOND

Body: 64′ 0″ × 8′ 6″ & 9′ 0″. Non-gangwayed, side doors to each seating bay

Weight: 32 tons **Seats: 2nd,** 76

1301	1305	1308	1311	1314	1317
1302	1306	1309	1312	1315	1318
1303	1307	1310	1313	1316	1319
1304					

B.R. ELECTRIC LOCOMOTIVES AND MULTIPLE-UNITS

ELECTRIC locomotives on British Railways are numbered in two series. Those built by British Railways as part of the modernisation programme carry the prefix "E" in a series ranging from E1000 for a.c. units and from E5000 for d.c. units. The first figure of the a.c. series, in addition to identifying the locomotive, also gives an indication of its horsepower—for example, E2001 for a unit in the 2,000 h.p. range and E3001 for a locomotive in the 3,000 h.p. range. Earlier locomotives built to S.R. or L.N.E.R. designs are numbered in the 20000 series.

The headings to each class show the type designation or class, principal manufacturer and wheel arrangement. Originally the type designation A or B was intended to be used to identify locomotives suited for passenger and freight haulage respectively, but subsequent experience has shown that locomotives need not be geared specially for freight working and the designation B may disappear.

Wheel arrangements of electric (and diesel) locomotives are described by a development of the Continental notation. This calculates by axles and not by wheels, and uses letters instead of numerals to denote driving axles ("A" = 1, "B" = 2, "C" = 3, etc.) and numerals only for non-powered axles. An indication of the grouping of axles is given, but powered and non-powered axles may be found in the same group. Thus British Railways' diesel-electric locomotive No. D5500 is described as an A1A-A1A, indicating that it is mounted on two six-wheel bogies, each of which has a non-powered axle in the centre and a motored axle at either end. Groups of axles are separated by a hyphen if they are quite independent of each other, but by a "plus" sign in cases where powered bogies are linked by an articulated joint to take certain stresses.

If all axles on a bogie or frame unit are individually powered, a suffix letter "o" is added to the descriptive letter. Thus B.R. electric locomotive No. E5001 is shown as a Bo-Bo, indicating that it has two four-wheel bogies, each axle of which has an individual traction motor.

Because several numbering schemes are in use, electric multiple-unit trains are listed Region by Region and sub-divided into areas or lines or, in the case of the S.R., into types of stock. It has been impossible to list m.u. stock in a single numerical sequence. Details of all the coaches in a particular set are listed together. Unit numbers, which are painted on the front and rear of each set, are listed where used by British Railways; otherwise individual coach numbers are shown.

A.E.I. Type A 3,300 h.p. 25kV a.c. Bo-Bo No. E3013 [*P. J. Sharpe*

English Electric Type A 3,300 h.p. 25kV a.c. Bo-Bo No. E3030 [*P. J. Sharpe*

General Electric Type A 3,300 h.p. 25kV a.c. Bo-Bo No. E3044 [*P. J. Sharpe*

ELECTRIC LOCOMOTIVES

Metropolitan Vickers A1A-A1A

Introduced
1958

Equipment
Four 625 h.p. Metropolitan-Vickers nose-suspended traction motors

Driving wheel diameter
3′ 8″

System
25 kV. a.c. overhead
(Rebuilt from former Gas Turbine Loco. No. 18100)

Total h.p.
2,500

Weight
109 tons 0 cwt

Maximum tractive effort
40,000 lb

E2001

Type A A.E.I. Bo-Bo (British Thomson-Houston)

Introduced
1959

Equipment
Four A.E.I. (B.T.H.) spring-borne d.c. traction motors of 847 h.p. (continuous) driving through Alsthom quill drive

Driving wheel diameter
4′ 0″

System
25 kV. a.c. overhead

Total h.p.
3,300

Weight
79 tons 12 cwt

Maximum tractive effort
48,000 lb

E3001	E3005	E3009	E3012	E3015	E3018	E3021
E3002	E3006	E3010	E3013	E3016	E3019	E3022
E3003	E3007	E3011	E3014	E3017	E3020	E3023
E3004	E3008					

Type A English Electric Bo-Bo

Introduced
1960

Equipment
Four English Electric spring-borne d.c. traction motors of 740 h.p. (continuous) driving through S.L.M. resilient drives

Driving wheel diameter
4′ 0″

System
25 kV. a.c. overhead

Total h.p.
3,300

Weight
73 tons 0 cwt

Maximum tractive effort
40,000 lb

Top: British Railways Type A 3,300 h.p. 25kV a.c. Bo-Bo No. E3069 [*P. J. Sharpe*

Centre: English Electric Type A 3,300 h.p. 25kV a.c. Bo-Bo No. E3100 (fitted with stepless supply voltage control) [*J. Duncan*

Left: Brush 630V d.c. Bo-Bo No. 26501 (in North Eastern Railway livery) [*D. J. Dippie*

E3024 E3026 E3028 E3030 E3032 E3034 E3035
E3025 E3027 E3029 E3031 E3033

Type A General Electric Bo-Bo

Introduced
1960

Equipment
Four G.E.C. spring-borne d.c. traction motors of 750 h.p. (continuous), driving through Brown-Boveri spring drives

Driving wheel diameter
4′ 0″

System
25 kV. a.c. overhead

Total h.p.
3,300

Weight
76 tons 10 cwt

Maximum tractive effort
50,000 lb

E3036 E3038 E3040 E3042 E3043 E3044 E3045
E3037 E3039 E3041

Type A A.E.I. (Metropolitan Vickers) Bo-Bo

Introduced
1960

Equipment
Four A.E.I. (M.V.) d.c. traction motors of 847 h.p. (continuous) driving through Alsthom quill drive

Driving wheel diameter
4′ 0″

System
25 kV. a.c. overhead

Total h.p.
3,300

Weight
78 tons 8 cwt

Maximum tractive effort
48,000 lb

E3046 E3048 E3050 E3052 E3053 E3054 E3055
E3047 E3049 E3051

Type A British Railways Bo-Bo

Introduced
1960

Equipment
Four A.E.I. (B.T.H.) d.c. traction motors of 847 h.p. (continuous) driving through Alsthom quill drive

Driving wheel diameter
4′ 0″

System
25 kV. a.c. overhead

Total h.p.
3,300

Weight
79 tons 0 cwt

Maximum tractive effort
48,000 lb

E3056	E3059	E3062	E3065	E3068	E3071	E3074
E3057	E3060	E3063	E3066	E3069	E3072	E3075
E3058	E3061	E3064	E3067	E3070	E3073	

Type A British Railways Bo-Bo

Introduced
1962

Equipment
B.T.H.

Driving wheel diameter
4′ 0″

System
25 kV. a.c. overhead

Total h.p.
3,300

Weight
80 tons 0 cwt

Maximum tractive effort
48,000 lb

E3076	E3079	E3082	E3085	E3088	E3091	E3094
E3077	E3080	E3083	E3086	E3089	E3092	E3095
E3078	E3081	E3084	E3087	E3090	E3093	

Type A English Electric Bo-Bo

Introduced
1961

Equipment
Four English Electric springborne d.c. traction motors of 740 h.p. (continuous) driving through S.L.M. resilient drives

Driving wheel diameter
4′ 0″

System
25 kV. a.c. overhead

Total h.p.
3,300

Weight
73 tons 0 cwt

Maximum tractive effort

E3098 E3099

Type A English Electric Bo-Bo

Introduced
1962

Equipment
As E3024. Adopted as the test locomotive for a stepless form of supply voltage control to the traction motors, using semi-conductor rectifiers. Equipped with rheostatic braking

Driving wheel diameter
4′ 0″

System
25 kV. a.c. overhead

Total h.p.
3,300

Weight

Maximum tractive effort

E3100

Type B A.E.I. Bo-Bo
(British Thomson-Houston)

To be introduced

Equipment
Four A.E.I. (B.T.H.) spring-borne d.c. traction motors of 847 h.p. (continuous) driving through Alsthom quill drive

Driving wheel diameter
4′ 0″

System
25 kV. a.c. overhead

Total h.p.
3,300

Weight
80 tons 0 cwt

Maximum tractive effort
60,000 lb

E3301 E3302

British Railways Bo-Bo

Introduced
1958

Equipment
Motor generator booster set and four 638 h.p. English Electric spring-borne traction motors driving through S.L.M. flexible drive

Driving wheel diameter
4′ 0″

System
750 V. d.c. 3rd rail and overhead

Total h.p.
2,552

Weight
77 tons 0 cwt

Maximum tractive effort
43,000 lb

E5001	E5005	E5009	E5013	E5016	E5019	E5022
E5002	E5006	E5010	E5014	E5017	E5020	E5023
E5003	E5007	E5011	E5015	E5018	E5021	E5024
E5004	E5008	E5012				

Electro-Diesel Bo-Bo
British Railways

Introduced
1962

Equipment
English Electric 4-cyl type 4 SRKT mark II 600 b.h.p. diesel engine; four English Electric 400 h.p. traction motors. These locomotives can work either direct from a 750 V. d.c. third rail supply or, when this is not available, with the diesel generator powering the traction motors, though at reduced horsepower

Driving wheel diameter
3′ 4″

System
750 V. d.c. 3rd rail or diesel

Total h.p.
Electric 1,600
Diesel 600

Weight
73 tons 0 cwt

Maximum tractive effort
42,000 lb

E6001 E6002 E6003 E6004 E6005 E6006

Above: British Railways Class EM1 1,868 h.p. 1,500V d.c. Bo-Bo No. 26055 *Prometheus*
[*I. G. Holt*

Left: British Railways Class EM2 2,490 h.p. 1,500V d.c. Co-Co No. 27002 *Aurora*
[*P J. Hurcum*

Below: British Railways 2,552 h.p. 750V d.c. Bo-Bo No. E5015
[*Alan Williams*

Top: British Railways 1,600/600 h.p. 750V d.c. electro-diesel Bo-Bo No. E6006 [*D. L. Percival*

Centre: Southern Railway 1,470 h.p. 750V d.c. Co-Co No. 20002 [*R. A. Panting*

Right: Southern Railway 1,470 h.p. 750V d.c. Co-Co No. 20003 [*R. A. Panting*

CC S.R. Co-Co

Introduced
1941
1948*

Equipment
Motor generator booster set and six 245 h.p. English Electric nose-suspended traction motors.

Driving wheel diameter
3′ 6″

System
750 V. d.c. 3rd rail and overhead

Total h.p.
1,470

Weight
99 tons 14 cwt
104 tons 14 cwt*

Maximum tractive effort
40,000 lb
45,000 lb*

20001 20002 20003*

EM1 Bo-Bo
L.N.E.R. & British Railways

Introduced
1941*
1950

Equipment
Four 467 h.p. Metropolitan-Vickers nose-suspended traction motors

Driving wheel diameter
4′ 2″

System
1,500 V. d.c. overhead

Total h.p.
1,868

Weight
87 tons 18 cwt

Maximum tractive effort
45,000 lb

26000* *Tommy*

26001	26008	26015	26022	26028	26034	26040
26002	26009	26016	26023	26029	26035	26041
26003	26010	26017	26024	26030	26036	26042
26004	26011	26018	26025	26031	26037	26043
26005	26012	26019	26026	26032	26038	26044
26006	26013	26020	26027	26033	26039	26045
26007	26014	26021				

26046 *Archimedes*
26047 *Diomedes*
26048 *Hector*
26049 *Jason*
26050 *Stentor*
26051 *Mentor*
26052 *Nestor*
26053 *Perseus*
26054 *Pluto*
26055 *Prometheus*
26056 *Triton*
26057 *Ulysses*

ES1 Brush Bo-Bo

Introduced
1902

Equipment
Four B.T.H. nose-suspended traction motors

Driving wheel diameter

System
630 V. d.c. overhead and 3rd rail

Total h.p.

Weight
46 tons 0 cwt

Maximum tractive effort
25,000 lb

26500 26501

EM2 British Railways Co-Co

Introduced
1954

Equipment
Six 415 h.p. Metropolitan-Vickers nose-suspended traction motors

Driving wheel diameter
4′ 2″

System
1,500 V. d.c. overhead

Total h.p.
2,490

Weight
102 tons 0 cwt

Maximum tractive effort
45,000 lb

27000 *Electra*
27001 *Ariadne*
27002 *Aurora*
27003 *Diana*
27004 *Juno*
27005 *Minerva*
27006 *Pandora*

DEPARTMENTAL LOCOMOTIVES

SOUTHERN REGION

Bo-Bo DS74

Bo DS75

LONDON MIDLAND REGION

Battery Electric L.M.S. Bo

Introduced
1914*
1917†

Equipment
*Two Dick Kerr traction motors
†Two B.T.H. traction motors

Driving wheel diameter
3′ 1″

Total h.p.
*44
†82

Weight
*18 tons
†17 tons

Maximum tractive effort

Bel 1*

Bel 2†

ELECTRIC MULTIPLE-UNITS

The dimensions shown are length and width over body and width overall.

The letter "L" in the headings indicates an open vehicle fitted with toilet facilities. "K" indicates a side corridor vehicle with toilet.

London Midland Region

SYSTEM: 630 VOLTS D.C. 3rd AND 4th RAIL

London District
Three-Car Compartment Sets

MOTOR BRAKE SECOND

Body: 59′ 0″ × 8′ 11″ & 9′ 6″ **Weight:** 56 tons **Seats: 2nd,** 84
Equipment: Four 280 h.p. G.E.C. or M.V. traction motors

M28001M M28006M M28010M M28014M M28018M M28022M
M28002M M28007M M28011M M28015M M28019M M28023M
M28003M M28008M M28012M M28016M M28020M M28024M
M28004M M28009M M28013M M28017M M28021M M28025M
M28005M

TRAILER SECOND

Body: 57′ 0″ × 8′ 11″ & 9′ 6″ **Weight:** 28 tons **Seats: 2nd,** 108

M29401M M29409M M29605M M29610M M29615M M29620M
M29402M M29600M M29606M M29611M M29616M M29621M
M29403M M29601M M29607M M29612M M29617M M29622M
M29404M M29602M M29608M M29613M M29618M M29624M
M29405M M29603M M29609M M29614M M29619M M29625M
M29406M M29604M

DRIVING TRAILER BRAKE SECOND

Body: 57′ 0″ × 8′ 11″ & 9′ 6″ **Weight:** 30 tons **Seats: 2nd,** 96

M28800M M28805M M28809M M28813M M28817M M28821M
M28801M M28806M M28810M M28814M M28818M M28822M
M28802M M28807M M28811M M28815M M28819M M28823M
M28803M M28808M M28812M M28816M M28820M M28824M
M28804M

Two L.M.R. London District B.R. Standard three-car sets passing Bushey troughs [G. M. Kichenside

L.M.R. London District three-car compartment set [G. M. Kichenside

L.M.R. Liverpool–Southport compartment and open sets, with Motor Brake Second M28307M nearest the camera [L. Sandler

London District Three-Car B.R. Sets

B.R. Standard design

MOTOR OPEN BRAKE SECOND

Body: 57′ 5″ × 9′ 0″ & 9′ 6″ **Weight:** 47 tons **Seats:** 2nd, 74
Equipment: Four 185 h.p. G.E.C. traction motors

M61133	M61143	M61153	M61163	M61172	M61181
M61134	M61144	M61154	M61164	M61173	M61182
M61135	M61145	M61155	M61165	M61174	M61183
M61136	M61146	M61156	M61166	M61175	M61184
M61137	M61147	M61157	M61167	M61176	M61185
M61138	M61148	M61158	M61168	M61177	M61186
M61139	M61149	M61159	M61169	M61178	M61187
M61140	M61150	M61160	M61170	M61179	M61188
M61141	M61151	M61161	M61171	M61180	M61189
M61142	M61152	M61162			

TRAILER SECOND

Body: 57′ 1″ × 9′ 0″ & 9′ 6″ **Weight:** 29 tons **Seats:** 2nd, 108

M70133	M70143	M70153	M70163	M70172	M70181
M70134	M70144	M70154	M70164	M70173	M70182
M70135	M70145	M70155	M70165	M70174	M70183
M70136	M70146	M70156	M70166	M70175	M70184
M70137	M70147	M70157	M70167	M70176	M70185
M70138	M70148	M70158	M70168	M70177	M70186
M70139	M70149	M70159	M70169	M70178	M70187
M70140	M70150	M70160	M70170	M70179	M70188
M70141	M70151	M70161	M70171	M70180	M70189
M70142	M70152	M70162			

DRIVING TRAILER OPEN BRAKE SECOND

Body: 57′ 5″ × 9′ 0″ & 9′ 6″ **Weight:** 30 tons **Seats:** 2nd, 74

M75133	M75143	M75153	M75163	M75172	M75181
M75134	M75144	M75154	M75164	M75173	M75182
M75135	M75145	M75155	M75165	M75174	M75183
M75136	M75146	M75156	M75166	M75175	M75184
M75137	M75147	M75157	M75167	M75176	M75185
M75138	M75148	M75158	M75168	M75177	M75186
M75139	M75149	M75159	M75169	M75178	M75187
M75140	M75150	M75160	M75170	M75179	M75188
M75141	M75151	M75161	M75171	M75180	M75189
M75142	M75152	M75162			

Liverpool-Southport Two- and Three-Car Compartment Sets

MOTOR BRAKE SECOND

Body: 59′ 0″ × 8′ 11″ & 9′ 3″ **Weight:** 56 tons **Seats:** 2nd, 84
Equipment: Four 265 h.p. Metropolitan Vickers traction motors

M28301M M28303M M28305M M28307M M28309M M28310M
M28302M M28304M M28306M M28308M

TRAILER COMPOSITE

Body: 57′ 0″ × 8′ 11″ & 9′ 3″ **Weight:** 28 tons **Seats:** 1st, 24; 2nd, 72

M29800M M29802M M29804M M29806M M29808M M29810M
M29801M M29803M M29805M M29807M M29809M M29811M

DRIVING TRAILER BRAKE SECOND

Body: 57′ 0″ × 8′ 11″ & 9′ 3″ **Weight:** 28 tons **Seats:** 2nd, 96

M29100M M29102M M29104M M29106M M29108M M29110M
M29101M M29103M M29105M M29107M M29109M

Liverpool-Southport Two- and Three-Car Open Sets

MOTOR OPEN BRAKE SECOND

Body: 66′ 6″ × 9′ 3″ & 9′ 5″ **Weight:** 41 tons **Seats:** 2nd, 88
Equipment: Four 235 h.p. English Electric traction motors

M28311M M28322M M28332M M28342M M28352M M28361M
M28312M M28323M M28333M M28343M M28353M M28362M
M28313M M28324M M28334M M28344M M28354M M28363M
M28314M M28325M M28335M M28345M M28355M M28364M
M28315M M28326M M28336M M28347M M28356M M28365M
M28316M M28327M M28337M M28348M M28357M M28366M
M28317M M28328M M28338M M28349M M28358M M28367M
M28318M M28329M M28339M M28350M M28359M M28368M
M28319M M28330M M28340M M28351M M28360M M28369M
M28321M M28331M M28341M

TRAILER OPEN SECOND

Body: 66′ 6″ × 9′ 3″ & 9′ 5″ **Weight:** 24 tons **Seats:** 2nd, 102

L.M.R. Liverpool–Southport motor open brake second M28350M
[*G. M. Kichenside*

L.M.R. Wirral and Mersey three-car open set v..... motor open brake second M28392M leading
[*P. J. Sharpe*

L.M.R. Wirral and Mersey driving trailer open second M29276M
[*P. J. Sharpe*

M29545M M29554M M29563M M29571M M29579M M29587M
M29546M M29555M M29564M M29572M M29580M M29588M
M29547M M29556M M29565M M29573M M29581M M29589M
M29548M M29557M M29566M M29574M M29582M M29590M
M29549M M29558M M29567M M29575M M29583M M29591M
M29550M M29559M M29568M M29576M M29584M M29592M
M29551M M29560M M29569M M29577M M29585M M29593M
M29552M M29561M M29570M M29578M M29586M M29594M
M29553M M29562M

TRAILER OPEN SECOND

(Built as Composite)

Body: 66′ 6″ × 9′ 3″ & 9′ 5″ **Weight:** 24 tons **Seats: 2nd,** 82

M29812M M29814M M29816M M29818M M29819M M29820M
M29813M M29815M M29817M

DRIVING TRAILER OPEN COMPOSITE

Body: 66′ 6″ × 9′ 3″ & 9′ 5″ **Weight:** 25 tons **Seats: 1st,** 53; **2nd,** 25

M29866M M29872M M29878M M29884M M29890M M29895M
M29867M M29873M M29879M M29885M M29891M M29896M
M29868M M29874M M29880M M29886M M29892M M29897M
M29869M M29875M M29881M M29887M M29893M M29898M
M29870M M29876M M29882M M29888M M29894M M29899M
M29871M M29877M M29883M M29889M

Liverpool-Southport Single Units

MOTOR PARCELS VAN

Body: 59′ 0″ × 8′ 11″ & 9′ 3″* or 57′ 0″ × 8′ 11″ & 9′ 3″† **Weight:**
Equipment: Two 265 h.p. Metropolitan-Vickers nose-suspended traction motors

M28496M* M28497M†

B.R. Standard design

MOTOR PARCELS VAN

Body: 64′ 5″ × 9′ 0″ & 9′ 3″ **Weight:** 49 tons
Equipment: Four 250 h.p. English Electric traction motors

M68000

SYSTEM: 650 VOLTS D.C. 3rd RAIL

Wirral & Mersey Three-Car Open Sets

MOTOR OPEN BRAKE SECOND

Body: 58′ 0″ × 8′ 8″ & 9′ 11″ **Weight:** 36 tons **Seats: 2nd,** 58
Equipment: Four 135 h.p. B.T.H. traction motors

M28371M	M28379M	M28387M	M28394M	M28677M	M28684M
M28372M	M28380M	M28388M		M28678M	M28685M
M28373M	M28381M	M28389M	M28672M	M28679M	M28686M
M28374M	M28382M	M28390M	M28673M	M28680M	M28687M
M28375M	M28383M	M28391M	M28674M	M28681M	M28688M
M28376M	M28384M	M28392M	M28675M	M28682M	M28689M
M28377M	M28385M	M28393M	M28676M	M28683M	M28690M
M28378M	M28386M				

TRAILER OPEN COMPOSITE

Body: 56′ 0″ × 8′ 8″ & 9′ 11″ **Weight:** 20 tons **Seats: 1st,** 40; **2nd,** 15

M29702M	M29710M	M29718M	M29825M	M29833M	M29840M
M29703M	M29711M	M29719M	M29826M	M29834M	M29841M
M29704M	M29712M	M29720M	M29827M	M29835M	M29842M
M29705M	M29713M		M29828M	M29836M	M29843M
M29706M	M29714M	M29821M	M29829M	M29837M	M29844M
M29707M	M29715M	M29822M	M29830M	M29838M	M29845M
M29708M	M29716M	M29823M	M29831M	M29839M	M29846M
M29709M	M29717M	M29824M	M29832M		

DRIVING TRAILER OPEN SECOND

Body: 58′ 0″ × 8′ 8″ & 9′ 11″ **Weight:** 21 tons **Seats: 2nd,** 68

M29131M	M29139M	M29147M	M29155M	M29276M	M29283M
M29132M	M29140M	M29148M	M29156M	M29277M	M29284M
M29133M	M29141M	M29149M		M29278M	M29285M
M29134M	M29142M	M29150M	M29271M	M29279M	M29286M
M29135M	M29143M	M29151M	M29272M	M29280M	M29287M
M29136M	M29144M	M29152M	M29273M	M29281M	M29288M
M29137M	M29145M	M29153M	M29274M	M29282M	M29289M
M29138M	M29146M	M29154M	M29275M		

SYSTEM: 1,200 VOLTS D.C. SIDE CONTACT 3rd RAIL

Manchester-Bury Two-Car B.R. Sets

B.R. Standard design

MOTOR OPEN BRAKE SECOND

Body: 63′ 11½″ × 9′ 0″ & 9′ 3″ **Weight:** **Seats: 2nd,** 84
Equipment: Two 141 h.p. English Electric traction motors

M65436	M65441	M65446	M65450	M65454	M65458
M65437	M65442	M65447	M65451	M65455	M65459
M65438	M65443	M65448	M65452	M65456	M65460
M65439	M65444	M65449	M65453	M65457	M65461
M65440	M65445				

Two L.M.R. Manchester–Bury two-car sets with driving trailer second M77177 leading [*G. M. Kichenside*

L.M.R. Lancaster–Morecambe–Heysham motor open brake second M28221M [*P. J. Sharpe*

L.M.R. Lancaster–Morecambe–Heysham driving trailer open second M29023M [*P. J. Sharpe*

Left: L.M.R. Manchester–Altrincham three-car set with driving trailer second M29237M leading

[*P. J. Sharpe*

Centre: L.M.R. Manchester–Altrincham motor brake second M28584M

[*P. J. Sharpe*

Bottom: L.M.R. Manchester–Altrincham motor brake second M28575M (with modified side ventilator louvres)

[*P. J. Sharpe*

DRIVING TRAILER SECOND

Body: 63′ 11½″ × 9′ 0″ & 9′ 3″ **Weight:** **Seats: 2nd, 102**

M77157	M77162	M77167	M77171	M77175	M77179
M77158	M77163	M77168	M77172	M77176	M77180
M77159	M77164	M77169	M77173	M77177	M77181
M77160	M77165	M77170	M77174	M77178	M77182
M77161	M77166				

SYSTEM: 1,500 VOLTS D.C. OVERHEAD

Manchester-Altrincham Three-Car Sets

MOTOR BRAKE SECOND

Body: 58′ 1″ × 8′ 11″ & 9′ 3″ **Weight:** 57 tons **Seats: 2nd, 72**
Equipment: Four 330 h.p. traction motors

M28571M	M28575M	M28579M	M28583M	M28587M	M28591M
M28572M	M28576M	M28580M	M28584M	M28588M	M28592M
M28573M	M28577M	M28581M	M28585M	M28589M	M28593M
M28574M	M28578M	M28582M	M28586M	M28590M	M28594M

TRAILER COMPOSITE

Body: 57′ 1″ × 8′ 11″ & 9′ 3″ **Weight:** 30 tons **Seats: 1st, 24; 2nd, 72**

M29396M	M29652M	M29656M	M29660M	M29664M	M29668M
	M29653M	M29657M	M29661M	M29665M	M29669M
M29650M	M29654M	M29658M	M29662M	M29666M	M29670M
M29651M	M29655M	M29659M	M29663M	M29667M	M29671M

DRIVING TRAILER SECOND

Body: 58′ 1″ × 8′ 11″ & 9′ 3″ **Weight:** 31 tons **Seats: 2nd, 108**

M29231M	M29235M	M29239M	M29243M	M29247M	M29250M
M29232M	M29236M	M29240M	M29244M	M29248M	M29251M
M29233M	M29237M	M29241M	M29245M	M29249M	M29252M
M29234M	M29238M	M29242M	M29246M		

SYSTEM: 6,600 VOLTS A.C. 50 CYCLES OVERHEAD

Lancaster-Morecambe-Heysham Three-Car Open Sets

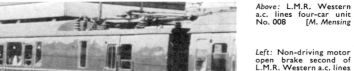

Above: L.M.R. Western a.c. lines four-car unit No. 008 [*M. Mensing*

Left: Non-driving motor open brake second of L.M.R. Western a.c. lines unit No. 022 [*P. J. Sharpe*

MOTOR OPEN BRAKE SECOND

Body: 57′ 0″ × 8′ 11″ & 9′ 6″ **Weight:** 57 tons **Seats:** 2nd, 28 (38*)
Equipment: Four 215 h.p. English Electric traction motors. (*Four 215 h.p. Metropolitan-Vickers traction motors)

M28219M M28220M M28221M M28222M*

TRAILER OPEN SECOND

Body: 57′ 0″ × 8′ 11″ & 9′ 6″ **Weight:** 26 tons **Seats:** 2nd, 62

M29721M M29722M M29723M M29724M

DRIVING TRAILER OPEN SECOND

Body: 57′ 0″ × 8′ 11″ & 9′ 6″ **Weight:** **Seats:** 2nd, 56

M29021M M29022M M29023M M29024M

SYSTEM: 1500 VOLTS D.C. OVERHEAD

Manchester-Glossop-Hadfield Three-Car Open Sets

MOTOR OPEN BRAKE SECOND

Body: 60′ 4½″ × 9′ 0″ & 9′ 3″ **Weight:** 50 tons 12 cwt **Seats:** 2nd, 52
Equipment: Four 185 h.p. G.E.C. traction motors

M59401 M59403 M59405 M59406 M59407 M59408
M59402 M59404

TRAILER OPEN SECOND

Body: 55′ 0½″ × 9′ 0″ & 9′ 3″ **Weight:** 26 tons 8 cwt **Seats:** 2nd,

M59501 M59503 M59505 M59506 M59507 M59508
M59502 M59504

DRIVING TRAILER OPEN SECOND

Body: 55′ 4½″ × 9′ 0″ & 9′ 3″ **Weight:** 27 tons 9 cwt **Seats:** 2nd, 60

M59601 M59603 M59605 M59606 M59607 M59608
M59602 M59604

SYSTEM: 25 kV. A.C. 50 CYCLES OVERHEAD

Western Lines Four-Car Units

Manchester, Liverpool, Crewe and Stafford (some units are temporarily running on GE line services from Liverpool Street)

B.R. Standard design

Scottish Region Glasgow suburban non-driving motor open brake second of unit No. 043 *[P. J. Sharpe*

Scottish Region Glasgow suburban driving trailer open second SC75598 of unit No. 033 *[P. J. Sharpe*

L.M.R. Manchester–Glossop three-car set at Hyde *[P. J. Sharpe*

Two L.M.R. Manchester–Glossop three-car sets, with driving trailer open second M59603 in the foreground [*P. J. Sharpe*

E.R. Liverpool Street–Shenfield three-car unit No. 001 [*P. J. Sharpe*

Trailer open brake second E65469 of an E.R. Liverpool Street–Shenfield three-car unit [*P. J. Sharpe*

DRIVING TRAILER OPEN BRAKE SECOND

Body: 64′ 0⅝″ × 9′ 0″ & 9′ 3″ **Weight:** 31 tons 8 cwt **Seats: 2nd,** 82

TRAILER COMPOSITE (L)

Body: 63′ 6¼″ × 9′ 0″ & 9′ 3″ **Weight:** 31 tons 5 cwt
Seats: 1st, 19; **2nd,** 60

NON-DRIVING MOTOR BRAKE SECOND (OPEN*)

Body: 63′ 6¼″ × 9′ 0″ & 9′ 3″ **Weight:** 53 tons 12 cwt **Seats: 2nd,** 96 (72*)
Equipment: Four A.E.I. 207 h.p. axle-hung nose-suspended d.c. traction motors

DRIVING TRAILER OPEN SECOND (L)

Body: 64′ 0⅝″ × 9′ 0″ & 9′ 3″ **Weight:** 35 tons 12 cwt **Seats: 2nd,** 80

UNIT Nos.

001	007	013	019*	025*	031*	036*	041*
002	008	014	020*	026*	032*	037*	042*
003	009	015	021*	027*	033*	038*	043*
004	010	016*	022*	028*	034*	039*	044*
005	011	017*	023*	029*	035*	040*	045*
006	012	018*	024*	030*			

Eastern Region

SYSTEM: 25 kV. A.C. 50 CYCLES OVERHEAD

(All Eastern Region 25kV multiple-units are interchangeable, and may be used on all G.E. and L.T. & S. a.c. electric lines.)

Liverpool St.-Shenfield Three-Car Open Units

These units were converted for working on 25,000 volts a.c. from 1,500 volts d.c. The centre trailers were altered to include the guard's compartment and pantograph, and part of the passenger saloon thus displaced transferred to the existing motor coach. The centre trailer now carries the transformer and rectifier to feed the existing d.c. control equipment and traction motors on the original motor coach.

MOTOR OPEN SECOND

Body: 60′ 4½″ × 9′ 0″ & 9′ 6″ **Weight:** 50 tons 17 cwt **Seats: 2nd,** 62
Equipment: Four 157 h.p. nose-suspended d.c. traction motors

TRAILER OPEN BRAKE SECOND

(with transformer and rectifier)

Body: 55′ 0½″ × 9′ 0″ & 9′ 6″ **Weight:** 26 tons **Seats: 2nd, 46**

DRIVING TRAILER OPEN SECOND

Body: 55′ 4″ × 9′ 0″ & 9′ 6″ **Weight:** 27 tons 10 cwt **Seats: 2nd, 60**

UNIT Nos.

001	013	025	037	049	060	071	082
002	014	026	038	050	061	072	083
003	015	027	039	051	062	073	084
004	016	028	040	052	063	074	085
005	017	029	041	053	064	075	086
006	018	030	042	054	065	076	087
007	019	031	043	055	066	077	088
008	020	032	044	056	067	078	089
009	021	033	045	057	068	079	090
010	022	034	046	058	069	080	091
011	023	035	047	059	070	081	092
012	024	036	048				

G.E. Outer Suburban Four-Car Units

These units have been converted for working on 25,000 volts a.c. from 1,500 volts d.c. A new pantograph, transformer and rectifier mounted on one of the original driving trailers feeds the existing d.c. control and traction equipment on the motor coach. The original guard's compartment has been rebuilt in the driving trailer now carrying the pantograph and the compartments thus displaced transferred to the motor coach.

B.R. Standard design

DRIVING TRAILER BRAKE SECOND

(with transformer and rectifier)

Body: 63′ 11½″ × 9′ 0″ & 9′ 3″ **Weight:** **Seats: 2nd, 84**

NON-DRIVING MOTOR SECOND

Body: 63′ 6″ × 9′ 0″ & 9′ 3″ **Weight:** **Seats: 2nd, 120**
Equipment: Four G.E.C. 174 h.p. axle-hung nose-suspended d.c. traction motors

TRAILER COMPOSITE (L)

Body: 63′ 6″ × 9′ 0″ & 9′ 3″ **Weight:** 30 tons **Seats: 1st, 19; 2nd, 60**

DRIVING TRAILER OPEN SECOND (L)

Body: 63′ 11½″ × 9′ 0″ & 9′ 3″ **Weight:** **Seats: 2nd, 80**

Above: Driving trailer open second E75108 of E.R. Great Eastern outer suburban unit No. 108 [*P. J. Sharpe*

Left: Trailer composite E70131 of an E.R. Fenchurch Street–Shoeburyness line four-car unit [*G. M. Kichenside*

Below: E.R. original Fenchurch Street–Shoeburyness line four-car unit No. 229 [*G. M. Kichenside*

UNIT Nos.

101	105	109	113	117	121	125	129
102	106	110	114	118	122	126	130
103	107	111	115	119	123	127	131
104	108	112	116	120	124	128	132

G.E. Outer Suburban Four-Car Units

B.R. Standard design

DRIVING TRAILER SECOND

Body: 64′ 0½″ × 9′ 0″ & 9′ 3″ **Weight:** 32 tons **Seats: 2nd,** 108

TRAILER COMPOSITE (L)

Body: 63′ 6″ × 9′ 0″ & 9′ 3″ **Weight:** 31 tons **Seats: 1st,** 19; **2nd,** 60

NON-DRIVING MOTOR BRAKE SECOND

Body: 63′ 6″ × 9′ 0″ & 9′ 3″ **Weight:** 54 tons **Seats: 2nd,** 96
Equipment: Four English Electric 200 h.p. axle-hung nose-suspended d.c. traction motors

DRIVING TRAILER OPEN SECOND (L)

Body: 64′ 0½″ × 9′ 0″ & 9′ 3″ **Weight:** 36 tons **Seats: 2nd,** 80

UNIT Nos.

133	138	142	146	150	154	158	162
134	139	143	147	151	155	159	163
135	140	144	148	152	156	160	164
136	141	145	149	153	157	161	165
137							

Fenchurch St.-Shoeburyness Four-Car Units

B.R. Standard design

DRIVING TRAILER SECOND

Body: 63′ 11½″ × 9′ 0″ & 9′ 3″ **Weight:** 32 tons **Seats: 2nd,** 108

TRAILER COMPOSITE (L)

Body: 63′ 6″ × 9′ 0″ & 9′ 3″ **Weight:** 31 tons **Seats: 1st,** 19; **2nd,** 60

NON-DRIVING MOTOR BRAKE SECOND

Body: 63′ 6″ × 9′ 0″ & 9′ 3″ **Weight:** 56 tons 10 cwt **Seats: 2nd,** 96
Equipment: Four 192 h.p. English Electric nose-suspended traction motors

Above: Non-driving motor brake second E61208 of an E.R. original Fenchurch Street–Shoeburyness line four-car unit [*G. M. Kichenside*

Left: Non-driving motor luggage van E68017 of a later Fenchurch Street Shoeburyness line four-car unit [*G. M. Kichenside*

Below: Non-driving motor brake open second E61441 of Liverpool Street–Enfield and Chingford three car unit No. 413 [*P. J. Sharpe*

DRIVING TRAILER OPEN SECOND (L)

Body: 63′ 11½″ × 9′ 0″ & 9′ 3″ **Weight:** 36 tons **Seats: 2nd, 80**

UNIT Nos.

201	215	229	243	257	271	285	299
202	216	230	244	258	272	286	300
203	217	231	245	259	273	287	301
204	218	232	246	260	274	288	302
205	219	233	247	261	275	289	303
206	220	234	248	262	276	290	304
207	221	235	249	263	277	291	305
208	222	236	250	264	278	292	306
209	223	237	251	265	279	293	307
210	224	238	252	266	280	294	308
211	225	239	253	267	281	295	309
212	226	240	254	268	282	296	310
213	227	241	255	269	283	297	311
214	228	242	256	270	284	298	312

Fenchurch St.-Shoeburyness Four-Car Units

B.R. Standard design

DRIVING TRAILER SECOND

Body: 63′ 11½″ × 9′ 0″ & 9′ 3″ **Weight:** 32 tons **Seats: 2nd, 108**

TRAILER COMPOSITE (L)

Body: 63′ 6″ × 9′ 0″ & 9′ 3″ **Weight:** 31 tons **Seats: 1st, 19; 2nd, 60**

NON-DRIVING MOTOR LUGGAGE VAN

Body: 63′ 6″ × 9′ 0″ & 9′ 3″ **Weight:** 51 tons 12 cwt
Equipment: Four 192 h.p. English Electric nose-suspended traction motors

DRIVING TRAILER OPEN SECOND (L)

Body: 63′ 11½″ × 9′ 0″ & 9′ 3″ **Weight:** 36 tons **Seats: 2nd, 80**

UNIT Nos.

313	315	316	317	318	319	320	321
314							

Liverpool St.-Enfield and Chingford Three-Car Units

B.R. Standard design

DRIVING TRAILER OPEN SECOND

Body: 63′ 11½″ × 9′ 0″ & 9′ 3″ **Weight:** **Seats:** 2nd, 94

NON-DRIVING MOTOR OPEN BRAKE SECOND

Body: 63′ 6″ × 9′ 0″ & 9′ 3″ **Weight:** **Seats:** 2nd, 84
Equipment: Four G.E.C. 200 h.p. axle-hung nose-suspended d.c. traction motors

DRIVING TRAILER OPEN SECOND

Body: 63′ 11½″ × 9′ 0″ & 9′ 3″ **Weight:** **Seats:** 2nd, 94

UNIT Nos.

401	408	415	422	429	436	443	450
402	409	416	423	430	437	444	451
403	410	417	424	431	438	445	452
404	411	418	425	432	439	446	453
405	412	419	426	433	440	447	454
406	413	420	427	434	441	448	455
407	414	421	428	435	442	449	

G.E. Outer Suburban Four-Car Units

B.R. Standard design

DRIVING TRAILER SECOND

Body:64′ 0½″ × 9′ 0″ & 9′ 3″ **Weight:** 32 tons **Seats:** 2nd, 108

TRAILER COMPOSITE (L)

Body: 63′ 6″ × 9′ 0″ & 9′ 3″ **Weight:** 31 tons **Seats:** 1st, 19; 2nd, 60

NON-DRIVING MOTOR BRAKE SECOND

Body: 63′ 6″ × 9′ 0″ & 9′ 3″ **Weight:** 54 tons **Seats:** 2nd, 96
Equipment: Four G.E.C. 200 h.p. axle-hung nose-suspended d.c. traction motors

DRIVING TRAILER OPEN SECOND (L)

Body: 64′ 0½″ × 9′ 0″ & 9′ 3″ **Weight:** 36 tons **Seats:** 2nd, 80

D 1501
1N62

Above: A three-car Birmingham R.C. W. & unit r

Previous page: Brush Type 4 2,7

Next page: B.R., Doncaster 2,

:on Salmon on a Manchester-York special working

diesel-electric Co-Co No. D1501

750V d.c. locomotive No. E5015
[*From paintings by V. Welch*

46
GOLDEN ARROW
E 5015
E5015

UNIT Nos.

501	504	507	510	512	514	516	518
502	505	508	511	513	515	517	519
503	506	509					

Liverpool St.-Clacton and Walton Two-Car Units

B.R. Standard design

Gangwayed throughout

MOTOR BRAKE SECOND (L)

Body: 64′ 9¾″ × 9′ 0″ & 9′ 3″ **Weight:** 59 tons 6 cwt **Seats: 2nd, 48**
Equipment: Four 282 h.p. G.E.C. traction motors

DRIVING TRAILER OPEN SECOND (L)

Body: 64′ 9¾″ × 9′ 0″ & 9′ 3″ **Weight:** 39 tons 11 cwt **Seats: 2nd, 60**

UNIT Nos.

601 602 603 604 605 606 607 608

Liverpool St.-Clacton and Walton Four-Car Buffet Units

B.R. Standard design

Gangwayed throughout

DRIVING TRAILER SEMI-OPEN COMPOSITE (L)

Body: 64′ 9¾″ × 9′ 0″ & 9′ 3″ **Weight:** 39 tons 7 cwt **Seats: 1st, 18; 2nd, 32**

NON-DRIVING MOTOR BRAKE SECOND (L)

Body: 64′ 6″ × 9′ 0″ & 9′ 3″ **Weight:** 56 tons 16 cwt **Seats: 2nd, 48**
Equipment: Four 282 h.p. G.E.C. traction motors

TRAILER GRIDDLE/BUFFET CAR

Body: 64′ 6″ × 9′ 0″ & 9′ 3″ **Weight:** 35 tons 16 cwt **Seats: Buffet, 32**

DRIVING TRAILER OPEN COMPOSITE (L)

Body: 64′ 9¾″ × 9′ 0″ & 9′ 3″ **Weight:** 36 tons 1 cwt **Seats: 1st, 18; 2nd, 32**

UNIT Nos.

611 612 613 614 615 616 617 618

Liverpool St.-Clacton and Walton Four-Car Units

B.R. Standard design

Gangwayed throughout

DRIVING TRAILER SEMI-OPEN COMPOSITE (L)

Body: 64′ 9¾″ × 9′ 0″ & 9′ 3″ **Weight:** 39 tons 7 cwt **Seats:** **Ist,** 18; **2nd,** 32

NON-DRIVING MOTOR BRAKE SECOND (L)

Body: 64′ 6″ × 9′ 0″ & 9′ 3″ **Weight:** 56 tons 16 cwt **Seats: 2nd, 48**
Equipment: Four 282 h.p. G.E.C. traction motors

TRAILER OPEN SECOND (L)

Body: 64′ 6″ × 9′ 0″ & 9′ 3″ **Weight:** 34 tons 8 cwt **Seats: 2nd, 64**

DRIVING TRAILER SEMI-OPEN COMPOSITE (L)

Body: 64′ 9¾″ × 9′ 0″ & 9′ 3″ **Weight:** 36 tons 15 cwt **Seats:** **Ist,** 18; **2nd,** 32

UNIT Nos.

621 622 623 624 625 626 627

North Eastern Region

SYSTEM: 600 VOLTS D.C. 3rd RAIL

South Tyneside Two-Car Units

B.R. Standard design

MOTOR OPEN BRAKE SECOND

Body: 63′ 11½″ × 9′ 0″ & 9′ 3″ **Weight:** 40 tons **Seats: 2nd, 74**
Equipment: Two 250 h.p. English Electric traction motors

E65311	E65314	E65317	E65320	E65322	E65324
E65312	E65315	E65318	E65321	E65323	E65325
E65313	E65316	E65319			

Top: Driving trailer open second E75495 of Liverpool Street–Enfield and Chingford three-car unit No. 434
[*P. J. Sharpe*

Centre: E.R. Fenchurch Street–Shoeburyness four-car unit No. 315
[*G. M. Kichenside*

Right: Driving trailer composite of E.R. Liverpool Street–Clacton and Walton four-car unit No. 627
[*G. M. Kichenside*

Above: Driving trailer open second E29323E of an N.E.R. North Tyneside articulated unit [*M. Mensing*

Left: N.E.R. North Tyneside motor parcels van E29467E [*J. N. Faulkner*

Below: Motor open brake second E29124E of an N.E.R. North Tyneside articulated unit [*P. J. Sharpe*

DRIVING TRAILER SECOND

Body: 63′ 11½″ × 9′ 0″ & 9′ 3″ **Weight:** 30 tons **Seats:** **2nd,**

E77100	E77103	E77106	E77109	E77111	E77113
E77101	E77104	E77107	E77110	E77112	E77114
E77102	E77105	E77108			

(The above South Tyneside units have been withdrawn from service and transferred to the Southern Region. Details of alterations were not to hand as this edition closed for press)

North Tyneside Articulated Twin Units

MOTOR OPEN BRAKE SECOND

Body: 55′ 0″ × 9′ 0½″ & 9′ 3″ **Combined weight with trailer:** 54 tons 19 cwt
Seats: 2nd, 52
Equipment: Two 154 h.p. Crompton Parkinson traction motors

DRIVING TRAILER OPEN SECOND

Body: 55′ 0″ × 9′ 0½ & 9′ 3″ **Seats: 2nd,** 76

Motor Coaches			*Driving Trailers*		
E29101E	E29105E	E29109E	E29301E	E29305E	E29309E
E29102E	E29106E	E29110E	E29302E	E29306E	E29310E
E29103E	E29107E	E29111E	E29303E	E29307E	E29311E
E29104E	E29108E		E29304E	E29308E	

MOTOR OPEN BRAKE SECOND

Body: 55′ 0″ × 9′ 0½′ & 9′ 3″ **Combined weight with trailer:** 55 tons 7 cwt
Seats: 2nd, 52
Equipment: Two 154 h.p. Crompton Parkinson traction motors

DRIVING TRAILER OPEN SECOND

Body: 55′ 0″ × 9′ 0½″ & 9′ 3″ **Seats: 2nd,** 60

Motor Coaches			*Driving Trailers*		
E29113E	E29119E	E29124E	E29313E	E29319E	E29324E
E29114E	E29120E	E29125E	E29314E	E29320E	E29325E
E29115E	E29121E	E29126E	E29315E	E29321E	E29326E
E29116E	E29122E	E29127E	E29316E	E29322E	E29327E
E29117E	E29123E	E29128E	E29317E	E29323E	E29328E
E29118E			E29318E		

MOTOR OPEN BRAKE SECOND

Body: 55′ 0″ × 9′ 0½″ & 9′ 3″ **Combined weight with trailer:** 53 tons 12 cwt
Seats: 2nd, 52
Equipment: Two 154 h.p. Crompton Parkinson traction motors

TRAILER OPEN SECOND

Body: 55′ 0″ × 9′ 0½″ & 9′ 3″ **Seats:** **2nd,** 80

Motor Coaches			*Trailers*		
E29129E	E29135E	E29141E	E29229E	E29235E	E29241E
E29130E	E29136E	E29142E	E29230E	E29236E	E29242E
E29131E	E29137E	E29143E	E29231E	E29237E	E29243E
E29132E	E29138E	E29144E	E29232E	E29238E	E29244E
E29133E	E29139E	E29145E	E29233E	E29239E	E29245E
E29134E	E29140E	E29146E	E29234E	E29240E	E29246E

MOTOR OPEN BRAKE SECOND

Body: 55′ 0″ × 9′ 0½″ & 9′ 3″ **Combined weight with trailer:** 54 tons 6 cwt
Seats: 2nd, 52
Equipment: Two 154 h.p. Crompton Parkinson traction motors

TRAILER OPEN SECOND

Body: 55′ 0″ × 9′ 0″ & 9′ 3″ **Seats: 2nd,** 64

Motor Coaches			*Trailers*		
E29147E	E29153E	E29159E	E29247E	E29253E	E29259E
E29148E	E29154E	E29160E	E29248E	E29254E	E29260E
E29149E	E29155E	E29161E	E29249E	E29255E	E29261E
E29150E	E29156E	E29162E	E29250E	E29256E	E29262E
E29151E	E29157E	E29163E	E29251E	E29257E	E29263E
E29152E	E29158E	E29164E	E29252E	E29258E	E29264E

North Tyneside Single Units

MOTOR OPEN BRAKE SECOND

Body: 59′ 0″ × 9′ 0½″ & 9′ 3″ **Weight:** 47 tons 5 cwt **Seats: 2nd,** 52
Equipment: Two 154 h.p. Crompton Parkinson traction motors

E29165E E29166E

DRIVING TRAILER OPEN SECOND

Body: 56′ 6″ × 9′ 0¾″ & 9′ 3″ **Weight:** 26 tons 10 cwt **Seats: 2nd,** 68

E29376E E29387E E29388E E29390E

MOTOR PARCELS VAN

Body: 59′ 0″ × 9′ 0½″ & 9′ 3″ **Weight:** 38 tons 15 cwt
Equipment: Four 154 h.p. Crompton Parkinson traction motors

E29467E E29468E

Scottish Region

SYSTEM: 25 kV. A.C. 50 CYCLES OVERHEAD

Glasgow Suburban Three-Car Units

B.R. Standard design

DRIVING TRAILER OPEN SECOND

Body: 63′ 11⅝″ × 9′ 3″ & 9′ 3″ **Weight:** 34 tons **Seats:** 2nd, 83

NON-DRIVING MOTOR OPEN BRAKE SECOND

Body: 63′ 6⅛″ × 9′ 3″ & 9′ 3″ **Weight:** 56 tons **Seats:** 2nd, 70
Equipment: Four A.E.I. (MV) 207 h.p. axle-hung nose-suspended d.c. traction motors

DRIVING TRAILER OPEN SECOND

Body: 63′ 11⅝″ × 9′ 3″ & 9′ 3″ **Weight:** 38 tons **Seats:** 2nd, 83

UNIT Nos.

001	013	025	037	048	059	070	081
002	014	026	038	049	060	071	082
003	015	027	039	050	061	072	083
004	016	028	040	051	062	073	084
005	017	029	041	052	063	074	085
006	018	030	042	053	064	075	086
007	019	031	043	054	065	076	087
008	020	032	044	055	066	077	088
009	021	033	045	056	067	078	089
010	022	034	046	057	068	079	090
011	023	035	047	058	069	080	091
012	024	036					

Southern Region

The numbers of Southern Electric units have been checked to February 6, 1963

(Numbers to be seen on front and rear of each unit)

SYSTEM: 750 VOLTS D.C. 3rd RAIL

Two-Car Units (2-BIL)

MOTOR BRAKE SECOND (K)

Body: 62′ 6″ × 9′ 0″ & 9′ 3″ **Weight:** 43 tons 10 cwt **Seats:** 2nd, 52 (56*)
Equipment: Two 275 h.p. English Electric traction motors

DRIVING TRAILER COMPOSITE (K)

Body: 62′ 6″ × 9′ 0″ & 9′ 3″ **Weight:** 31 tons 5 cwt
Seats: **1st, 24; 2nd,** 32

2001*	2021	2040	2059	2077	2096	2115	2135
2002*	2022	2041	2060	2078	2097	2116	2136
2003*	2023	2042	2061	2079	2098	2117	2137
2004*	2024	2043	2062	2080	2099	2118	2138
2005*	2025	2044	2063	2081	2100‡	2120	2139
2006*	2026	2045	2064	2082	2101	2121	2140
2007*	2027	2046	2065	2083	2103	2122	2141
2008*	2028	2047	2066	2084	2104	2123	2142
2009*	2029	2048	2067	2085	2105	2124	2143
2010*	2030	2049	2068	2086	2106	2125	2144
2011	2031	2050	2069‡	2087	2107	2126	2145
2012	2032	2051	2070	2089	2108	2127	2146
2013	2033	2052	2071	2090	2109	2128	2147
2015	2034	2053	2072	2091	2110	2129	2148
2016	2035	2054	2073	2092	2111	2130	2149
2017	2036	2055	2074	2093	2112	2132	2150
2018	2037	2056†	2075	2094	2113	2133‡	2151
2019	2038	2057	2076	2095	2114	2134	2152
2020	2039	2058					

† Unit 2056 has a BIL motor coach and a 1939-type HAL trailer.
‡ Units 2069, 2100 and 2133 have BIL motor coaches and post-war all-steel HAL trailers.

Two-Car Units (2-HAL) 1939-type

MOTOR BRAKE SECOND

Body: 62′ 6″ × 9′ 0″ & 9′ 3″ **Weight:** 44 tons **Seats: 2nd,** 70
Equipment: Two 275 h.p. English Electric nose-suspended traction motors

DRIVING TRAILER COMPOSITE (K)

Body: 62′ 6″ × 9′ 0″ & 9′ 3″ **Weight:** 32 tons
Seats: **1st,** 18 or 24; **2nd,** 40 or 32

2601	2613	2625	2636	2648	2659	2670	2682
2602	2614	2626	2637	2649	2660	2671	2683
2603	2615	2627	2638	2650	2661	2672	2684
2604	2616	2628	2639	2651	2662	2673	2685
2605	2617	2629	2640	2652	2663	2674	2686
2606	2618	2630	2641	2653*	2664	2675	2687
2607	2619	2631	2642	2654	2665	2676	2688
2608	2620	2632	2643	2655	2666	2677	2689
2609	2621	2633	2644	2656	2667	2678	2690
2610	2622	2634	2645	2657	2668	2679	2691
2611	2623	2635	2647	2658	2669	2681	2692
2612	2624						

* Unit 2653 has a post-war all-steel HAL trailer

Driving trailer composite of Southern Region 2-BIL unit No. 2085 [*Alan Williams*

Motor brake second of Southern Region 2-BIL unit No. 2017 [*P. J. Sharpe*

Southern Region 4-LAV unit No. 2936 [*P. J. Sharpe*

Two-Car Units (2-HAL) Post-war all-steel type

MOTOR BRAKE SECOND

Body: 62′ 6″ × 9′ 0″ & 9′ 3″ **Weight:** 42 tons **Seats: 2nd,** 84
Equipment: Two 275 h.p. English Electric nose-suspended traction motors

DRIVING TRAILER COMPOSITE (K)

Body: 62′ 6″ × 9′ 0″ & 9′ 3″ **Weight:** 31 tons **Seats: 1st,** 18; **2nd,** 40

2693 2694 2695 2696 2697 2698 2699

Two-Car Unit (2-HAL) Post-war all-steel type

MOTOR BRAKE SALOON SECOND

Body: 62′ 6″ × 9′ 0″ & 9′ 3″ **Weight:** 39 tons **Seats: 2nd,** 82
Equipment: Two 275 h.p. English Electric nose-suspended traction motors

DRIVING TRAILER COMPOSITE (K)

Body: 62′ 6″ × 9′ 0″ & 9′ 3″ **Weight:** 31 tons **Seats: 1st,** 24; **2nd,** 32

2700

Four-Car Units (4-LAV)

MOTOR BRAKE SECOND

Body: 62′ 6″ × 9′ 0″ & 9′ 3″ **Weight:** 41 tons (*†44 tons) **Seats: 2nd,** 70
Equipment: Two 275 h.p. Metropolitan-Vickers traction motors. (*† Two 275 h.p. English Electric traction motors)

TRAILER COMPOSITE

Body: 62′ 0″ × 9′ 0″ & 9′ 3″ **Weight:** 28 tons
Seats: 1st, 16; **2nd,** 70 *29 tons

TRAILER COMPOSITE (K) (†SECOND)

Body: 62′ 0″ × 9′ 0″ & 9′ 3″ **Weight:** 29 tons
Seats: 1st, 30; **2nd,** 24 *30 tons
†**2nd,** 120 †26 tons

MOTOR BRAKE SECOND

(As above)

2921	2926†	2931	2936	2940	2944	2948	2952
2922	2927	2932	2937	2941	2945	2949	2953
2923	2928	2933	2938	2942	2946	2950	2954*
2924	2929	2934	2939	2943	2947	2951	2955*
2925	2930	2935					

* 1939 Bulleid units.
†Unit 2926 has one 1939-type HAL motor coach and one all-steel SUB trailer compartment second.

Motor brake second of Southern Region 2-HAL unit No. 2632 [*P. J. Sharpe*

Driving trailer composite of Southern Region 2-HAL unit No. 2682 [*P. J. Sharpe*

Driving trailer composite of Southern Region post-war all-steel 2-HAL unit No. 2694 [*P. J. Sharpe*

Six-Car Units (6-PUL)

Gangwayed within set

MOTOR SALOON BRAKE SECOND

Body: 63′ 6″ × 9′ 0″ & 9′ 5″ **Weight:** 59 tons **Seats: 2nd, 52**
Equipment: Four 225 h.p. B.T.H. traction motors

TRAILER SECOND (K)

Body: 63′ 6″ × 9′ 0″ & 9′ 3″ **Weight:** 35 tons **Seats: 2nd, 68**

TRAILER COMPOSITE (K)

Body: 63′ 6″ × 9′ 0″ & 9′ 3″ **Weight:** 35 tons **Seats: 1st,** 30; **2nd,** 24

TRAILER COMPOSITE PULLMAN (L)

Body: 66′ 0″ × 8′ 11½″ & 8′ 11½″ **Weight:** 43 tons **Seats: 1st,** 12; **2nd,** 16

TRAILER COMPOSITE (K)

(As above)

MOTOR SALOON BRAKE SECOND

(As above)

3001	3004	3007	3010	3013	3015	3017	3019
3002	3005	3008	3011	3014*	3016	3018	3020
3003*	3006	3009	3012				

* One PAN motor coach.

Six-Car Units (6-PAN)

Gangwayed within set

MOTOR SALOON BRAKE SECOND

Body: 63′ 6″ × 9′ 0″ & 9′ 5″ **Weight:** 59 tons **Seats: 2nd, 52**
Equipment: Four 225 h.p. English Electric traction motors

TRAILER SECOND (K)

Body: 63′ 6″ × 9′ 0″ & 9′ 3″ **Weight:** 31 tons 10 cwt **Seats: 2nd, 68**

TRAILER FIRST (K)

Body: 59′ 0″ × 9′ 0″ & 9′ 3″ **Weight:** 31 tons **Seats: 1st, 42**

TRAILER PANTRY FIRST (K)

Body: 63′ 6″ × 9′ 0″ & 9′ 3″ **Weight:** 32 tons **Seats: 1st, 30**

Motor brake second of Southern Region 6-PUL unit No. 3020 [*P. J. Sharpe*

Trailer pantry first of Southern Region 6-PAN unit No. 3025 [*P. J. Sharpe*

Motor brake second of Southern Region 5-BEL unit No. 3052 [*P. J. Sharpe*

TRAILER SECOND (K)

(As Above)

MOTOR SALOON BRAKE SECOND

(As Above)

3021	3023	3025	3027	3029	3031	3034	3036
3022	3024	3026†	3028	3030	3033	3035	3037

† One PUL motor coach.

Six-Car Units (6-PUL)

Gangwayed within set

MOTOR SALOON BRAKE SECOND

Body: 63′ 6″ × 9′ 0″ & 9′ 5″ **Weight:** 57 tons (59 tons*) **Seats: 2nd,** 56 (52*)
Equipment: Four 225 h.p. B.T.H. traction motors

TRAILER SECOND (K)

Body: 59′ 0″ × 9′ 0″ & 9′ 3″ **Weight:** 34 tons **Seats: 2nd, 56**

TRAILER COMPOSITE (K)

Body: 59′ 0″ × 9′ 0″ & 9′ 3″ **Weight:** 34 tons **Seats: 1st,** 30; **2nd,** 16

TRAILER COMPOSITE PULLMAN (L)

Body: 66′ 0″ × 8′ 11½″ & 8′ 11½″ **Weight:** 43 tons **Seats: 1st,** 12; **2nd,** 16

TRAILER COMPOSITE (K)

(As Above)

MOTOR SALOON BRAKE SECOND

Body: 63′ 6″ × 9′ 0″ & 9′ 5″ **Weight:** 59 tons **Seats: 2nd, 52**
Equipment: Four 225 h.p. B.T.H. traction motors

3041 3042 3043*

Five-Car Pullman Units (5-BEL)

All-Pullman: Gangwayed within set

MOTOR BRAKE SECOND PULLMAN (L)

Body: 66′ 0″ × 8′ 11½″ & 8′ 11½″ **Weight:** 62 tons **Seats: 2nd, 48**
Equipment: Four 225 h.p, B.T.H. traction motors

TRAILER SECOND PULLMAN (L)

Body: 66′ 0″ × 8′ 11½″ & 8′ 11½″ **Weight:** 39 tons **Seats:** 2nd, 56

TRAILER KITCHEN FIRST PULLMAN (L)

Body: 66′ 0″ × 8′ 11½″ & 8′ 11½ **Weight:** 43 tons **Seats:** 1st, 20

TRAILER KITCHEN FIRST PULLMAN (L)

(As Above)

MOTOR BRAKE SECOND PULLMAN (L)

(As Above)

3051 3052 3053

Four-Car Units (4-RES)

Gangwayed throughout

MOTOR SALOON BRAKE SECOND

Body: 63′ 6″ × 9′ 0″ & 9′ 4½″ **Weight:** 46 tons 10 cwt **Seats:** 2nd, 52
Equipment: Two 225 h.p. English Electric traction motors

TRAILER FIRST (K)

Body: 63′ 6″ × 9′ 0″ & 9′ 3″ **Weight:** 33 tons
Seats: 1st, 30; 1st Dining, 12

TRAILER KITCHEN SECOND

*Trailer Buffet †Trailer Griddle Car

Body: 63′ 6″ × 9′ 0″ & 9′ 4½″ **Weight:** 35 tons, *35 tons, †34 tons **Seats:** 2nd Dining, 36, *36, †26

MOTOR SALOON BRAKE SECOND

(As Above)

3054	3056†	3059	3062	3065†	3067	3069	3071
3055	3057	3061	3064	3066	3068†	3070	3072*

Four-Car Units (4-BUF)

Gangwayed throughout

Trailer Kitchen Second of Southern Region 4-RES unit No. 3066
[*Alan Williams*

Trailer Buffet of Southern Region 4-BUF unit No. 3084 [*Alan Williams*

Trailer Griddle/Buffet of Southern Region 4-RES unit No. 3068
[*Alan Williams*

Motor brake second of Southern Region 4-COR unit No. 3124 [*Alan Williams*

Trailer second of Southern Region 4-COR unit No. 3147 [*P. J. Sharpe*

Trailer composite of Southern Region 4-COR unit No. 3142 [*Alan Williams*

MOTOR SALOON BRAKE SECOND

Body: 63′ 6″ × 9′ 0″ & 9′ 4½″ **Weight:** 46 tons 10 cwt **Seats: 2nd, 52**
Equipment: Two 225 h.p. English Electric traction motors

TRAILER COMPOSITE (K)

Body: 63′ 6″ × 9′ 0″ & 9′ 3″ **Weight:** 32 tons 12 cwt
Seats: **1st**, 30; **2nd**, 24

TRAILER BUFFET (L)

Body: 63′ 6″ × 9′ 0″ & 9′ 3″ **Weight:** 37 tons **Seats: Buffet, 26**

MOTOR SALOON BRAKE SECOND

(As Above)

3073	3075	3077	3079	3081	3083	3084	3085
3074	3076	3078	3080	3082			

Four-Car Units (4-COR)

Gangwayed throughout

MOTOR SALOON BRAKE SECOND

Body: 63′ 6″ × 9′ 0″ & 9′ 4½″ **Weight:** 46 tons 10 cwt **Seats: 2nd, 52**
Equipment: Two 225 h.p. English Electric traction motors

TRAILER SECOND (K)

Body: 63′ 6″ × 9′ 0″ & 9′ 3″ **Weight:** 32 tons 13 cwt **Seats: 2nd, 68**

TRAILER COMPOSITE (K)

Body: 63′ 6″ × 9′ 0″ & 9′ 3″ **Weight:** 32 tons 12 cwt (33 tons*)
Seats: **1st**, 30; **2nd**, 24 (16*)

MOTOR SALOON BRAKE SECOND

(As Above)

3101	3109	3117	3124	3131	3138	3145	3152
3102	3110	3118	3125	3132	3139	3146	3153
3103	3111	3119	3126	3133	3140	3147	3154
3104	3112	3120	3127	3134	3141	3148	3155
3105	3113	3121	3128	3135	3142	3149	3156
3106	3114	3122	3129	3136	3143	3150	3157
3107	3115	3123	3130	3137	3144	3151	3158*
3108	3116						

* Trailer composite in unit 3158 is a converted RES trailer first.

Four-Car Double Deck Suburban Units (4-DD)

MOTOR BRAKE SECOND

Body: 62′ 6″ × 9′ 0″ & 9′ 3″ **Weight:** 39 tons
Seats: **2nd,** Lower deck 55; Upper deck 55 (*plus* 10 tip-up)
Equipment: Two 250 h.p. English Electric traction motors

TRAILER SECOND

Body: 62′ 0″ × 9′ 0″ & 9′ 3″ **Weight:** 28 tons
Seats: **2nd,** Lower deck 78; Upper deck 66 (*plus* 12 tip-up)

TRAILER SECOND

(As Above)

MOTOR BRAKE SECOND

(As Above)

4001 4002

Four-Car Suburban Units (4-SUB)

MOTOR BRAKE SECOND

Seats: 62′ 6″ × 9′ 0″ & 9′ 3″ **Weight:** 43 tons **Seats: 2nd,** 102
Equipment: Two 275 h.p. English Electric traction motors

TRAILER SECOND

Body: 62′ 0″ × 9′ 0″ & 9′ 3″ **Weight:** 29 tons **Seats: 2nd,** 132

TRAILER SECOND

Body: 62′ 0″ × 9′ 0″ & 9′ 3″ **Weight:** 29 tons **Seats: 2nd,** 120

MOTOR BRAKE SECOND

(As Above)

4101 4103 4105 4106 4107 4108 4109 4110
4102 4104

Four-Car Suburban Units (4-SUB)

MOTOR BRAKE SECOND

Body: 62′ 6″ × 9′ 0″ & 9′ 3″ **Weight:** 43 tons **Seats: 2nd,** 96
Equipment: Two 275 h.p. English Electric traction motors

TRAILER SECOND

Body: 62′ 0″ × 9′ 0″ & 9′ 3″ **Weight:** 28 tons **Seats: 2nd, 108**

TRAILER SECOND

Body: 62′ 0″ × 9′ 0″ & 9′ 3″ **Weight:** 28 tons **Seats: 2nd, 120**

MOTOR BRAKE SECOND

(As Above)

4111 4113 4114 4115 4116 4117 4118 4119
4112

Four-Car Suburban Unit (4-SUB)

MOTOR BRAKE SECOND

Body: 62′ 6″ × 9′ 0″ & 9′ 3″ **Weight:** 43 tons **Seats: 2nd, 96**
Equipment: Two 275 h.p. English Electric traction motors

TRAILER SECOND

Body: 62′ 0″ × 9′ 0″ & 9′ 3″ **Weight:** 28 tons **Seats: 2nd, 108**

TRAILER SECOND

Body: 62′ 0″ × 9′ 0″ & 9′ 3″ **Weight:** 28 tons **Seats: 2nd, 120**

MOTOR SALOON BRAKE SECOND

Body: 62′ 6″ × 9′ 0″ & 9′ 3″ **Weight:** 39 tons **Seats: 2nd, 82**
Equipment: Two 250 h.p. English Electric traction motors

4120

Four-Car Suburban Units (4-SUB)

MOTOR BRAKE SECOND (SEMI-SALOON)

Body: 62′ 6″ × 9′ 0″ & 9′ 3″ **Weight:** 43 tons **Seats: 2nd, 84**
Equipment: Two 275 h.p. English Electric traction motors

TRAILER SECOND

Body: 62′ 0″ × 9′ 0″ & 9′ 3″ **Weight:** 28 tons **Seats: 2nd, 108**

TRAILER SECOND (SEMI-SALOON)

Body: 62′ 0″ × 9′ 0″ & 9′ 3″ **Weight:** 28 tons **Seats: 2nd, 106**

MOTOR BRAKE SECOND (SEMI-SALOON)

(As Above)

4121 4123 4125 4126 4127 4128 4129 4130
4122 4124

Four-Car Suburban Units (4-SUB)

MOTOR SALOON BRAKE SECOND

Body: 62′ 6″ × 9′ 0″ & 9′ 3″ **Weight:** 39 tons **Seats:** 2nd, 82
Equipment: Two 250 h.p. English Electric traction motors

TRAILER SECOND

Body: 62′ 0″ × 9′ 0″ & 9′ 3″ **Weight:** 28 tons **Seats:** 2nd, 120

TRAILER SALOON SECOND

Body: 62′ 0″ × 9′ 0″ & 9′ 3″ **Weight:** 28 tons **Seats:** 2nd, 102

MOTOR SALOON BRAKE SECOND

(As Above)

4277 4280 4283 4286 4289 4292 4295 4298
4278 4281 4284 4287 4290 4293 4296 4299
4279 4282 4285 4288 4291 4294 4297

Four-Car Suburban Units (4-SUB)

MOTOR BRAKE SECOND

Body: 62′ 6″ × 9′ 0″ & 9′ 3″ **Weight:** 43 tons **Seats:** 2nd, 96
Equipment: Two 275 English Electric traction motors

TRAILER SECOND

Body: 62′ 0″ × 9′ 0″ & 9′ 3″ **Weight:** 28 tons **Seats:** 2nd, 120

TRAILER SECOND

(As Above)

MOTOR BRAKE SECOND

(As Above)

4355 4357 4358 4359 4360 4361 4362 43 63
4356

Four-Car Suburban Units (4-SUB)

MOTOR BRAKE SECOND

Body: 62′ 6″ × 9′ 0″ & 9′ 3″ **Weight:** 43 tons **Seats:** 2nd, 96
Equipment: Two 275 h.p. English Electric traction motors

TRAILER SECOND

Body: 62′ 0″ × 9′ 0″ & 9′ 3″ **Weight:** 28 tons **Seats:** 2nd, 108

TRAILER SECOND

Body: 62′ 0″ × 9′ 0″ & 9′ 3″ **Weight:** 28 tons **Seats: 2nd,** 120

MOTOR BRAKE SECOND

(As Above)

4364 4366 4368 4370 4372 4374 4375 4376
4365 4367 4369 4371 4373

Four-Car Suburban Unit (4-SUB)

MOTOR BRAKE SECOND

Body: 62′ 6″ × 9′ 0″ & 9′ 3″ **Weight:** **Seats: 2nd,** 96
Equipment: Two 275 h.p. English Electric traction motors

TRAILER SECOND

Body: 62′ 0″ × 9′ 0″ & 9′ 3″ **Weight:** 28 tons **Seats: 2nd,** 108

TRAILER SALOON SECOND

Body: 62′ 0″ × 9′ 0″ & 9′ 3″ **Weight:** 28 tons **Seats: 2nd,** 102

MOTOR BRAKE SECOND

(As Above)

4377

Four-Car Suburban Units (4-SUB)

MOTOR SALOON BRAKE SECOND

Body: 62′ 6″ × 9′ 0″ & 9′ 3″ **Weight:** 42 tons **Seats: 2nd,** 82
Equipment: Two 275 h.p. English Electric traction motors

TRAILER SECOND

Body: 62′ 0″ × 9′ 0″ & 9′ 3″ **Weight:** 28 tons **Seats: 2nd,** 120

TRAILER SALOON SECOND

Body: 62′ 0″ × 9′ 0″ & 9′ 3″ **Weight:** 28 tons **Seats: 2nd,** 102

MOTOR SALOON BRAKE SECOND

(As Above)

4378 4380 4382 4383 4384 4385 4386 4387
4379 4381

Four-Car Suburban Units (4-SUB)

MOTOR SALOON BRAKE SECOND

Body: 62′ 6″ × 9′ 0″ & 9′ 3″ **Weight:** 39 tons **Seats: 2nd,** 82
Equipment: Two 250 h.p. English Electric traction motors

Original 1942-type Southern Region all-steel 4-SUB unit No. 4105 [*P. J. Sharpe*

Later 1946-type Southern Region all-steel 4-SUB unit No. 4690
[*Alan Williams*

Southern Region 4-EPB unit No. 5209 [*Alan Williams*

TRAILER SECOND

Body: 62′ 0″ × 9′ 0″ & 9′ 3″ **Weight:** 28 tons **Seats: 2nd,** 120

TRAILER SECOND

(As Above)

MOTOR SALOON BRAKE SECOND

(As Above)

4601 4602 4603 4604 4605 4606 4607

Four-Car Suburban Units (4-SUB)

MOTOR SALOON BRAKE SECOND

Body: 62′ 6″ × 9′ 0″ & 9′ 3″ **Weight:** 39 tons **Seats: 2nd,** 82
Equipment: Two 250 h.p. English Electric traction motors

TRAILER SECOND

Body: 62′ 0″ × 9′ 0″ & 9′ 3″ **Weight:** 28 tons (27 tons*)
Seats: 2nd, 120 (108*)

TRAILER SALOON SECOND

Body: 62′ 0″ × 9′ 0″ & 9′ 3″ **Weight:** 26 tons (28 tons) **Seats: 2nd,** 102

MOTOR SALOON BRAKE SECOND

(As Above)

4621	4638	4656	4673	4690	4707	4723*	4739*
4622	4639	4657	4674	4691	4708	4724	4740
4623	4640	4658	4675	4692	4709	4725	4741
4624	4641	4659	4676	4693	4710	4726	4742
4625	4642	4660	4677	4694	4711	4727	4743
4626	4643	4661	4678	4695	4712	4728*	4744
4627	4644	4662	4679	4696*	4713	4729	4745
4628	4645	4663	4680	4697	4714	4730	4746
4629	4646	4664	4681	4698	4715	4731	4747
4630	4647	4665	4682	4699	4716	4732	4748
4631	4648	4666	4683	4700	4717	4733*	4749
4632	4649	4667	4684	4701	4718	4734	4750
4633	4650	4668	4685	4702	4719	4735	4751
4634	4651	4669	4686	4703	4720	4736	4752
4635	4653	4670	4687	4704	4721	4737	4753
4636	4654	4671	4688*	4705	4722	4738	4754
4637	4655	4672	4689	4706			

Four-Car Suburban Units (4-EPB)

MOTOR SALOON BRAKE SECOND

Body: 62′ 6″ × 9′ 0″ & 9′ 3″ **Weight:** 40 tons **Seats:** 2nd, 82
Equipment: Two 250 h.p. English Electric traction motors

TRAILER SECOND

Body: 62′ 0″ × 9′ 0″ & 9′ 3″ **Weight:** 28 tons **Seats:** 2nd, 120 (108*)

TRAILER SALOON SECOND

Body: 62′ 0″ × 9′ 0″ & 9′ 3″ **Weight:** 27 tons **Seats:** 2nd, 102

MOTOR SALOON BRAKE SECOND

(As Above)

5001	5029	5103	5129	5156	5182	5209	5235
5002	5030	5104	5130	5157	5183	5210	5236
5003	5031	5105	5131	5158	5184	5211	5237
5004	5032	5106	5132	5159	5185	5212	5238
5005*	5033	5107	5133	5160	5186	5213	5239
5006	5034	5108	5134	5161	5187	5214	5240
5007	5035	5109	5135	5162	5188	5215	5241
5008	5036	5110	5136	5163	5189	5216	5242
5009	5037	5111	5137	5164	5190	5217	5243
5010	5038	5112	5138	5165	5191	5218	5244
5011	5039	5113	5139	5166	5192	5219	5245†
5012	5040	5114	5140	5167	5193	5220*	5246
5013	5041	5115	5142	5168	5194	5221	5247
5014	5042	5116	5143	5169	5195	5222	5248
5015	5043	5117	5144	5170	5196	5223	5249
5016	5044	5118	5145	5171	5197	5224	5250
5017	5045	5119	5146	5172	5198	5225	5251
5018	5046	5120	5147	5173	5199	5226	5252
5019	5047	5121	5148	5174	5200	5227	5253
5020	5048	5122	5149	5175	5201	5228	5254
5021	5049	5123	5150	5176	5202	5229	5255
5022	5050	5124	5151	5177	5203	5230	5256
5024	5051	5125	5152	5178	5205	5231	5257
5025	5052	5126	5153	5179	5206	5232	5258
5026	5053	5127	5154	5180	5207	5233	5259
5027	5101	5128	5155	5181	5208	5234	5260
5028	5102						

Unit 5245 has two trailer compartment seconds

Four-Car Suburban Units (4-EPB)

B.R. Standard design

MOTOR SALOON BRAKE SECOND

Body: 63′ 11½″ × 9′ 0″ & 9′ 3″ **Weight:** 39 tons or 40 tons
Seats: 2nd, 82
Equipment: Two 250 h.p. English Electric traction motors

TRAILER SECOND (SEMI-COMPARTMENT)

Body: 63′ 6″ × 9′ 0″ & 9′ 3″ **Weight:** 29 tons **Seats:** 2nd, 112

TRAILER SECOND (SEMI-COMPARTMENT)

(As Above)

MOTOR SALOON BRAKE SECOND

(As Above)

5301*	5310	5319	5328	5337	5346	5355	5363
5302*	5311	5320	5329	5338	5347	5356	5364
5303	5312	5321	5330	5339	5348	5357	5365
5304	5313	5322	5331	5340	5349	5358	5366
5305	5314	5323	5332	5341	5350	5359	5367
5306	5315	5324	5333	5342	5351	5360	5368
5307	5316	5325	5334	5343	5352	5361	5369
5308	5317	5326	5335	5344	5353	5362	5370
5309	5318	5327	5336	5345	5354		

* Both trailer seconds in units 5301/2 are S.R. type vehicles on 62′ 0″ underframes, weights as 5001–5260.

Two-Car Units (2-HAP)

MOTOR BRAKE SECOND (SEMI-SALOON)

Body: 62′ 6″ × 9′ 0″ & 9′ 3″ **Weight:** 40 tons **Seats:** 2nd, 84
Equipment: Two 250 h.p. English Electric traction motors

DRIVING TRAILER COMPOSITE (K)

Body: 62′ 6″ × 9′ 0″ & 9′ 3″ **Weight:** 32 tons **Seats:** 1st, 18; 2nd, 36

5601	5606	5611	5616	5621	5625	5629	5633
5602	5607	5612	5617	5622	5626	5630	5634
5603	5608	5613	5618	5623	5627	5631	5635
5604	5609	5614	5619	5624	5628	5632	5636
5605	5610	5615	5620				

Southern Region 2-HAP unit No. 5604 *[P. Ransome-Wallis*

Southern Region 2-EPB unit No. 5664 *[P. J. Sharpe*

Motor brake second of Southern Region B.R. Standard 2-EPB unit No. 5775 *[P. J. Sharpe*

Two-Car Suburban Units (2-EPB)

MOTOR BRAKE SECOND (SEMI-SALOON)

Body: 62′ 6″ × 9′ 0″ & 9′ 3″ **Weight:** 40 tons **Seats:** 2nd, 84
Equipment: Two 250 h.p. English Electric traction motors

DRIVING TRAILER SECOND (SEMI-SALOON)

Body: 62′ 6″ × 9′ 0″ & 9′ 3″ **Weight:** 30 tons **Seats:** 2nd, 94

5651	5656	5661	5665	5669	5673	5677	5681
5652	5657	5662	5666	5670	5674	5678	5682
5653	5658	5663	5667	5671	5675	5679	5683
5654	5659	5664	5668	5672	5676	5680	5684
5655	5660						

Two-Car Suburban Units (2-EPB)

B.R. Standard design

MOTOR BRAKE SECOND (SEMI-SALOON)

Body: 63′ 11½″ × 9′ 0″ & 9′ 3″ **Weight:** 40 tons **Seats:** 2nd, 84
Equipment: Two 250 h.p. English Electric traction motors

DRIVING TRAILER SECOND (SEMI-COMPARTMENT)

Body: 63′ 11½″ × 9′ 0″ & 9′ 3″ **Weight:** 30 tons (31 tons*) **Seats:** 2nd, 102

5701	5711	5721	5731	5741	5751	5761	5772
5702	5712	5722	5732	5742	5752	5762	5773
5703	5713	5723	5733	5743	5753	5763	5774
5704	5714	5724	5734	5744	5754	5764	5775
5705	5715	5725	5735	5745	5755	5765	5776
5706	5716	5726	5736	5746	5756	5767	5777
5707	5717	5727	5737	5747	5757	5768	5778
5708	5718	5728	5738	5748	5758	5769	5779
5709	5719	5729	5739	5749	5759	5770	5800*
5710	5720	5730	5740	5750	5760	5771	

Two-Car Units (2-HAP)

B.R. Standard design

MOTOR BRAKE SECOND (SEMI-SALOON)

Body: 63′ 11½″ × 9′ 0″ & 9′ 3″ **Weight:** 40 tons **Seats:** 2nd, 84
Equipment: Two 250 h.p. English Electric traction motors

DRIVING TRAILER COMPOSITE (L)

Body: 63′ 11½″ × 9′ 0″ & 9′ 3″ **Weight:** 30 tons **Seats:** 1st, 19; 2nd, 50

6001	6020	6039	6057	6075	6093	6111	6129
6002	6021	6040	6058	6076	6094	6112	6130
6003	6022	6041	6059	6077	6095	6113	6131
6004	6023	6042	6060	6078	6096	6114	6132
6005	6024	6043	6061	6079	6097	6115	6133
6006	6025	6044	6062	6080	6098	6116	6134
6007	6026	6045	6063	6081	6099	6117	6135
6008	6027	6046	6064	6082	6100	6118	6136
6009	6028	6047	6065	6083	6101	6119	6137
6010	6029	6048	6066	6084	6102	6120	6138
6011	6030	6049	6067	6085	6103	6121	6139
6012	6031	6050	6068	6086	6104	6122	6140
6013	6032	6051	6069	6087	6105	6123	6141
6014	6033	6052	6070	6088	6106	6124	6142
6015	6034	6053	6071	6089	6107	6125	6143
6016	6035	6054	6072	6090	6108	6126	6144
6017	6036	6055	6073	6091	6109	6127	6145
6018	6037	6056	6074	6092	6110	6128	6146
6019	6038						

Four-Car Units (4-BEP)

B.R. Standard design

Gangwayed throughout

MOTOR SALOON BRAKE SECOND

Body: 64′ 6″ × 9′ 0″ & 9′ 3″ **Weight:** 41 tons (40 tons*) **Seats:** 2nd, 56
Equipment: Two 250 h.p. English Electric traction motors

TRAILER COMPOSITE (K)

Body: 64′ 6″ × 9′ 0″ & 9′ 3″ **Weight:** 33 tons (31 tons*)
Seats: 1st, 24; 2nd, 24

TRAILER BUFFET

Body: 64′ 6″ × 9′ 0″ & 9′ 3″ **Weight:** 36 tons (35 tons*) **Seats:** Buffet, 21

MOTOR SALOON BRAKE SECOND

(As Above)

Southern Region B.R. Standard 2-HAP unit No. 6024 [*Alan Williams*

Southern Region B.R. Standard 4-CEP unit No. 7179 [*Alan Williams*

Trailer buffet of Southern Region B.R. Standard 4-BEP unit No. 7019 [*Alan Williams*

7001*	7004	7007	7010	7013	7016	7019	7021
7002*	7005	7008	7011	7014	7017	7020	7022
7003	7006	7009	7012	7015	7018		

Four-Car Units (4-CEP)

B.R. Standard design

Gangwayed throughout

MOTOR SALOON BRAKE SECOND

Body: 64′ 6″ × 9′ 0″ & 9′ 3″ **Weight:** 41 tons (40 tons*) **Seats: 2nd,** 56
Equipment: Two 250 h.p. English Electric traction motors

TRAILER COMPOSITE (K)

Body: 64′ 6″ × 9′ 0″ & 9′ 3″ **Weight:** 33 tons (31 tons*)
Seats: 1st, 24; **2nd,** 24

TRAILER SECOND (K)

Body: 64′ 6″ × 9′ 0″ & 9′ 3″ **Weight:** 32 tons (31 tons*) **Seats: 2nd,** 64

MOTOR SALOON BRAKE SECOND

(As Above)

7101*	7115	7129	7143	7157	7171	7185	7199
7102*	7116	7130	7144	7158	7172	7186	7200
7103*	7117	7131	7145	7159	7173	7187	7201
7104*	7118	7132	7146	7160	7174	7188	7202
7105	7119	7133	7147	7161	7175	7189	7203
7106	7120	7134	7148	7162	7176	7190	7204
7107	7121	7135	7149	7163	7177	7191	7205
7108	7122	7136	7150	7164	7178	7192	7206
7109	7123	7137	7151	7165	7179	7193	7207
7110	7124	7138	7152	7166	7180	7194	7208
7111	7125	7139	7153	7167	7181	7195	7209
7112	7126	7140	7154	7168	7182	7196	7210
7113	7127	7141	7155	7169	7183	7197	7211
7114	7128	7142	7156	7170	7184	7198	

Single Units

MOTOR LUGGAGE VAN

Body: 64′ 6″ × 9′ 0″ & 9′ 3″ **Weight:** 45 tons
Equipment: Two 250 h.p. English Electric traction motors

Note: These vehicles can work singly, hauling a limited load, or in multiple with EP-type stock. They are equipped with traction batteries for working on non-electrified quay lines at Dover and Folkestone

COACH Nos.

S68001	S68003	S68005	S68007	S68009	S68010
S68002	S68004	S68006	S68008		

Waterloo & City One- or Five-Car Units

(Tube size vehicles with air-operated sliding doors. Trains are formed of a single motor car or up to five-car units comprising two motor cars and three trailers)

MOTOR SALOON BRAKE SECOND

Body: 47′ 0″×8′ 7¾″ **Weight:** **Seats 2nd:** 40
Equipment: Two 190 h.p. English Electric traction motors

51	53	55	57	59	61
52	54	56	58	60	62

TRAILER SALOON SECOND

Body: 47′ 0″×8′ 7¾″ **Weight:** 18 tons 14 cwt **Seats 2nd:** 52

71	74	77	80	83	85
72	75	78	81	84	86
73	76	79	82		

Two-Car Departmental Motor De-Icing Units

Gangwayed within set

(Formed of the motor coaches from withdrawn Eastern Section 1925 4-SUB units; fitted with conductor rail scraping and spraying equipment)

MOTOR BRAKE

Body: 62′ 6″×8′ 6″ & 9′ 0″ **Weight:**
Equipment: Two 275 h.p. English Electric traction motors

MOTOR BRAKE

(As Above)

92	94	96	98	100	101
93	95	97	99		

LOCOMOTIVES SCHEDULED FOR PRESERVATION

Locomotives Preserved by the Railway Companies before 1948

Date Built	Previous Owner	Locomotive
*1822	Hetton Colliery	0-4-0.
†1825	Stockton & Darlington	0-4-0 *Locomotion.*
¶1837	G.W.R.	2-2-2 *North Star.*
	*Grand Junction	2-2-2 No. 45 *Columbine.*
†1845	Stockton & Darlington	0-6-0 No. 25 *Derwent.*
††1846	Furness R.	0-4-0 No. 3 *Coppernob.*
§1847	L.N.W.R.	2-2-2 No. 173 *Cornwall.*
1857	Wantage Tramway	0-4-0WT No. 5 *Shannon.*
§1865	L.N.W.R.	0-4-0T Narrow Gauge *Pet.*
1868	S. Devon R.	0-4-0T Broad Gauge *Tiny.*
*1869	N.E.R.	2-2-4T No. 66 *Aerolite.*
*1870	G.N.R.	4-2-2 Stirling 8ft class No. 1.
1874	N.E.R.	0-6-0 No. 1275.
*1875	N.E.R.	2-4-0 901 class No. 910.
‖1880	L.B.S.C.R.	0-6-0T Class A No. 82 *Boxhill.*
*1885	N.E.R.	2-4-0 1463 class No. 1463.
1886	C.R.	4-2-2 No. 123.
§1892	L.N.W.R.	2-4-0 "Precedent" class No. 790 *Hardwicke.*
*1893	N.E.R.	4-4-0 Class M1 No. 1621.
‖1893	L.S.W.R.	4-4-0 Class T3 No. 563
1893	Shropshire & Montgomeryshire	0-4-0WT *Gazelle.*
1894	H.R.	4-6-0 No. 103.
*1898	G.N.R.	4-4-2 No. 990 *Henry Oakley.*
‡1899	M.R.	4-2-2 115 class No. 118.
*1902	G.N.R.	4-4-2 Class C1 No. 251.
¶1903	G.W.R.	4-4-0 "City" class No. 3717 *City of Truro.*

Locomotives Preserved by the British Transport Commission

Date Built	Previous Owner	Locomotive
‡1866	M.R.	2-4-0 Class 1 No. 158A.
‖1866	Met. R.	4-4-0T Class A No. 23.
††1889	L.Y.R.	2-4-2T Class K2 No. 1008.
‖1895	G.E.R.	2-4-0 Class T26 No. 490.
¶1897	G.W.R.	0-6-0 2301 class No. 2516.
1899	L.S.W.R.	4-4-0 Class T9 No. 120.
‖1901	S.E.C.R.	4-4-0 Class D No. 737.
‡1902	M.R.	4-4-0 Class 4 No. 1000.
‖1904	G.E.	0-6-0T Class S56 No. 87.
¶1907	G.W.R.	4-6-0 "Star" class No. 4003 *Lode Star.*
‡1909	L.T.S.R.	4-4-2T 79 class No. 80 *Thundersley.*
1913	N.B.R.	4-4-0 "Glen" class No. 256 *Glen Douglas.*
1920	G.N.S.R.	4-4-0 Class F No. 49 *Gordon Highlander.*
1920	G.C.R.	4-4-0 Class 11F No. 506 *Butler-Henderson.*
**1923	G.W.R.	4-6-0 "Castle" class No. 4073 *Caerphilly Castle.*
¶1947	G.W.R.	0-6-0PT 94XX class No. 9400

Locomotives Donated since 1953

Date Built	*Previous Owner*	*Locomotive*
§1865	L.N.W.R.	0-4-0ST No. 1439.
‖1872	Met. R.	0-4-0 Tram Loco No. 807.
*1882	L.B.S.C.R.	0-4-2 Class B1 No. 214 *Gladstone.*
‡1885	Mersey R.	0-6-4T No. 5 *Cecil Raikes.*

Locomotives Scheduled for Preservation

Date Built	*Previous Owner*	*Locomotive*
1874	L.S.W.R.	2-4-0WT 0298 class.
1891	N.E.R.	0-6-0 Class C No. 1576.
1897	L.S.W.R.	0-4-4T Class M7.
1898	H.R.	4-4-0 "Small Ben" class No. 2 *Ben Alder.*
1903	G.W.R.	2-8-0 28XX Class
1911	G.C.R.	2-8-0 Class O4.
1919	N.E.R.	0-8-0 Class T3.
1921	L.N.W.R.	0-8-0 Class G2.
1924	L.M.S.R.	0-6-0 Class 4F.
1925	S.R.	4-6-0 "King Arthur" class.
1926	S.R.	4-6-0 "Lord Nelson" class.
1926	L.M.S.R.	2-6-0 Class 5.
1927	G.W.R.	4-6-0 "King" class No. 6000 *King George V.*
1930	S.R.	4-4-0 "Schools" class.
1934	L.M.S.R.	4-6-0 Class 5.
1935	L.M.S.R.	2-6-4T Class 4 (3-cyl.). No. 2500
1936	L.N.E.R.	2-6-2 Class V2.
1937	L.M.S.R.	4-6-2 Class 7P No. 6235 *City of Birmingham.*
1938	L.N.E.R.	4-6-2 Class A4 No. 4468 *Mallard.*
1942	S.R.	0-6-0 Class Q1.
1945	S.R.	4-6-2 "West Country" or "Battle of Britain"
1951	B.R.	4-6-2 Class 7 No. 70000 *Britannia.*
1954	B.R.	4-6-2 Class 8 No. 71000 *Duke of Gloucester.*
1956	B.R.	4-6-0 Class 5 (with Caprotti valve gear).
1960	B.R.	2-10-0 Class 9 No. 92220 *Evening Star.*

* York Railway Museum.
† Darlington Bank Top Station.
¶ Swindon Museum
** Science Museum, London
†† Horwich Works
‖ Clapham Museum
§ Crewe Works
‡ Derby Works

(†† Horwich Works, ‖ Clapham Museum, § Crewe Works, ‡ Derby Works:) Not on public view.

PULLMAN CARS RUNNING ON BRITISH RAILWAYS

K—Kitchen Car
B—Brake Car
P—Parlour Car

LOCOMOTIVE HAULED CARS

First Class

ADRIAN	(K)	GARNET	(P)	PERSEUS	(P)
AGATHA	(P)	HAWK	(K)	PHILOMEL	(K)
AMBER	(P)	HERCULES	(P)	PHOENIX	(P)
AMETHYST	(P)	HERON	(K)	PHYLLIS	(K)
AQUILA	(K)	IBIS	(K)	PLATO	(K)
ARGUS	(K)	IOLANTHE	(K)	RAVEN	(K)
ARIES	(K)	IONE	(K)	ROBIN	(K)
ATHENE	(B)	IRENE	(B)	ROSAMUND	(K)
AURELIA	(K)	ISLE OF THANET	(B)	ROSEMARY	(P)
AVON	(P)	JOAN	(K)	RUBY	(P)
BELINDA	(K)	JUANA	(P)	SAPPHO	(K)
CARINA	(K)	LORAINE	(K)	SEVERN	(K)
CASSANDRA	(K)	LUCILLE	(P)	SHEILA	(P)
CECILIA	(K)	LYDIA	(K)	SNIPE	(K)
CHLORIA	(K)	MAGPIE	(K)	STORK	(K)
CYGNUS	(P)	MEDUSA	(K)	SWIFT	(K)
CYNTHIA	(K)	MINERVA	(B)	THAMES	(K)
DIAMOND BAR	(K)	NILAR	(K)	THELMA	(K)
EAGLE	(K)	NIOBE	(B)	THRUSH	(K)
EMERALD	(P)	OCTAVIA	(K)	TOPAZ	(P)
EUNICE	(P)	ONYX	(P)	URSULA	(P)
EVADNE	(K)	OPAL	(P)	WREN	(K)
FALCON	(K)	ORION	(K)	WYE	(P)
FINCH	(K)	PEARL	(P)	ZENA	(P)
FINGALL	(K)	PEGASUS BAR		ZENOBIA	(K)
FORTUNA	(B)	PENELOPE	(K)		

Second Class

Car No. 27	(B)	Car No. 65	(B)	Car No. 78	(B)
" " 31	(K)	" " 67	(B)	" " 79	(B)
" " 32	(K)	" " 68	(B)	" " 80	(B)
" " 33	(K)	" " 69	(B)	" " 81	(B)
" " 34	(P)	" " 70	(B)	" " 82	(B)
" " 36	(B)	" " 71	(B)	" " 83	(P)
" " 54	(B)	" " 72	(B)	" " 84	(P)
" " 55	(B)	" " 73	(P)	" " 95	(B)
" " 58	(K)	" " 74	(P)	" " 105	(K)
" " 62	(B)	" " 75	(P)	" " 106	(K)
" " 63	(B)	" " 76	(P)	" " 107	(K)
" " 64	(P)	" " 77	(B)		

LOCOMOTIVE-HAULED—(cont.)

Car No. 166	(K)	Car No. 335	(K)	Car No. 345	(K)
„ „ 167	(K)	„ „ 336	(K)	„ „ 346	(K)
„ „ 169	(K)	„ „ 337	(K)	„ „ 347	(P)
„ „ 171	(K)	„ „ 338	(K)	„ „ 348	(P)
„ „ 208	(B)	„ „ 339	(K)	„ „ 349	(P)
„ „ 249	(K)	„ „ 340	(K)	„ „ 350	(P)
„ „ 303	(K)	„ „ 341	(K)	„ „ 351	(P)
„ „ 332	(K)	„ „ 342	(K)	„ „ 352	(P)
„ „ 333	(K)	„ „ 343	(K)	„ „ 353	(P)
„ „ 334	(K)	„ „ 344	(K)	*Hadrian Bar*	(K)

ELECTRIC MULTIPLE-UNIT CARS

First Class

AUDREY	(K)	GWEN	(K)	MONA	(K)
DORIS	(K)	HAZEL	(K)	VERA	(K)

Second Class

Car No. 85	(P)	Car No. 88	(B)	Car No. 91	(B)
„ „ 86	(P)	„ „ 89	(B)	„ „ 92	(B)
„ „ 87	(P)	„ „ 90	(B)	„ „ 93	(B)

Composite First and Second Class

ALICE	(K)	ETHEL	(K)	NAOMI	(K)
ANNE	(K)	GRACE	(K)	OLIVE	(K)
BERTHA	(K)	GWLADYS	(K)	PEGGY	(K)
BRENDA	(K)	IDA	(K)	RITA	(K)
CLARA	(K)	IRIS	(K)	ROSE	(K)
DAISY	(K)	JOYCE	(K)	RUTH	(K)
ELINOR	(K)	LORNA	(K)	VIOLET	(K)
ENID	(K)	MAY	(K)		

First published 2006

ISBN (10) 0 7110 3168 1
ISBN (13) 978 0 7110 3168 5

Published by Ian Allan Publishing

an imprint of Ian Allan Publishing Ltd, Hersham, Surrey KT12 4RG.
Printed in England by Ian Allan Printing Ltd, Hersham, Surrey KT12 4RG.

Code: 0602/B2

Visit the Ian Allan Publishing website at www.ianallanpublishing.com